Poynter Institute for Media Studies
Library

APR 17 '86

Magazine Editing in the '80s

TEXT AND EXERCISES

William L. Rivers

Stanford University

Wadsworth Publishing Company
Belmont, California
A Division of Wadsworth, Inc.

Communications Editor: Rebecca Hayden
Production Editor: Robin Lockwood
Designer: Hal Lockwood
Copy Editor: Julie Segedy
Technical Illustrator: Brenda Booth

Cover photos of *Sunset* magazine, Menlo Park, California, by Richard Wheeler.

© 1983 by Wadsworth, Inc. All rights reserved. No part of this book may be reproduced, stored in a retrieval system, or transcribed, in any form or by any means, electronic, mechanical, photocopying, recording, or otherwise, without the prior written permission of the publisher, Wadsworth Publishing Company, Belmont, California 94002, a division of Wadsworth, Inc.

Printed in the United States of America

1 2 3 4 5 6 7 8 9 10—87 86 85 84 83

ISBN 0-534-01266-3

Library of Congress Cataloging in Publication Data
Rivers, William L.
  Magazine editing in the '80s.
  (Wadsworth series in mass communication)
  Includes index.
  1. Journalism—Editing. I. Title. II. Title:
Magazine editing in the eighties.
PN4778.R53   1983   070.4'1   82-17531
ISBN 0-534-01266-3

Preface

Magazine Editing in the '80s is designed to show you the various tasks of a magazine editor and to let you experience those tasks through the eyes of actual working editors, who describe in their own words what they do. All aspects of magazine editing are covered as concisely as possible, and because this book is both a text *and* a workbook, you can sharpen your magazine editing skills by doing the many exercises at the ends of chapters.

In this book you will find that, in spite of some similarities, magazine editing is in fact quite different from newspaper editing. This is so, in part, because magazines must appeal to a wide audience, whereas most newspapers have a built-in readership. In the introduction, you will find that magazines have definite purposes and readerships, and you will probably be surprised at the great number of magazines that exist in the United States today.

Chapter 1 is divided into four sections: The first quotes a successful editor; the second shows how three types of magazines were started; the third describes editors' duties; and the last chronicles the revival of a once-successful magazine. In Chapter 2, writer-editor relationships are explained in detail. Chapter 3 deals with copy editing and gives examples of professional and student work. Chapter 4 explains the best ways to edit words, sentences, and paragraphs for magazines. Again, both professional and student examples are cited. Chapter 5 teaches how to write magazine headlines, titles, and subtitles and discusses specific pitfalls to avoid. Chapter 6 presents the complex subject of graphic arts, including typography, copyfitting, illustration, and printing. Chapter 7 discusses picture editing and the use of color in magazines. The basic rules of layout and design are introduced in Chapter 8, where you will see, among other things, how to dummy a magazine. Chapter 9 develops your understanding of law and ethics in publishing magazines, focusing on the important issues of libel, copyright, obscenity, and pornography.

At the end of the book appear a glossary of terms used in the magazine field and a description of how *Newsweek* is prepared for publication. Also included are the American Society of Journalists and Authors Code of Ethics and Fair Practices, and important guidelines for avoiding sexism in writing and editing.

I wish to thank many people for their help in the creation of this book, but I am especially grateful to Bryce McIntyre, a graphics expert who helped with the graphic arts sections as well as at other points throughout the project. I am also grateful to John Boyle, who did the sketches for many of the illustrations. Finally, I would like to express my appreciation for the guidance of Tom Siegfried of Texas Christian University, especially in Chapter 8 on layout and design. I also thank the following reviewers, who offered many useful suggestions: Floyd L. Arpan, Indiana University; Karen Boyd, Arizona State University; Chet Hunt, San Antonio College; and Howard M. Ziff, University of Massachusetts.

Contents

Preface   iii
Introduction   1

Chapter 1   Magazine Editors and Their Work   11
    The Campus Magazine   13
    The Professional Magazine   17
        The Formula and Prospectus   19
        The Duties of the Editors of *Sea Frontiers*   19
    Reviving a Once-successful Magazine   22
    Exercises   25

Chapter 2   Writer-Editor Relationships   27
    Accepting an Article   29
    Editor-Writer Disagreements   35
    Defending the Editor   36
    Article Rejections   37

Critiquing Articles   38
An Editor-Writer Reversal   40
Why Magazines Need Editors   41
Exercises   43

Chapter 3   Magazine Copy Editing   51

Newspaper vs. Magazine Copy Editing   53
   Becoming a Magazine Copy Editor   53
   Functions of a Copy Editor   55
Marking Copy   61
   Preparing Copy   62
   Marking All-cap Articles   62
   Inserting New Material   64
Examples of Professional Editors' Work   64
Computerized Magazine Editing   68
Editorial Research   72
Exercises   77

Chapter 4   Correcting Words, Sentences, and Paragraphs   81

Editing Words   82
Editing Sentences   86
Editing Paragraphs   89
A Student Example   91
Professional Writing of a Paragraph   93
Exercises   97

Chapter 5   Writing Headlines and Titles   101

Magazine Headlines   102
   Counting Headlines   103
   Writing Headlines   104
   Headline Grammar   106
   Headlines to Avoid   107
Magazine Titles   107
   Writing Good Titles   108
   Writing Subtitles   109
   Subheads, Page Heads, Jump Heads, and Blurbs   110
Specifications for the Printer   114
Exercises   115

Chapter 6 *Graphic Arts* *121*
    The Printing Processes   123
    Typography   127
        Type Measurement   127
        Classifications of Type   129
    Choosing Type   135
    Copyfitting   137
        Estimating   137
        Fitting Copy   138
        Other Copyfitting Methods   139
    Titles and Illustrations   141
        Titles   141
        Illustrations   142
    Planning for the Press   143
        Exercises   145

Chapter 7 *Picture Editing and Using Color* *155*
    Editor-Photographer Relationships   156
    Writing to Pictures   159
    Writing to Picture Stories   160
    What to Do With Pictures   161
        Cropping   162
        Scaling   163
        Tone Butting and Runarounds   163
        Retouching   163
    Four Guidelines   166
    Color   166
        Classification of Color   166
        Spot Color   167
        Fake Color   167
        Process Color   168
        Preseparated Color   168
        Duotones and Posterizations   169
    Exercises   171

Chapter 8 *Layout and Design* *187*
    Basic Rules of Layout   188
        Elements   190

Other Layout Considerations 192
Layout of an Article 193
Laying Out a Magazine 196
Dummying Your Magazine 197
    Covers 200
    Back Covers 200
    Inside Covers 204
The Lead Article and Center Spread 204
Exercises 209

Chapter 9 Magazines: Law and Ethics 211

Defamation 213
Privacy 216
Public or Private Figures? 217
Cameras in the Courtroom 218
Stronger Restrictions 218
Obscenity and Pornography 219
Magazines and Copyright Law 220
Editors' Ethics 222
Code of Ethics and the Editor 223
Advertising and the Magazine 225
Control Through Support 226
Control by Photographers 227
Threat of What Control? 228
Exercises 229

Appendix A How *Newsweek* Is Prepared for Publication 231

Appendix B American Society of Journalists and Authors Code of Ethics and Fair Practices 241

Appendix C Guidelines for Magazine Writing about Women 245

Glossary 249

Index 255

Introduction

Let us begin with the most important problem: With 1,760 newspapers published and nearly 1,000 television stations, more than 5,000 radio stations, and almost 4,000 cable systems broadcasting daily, and with book companies publishing more than 35,000 titles each year, why should magazines continue to exist? Yet they *do* exist—about 37,000 various magazines move through the mails to meet the changing interests of the readers.

Editor and writer Edwin Diamond wrote in 1981: "Special-interest magazines include *Wet: The Magazine of Gourmet Bathing*; *The Razor's Edge*, which concerns itself with women sporting shaved heads; *The Pick-Up Times*, a self-spoofing guide to meeting women; and *The Chocolate News*, printed on paper that smells like its subject."

Although it is entirely possible that all of the above magazines will have disappeared by the time this book is published, other magazines will sprout to replace them. At least 200 new magazine ventures were started in 1981 alone; only about 20 of them survived the first year. Lewis Lapham, the editor-in-chief of *Harper's*, described the central reason why: "Twenty years ago, an issue of *Harper's* might have contained articles or essays on topics as miscellaneous as marine biology, toy railroads, the failure of U.S. foreign policy, the ecology of Yellowstone National Park, and the unhappiness of women. Now, each of these topics commands a magazine of its own."

The Thinker's Medium

An issue of *Saturday Review* once carried an article entitled "The Thinking Man's Medium." In it, Roy Larsen, the former vice-chairman of the board of directors of Time, Inc., pointed out that research has indicated that those who read significant magazines are "the thinking men and women of our time." "The magazine audience," he wrote, "includes the generals and captains and lieutenants of the Command Generation—and the top revolutionaries as well." This is not surprising. Although commercial magazines of large circulation often support the status quo, are imitative, and help the other mass media create their own version of reality, it is nonetheless true that magazines in America—including some of the largest commercial magazines—have long ranked with books as the media of thought.

By magazine standards, the newspapers, press associations, and the electronic media came quite late to interpretative reporting. But interpretative writing and its forerunner, the essay, have been central to magazines for centuries. To clarify, to explain, sometimes to promote—these are the *raisons d'être* of our magazines. One editor called them "the characteristic literary medium of our generation."

The Changing Magazine Public

Pasted on the wall at eye level above a typewriter in the office of a movie-fan magazine editor is a small picture of a young girl, a sales clerk in a Woolworth's store. The editor has never met her; he keeps the picture in view to remind him of his primary readership. When he is choosing and editing articles and photographs, he thinks of this young girl's tastes.

This story illustrates a basic fact about magazines: most are written and edited for particular audiences. Few editors actually restrict their view of the audience this severely, and many feel that anything more definite than a vague picture of their audience is impossible. Nothing is more obvious, however, than the fact that most magazines, unlike newspapers and broadcasting, do *not* attempt to appeal simultaneously to the bank president and the janitor, to the teller and his 11-year-old son.

Magazine editors and writers know well that it is folly to think of the public as "one great mass." There are as many publics as there are levels of income, education, taste, and civic awareness; as many as there are political allegiances and religious loyalties. What concerns one public may be trivia to another.

During the first half of the twentieth century, the big general magazines—like *Collier's, Saturday Evening Post,* and *Coronet*—were able to lure several million subscribers by shrewdly appealing to different publics. They were able to do so because, as Theodore White once observed,

> The whole country is one market; you can make one brand image for the nation and deliver—but only if you can find a way of talking to the whole country at once. They need a big horn—a horn that will reach everybody.

The big general magazines were successful also because advertising paid most of their costs. This became painfully clear when television became the chief medium for general information and entertainment, and lured advertising away from the general magazine. Lewis Gillenson, the last editor of *Coronet*, one of the many mass magazines that died, pointed out:

> Contemplate the cost of a subscription. A giant weekly publisher begs you to sign up for a year with an enticing "9 cents a copy" offer. The magazine sells weekly on the newsstand for 25 cents. The following are, roughly, average costs for the publisher: production, 40 cents; mailing, 4 cents; fulfillment, billing, delinquency, 3 cents. Total, 47 cents. In all, the magazine is behind 38 cents on subscriptions, or about $20 for the year. Multiply this figure by 3 million, a reasonable estimate of the number of cut-rate subscribers a big magazine might carry, and you begin to get an idea of the deficit that must be made up by advertising.

Before midcentury, there were a dozen weekly magazines of general appeal. Now there are almost none. *Look* was among the last to go. After several years of operating in the red, it finally ceased publication in the early 1970s.

This is not to say that all magazines are moribund, just general magazines. In fact, some evidence suggests that the magazine world is stronger than ever. As the general weeklies have weakened and disappeared, the magazines of special interest that seek out the individual public have become far stronger. The greatest new successes in publishing during the last 25 years have been special-interest magazines: *Sports Illustrated, American Heritage, TV Guide, Scientific American,* and many others. The change is described by a veteran editor, Robert Stein:

> It used to be that we could cover almost any subject in a popular magazine by assigning a very good writer to go to a number of obvious sources, get the necessary facts and figures, and dramatize them with a few anecdotes or individual experiences, then put it all together in a neat, well-rounded way. The result would be that the reader would be superficially informed, would quite possibly be entertained, but would be left with very little of real value to him.
>
> Now, on some of the most serious subjects, we find that we are investing as much as two years of time; that we're using not only writers, but (often) teams of researchers to help them. In some cases we're working with research organizations to do basic research which goes far beyond reporting, simply to find out what the reality of the situation is before we can figure out what we're going to say about it, how we're going to treat it in a magazine. This is a growing trend because readers can discern the difference between an exploitation of their interest on the part of the magazine and the magazine's desire to serve their interest by clarifying confusion about issues that are important to them.
>
> When I first started writing magazine articles on almost any subject of direct concern to the reader, I finished with ten rules on how to handle the subject. Well, the ten-easy-rules days are over, because any issue that can be treated with ten easy rules isn't worth considering in the first place.*

The last fifteen years have proven that the modern network of mass media has no place for magazines that attempt to reach everyone simultaneously. *Reader's Digest*, which has the largest subscription list of any publication in the world, appeals to the general masses at the expense of the intellectual audience. More important in judging total readership is the fact that the *Digest* does not reach millions of others who think of it as too serious, *too intellectual*. Other, smaller magazines reach audiences that the *Digest* misses but cannot hope to duplicate in its broad appeal.

---

*Courtesy, Robert Stein.

Types of Magazines

Magazines were first introduced in France in the seventeenth century. The term "magazine" originates from the French word *magasin*, meaning "storehouse." From the beginning, the chief distinguishing characteristic was a *variety* of writing—essays, poetry, and plays. In fact, for many years publications in newspaper format that offered a variety of writing genres were known as "magazines." The late Frank Luther Mott, considered the foremost historian of American journalism, once defined a magazine as "a bound pamphlet issued more or less regularly and containing a variety of reading matter." Now, however, magazines are distinguished from newspapers and books by format and by their appeal to particular audiences.

Magazines can be categorized according to type and audience. *Writer's Market*, a leading guidebook for free-lance writers, lists more than 100 categories: general interest, women's poetry, sports and outdoor, and so on. But it is more useful for us to deal with magazines in four categories: mass magazines, news magazines, class magazines (including "little magazines"), and specialized magazines (including business publications).

The increase in postal rates that came in the early 1970s threatened most magazines, even some with loyal readers who were willing to pay more for their favorite publications. The increase was especially hard on the small political and literary magazines that appeal to a small segment of the market. The postal increase hurried the demise of some mass magazines that were already deep in trouble.

Mass Magazines

Mass magazines, as the name implies, are aimed at a large, general audience (although certainly not at everyone). Two features characterize the mass periodical: its huge circulation, usually in the millions, and its effort to bridge many levels of education, income, religion, and interest. The demise of *Look* came as no surprise to those who had been watching the magazine world for two decades. At the risk of oversimplifying, the birth of television signaled the slow death of general weekly magazines, which had long attempted to do what television could do better: entertain and inform a wide range of people at low cost to advertisers. There were, of course, other factors, but when the advertising dollars used to support magazines turned to television to reach many more millions of listeners than even the largest magazine, all the general weeklies and some of the monthlies died.

The general monthlies that survived decided quite early to raise subscription and newsstand prices—some to the point where their readers paid nearly all the costs of production and distribution, leaving most of their advertising revenue as profit. To continue to lure buyers, of course, it became necessary to create publications so attractive that readers could not resist them even at their higher rates.

The death of the *general* weekly, however, failed to mark the death of the mass magazine or the specialized weekly. Not only are many large monthlies and fortnightlies thriving—*Ms.*, *Rolling Stone*, *Cosmopolitan*, and *Playboy*, for example—but some weeklies that address particular interests of many readers now have mass circulations as well. *Sports Illustrated* is a prime example; *New York* is another; *TV Guide*, with a circulation of 18 million a week, sells more copies annually than any other magazine in history.

News Magazines

News magazines also try to bridge many levels of readership. Most news magazine readers, however, have a strong interest in contemporary affairs, which sets them apart from the majority of Americans. The three leading news magazines—*Time*, *Newsweek*, and *U.S. News & World Report*—all have circulations in the millions and all attempt to bridge several categories of readers. But even a cursory look at them indicates a different intent from other mass magazines.

The publication of the first issue of *Time* on March 3, 1923, was an important event in American journalism on many counts. Although it began with a circulation of only 12,000, *Time* now sells nearly 5 million copies each week. It is the keystone of one of the strongest magazine-publishing empires in the world, a complex corporation that includes *Fortune*, *Sports Illustrated*, and *Money*. It is no exaggeration to state that *Time* has altered the course of American journalism by turning journalistic interest toward the meaning and texture of the news. (Many professional reporters have an active disdain for it, particularly because its cleverness is sometimes carried to extremes to support the point of view of its editors.)

The founders of *Time*, Henry R. Luce and Briton Hadden, were originally interested in developing a magazine that would flesh out spot news. The prospectus ran:

> People in America are, for the most part, poorly informed. This is not the fault of the daily newspapers; they print all the news. It is not the fault of the

weekly reviews; they adequately develop and comment on the news. To say with the facile cynic that it is the fault of the people themselves is to beg the question. People are uninformed because no publication has adapted itself to the time which busy men are able to spend on merely keeping informed.

Luce and Hadden originally emphasized the newspaper aspect of their new publication, as indicated by one of the rules in the prospectus: no story was to be more than 400 words long.

There have been several changes in *Time* since its earliest days, among them longer stories and the gradual disappearance of many components of "Timestyle"—which was for years chiefly characterized by freshly coined, usually flippant words and inverted sentence structures. The narrative, or chronological, story structure emerged soon after the beginning of *Time*, and remains a dominant form.

One of the most distinctive changes, however, has been the evolution from news reporting and news interpretation to news feature treatment—an alteration that made *Time* more like conventional magazines. The long "cover stories," though they are usually built around personalities in the news, are often similar to articles published in magazines less concerned with timeliness. *Time* and the news magazines that came after it, *Newsweek* and *U.S. News & World Report*, bridge newspapers and magazines and contain elements of both.

Among the news magazines themselves are distinct differences. *Newsweek* seems similar to *Time* (and certainly might have been seen as "an imitator" during its earliest years), but *Newsweek* tends to be more objective in its news reports, with overt editorial comment restricted to signed columns.

U.S. News & World Report is a distant relation of *Time* and *Newsweek*. It grew out of an effort by the late David Lawrence, an outspoken conservative, to publish a national newspaper that he called the *United States Daily*. Curiously, *U.S. News* now has actually less newspaper flavor than the other weekly news magazines. It is made up largely of long "magazine-type" articles that are not always tied to news events.

Class Magazines

Class magazines or, as they are sometimes called, "quality magazines," are aimed at more educated audiences, who have a greater interest in public affairs and literature. The circulation of class magazines—including *Harper's, The Atlantic, The Nation, New Republic*, and *National Review*—will never reach a half-million. Because their readers are often opinion leaders, however, the class magazines usually wield more influence than do the mass news magazines.

Certainly class publications will never begin to challenge any national television program. The editor's chief concern is with winning a few more loyal readers and a little more advertising—just enough of each to make the economics of publishing a little less dismaying. William F. Buckley, Jr., editor of the right-wing political journal *National Review*, described the problem:

> When the cost of manufacturing goes up 10 percent, the mass periodical publisher seldom has to turn to his readers to demand a 10 percent increase in the subscription rate. He turns, instead, to the advertisers for an additional subsidy; and the advertisers absorb the increase as a cost of doing business, which is reflected, naturally, in the price of their product to the consumers. But the little magazine has no such buffer. Normal business enterprises turn immediately, as they must, to the consumer, to absorb an increase in the cost of production. But the consumers of periodical literature are accustomed to being heavily subsidized, and hence partially relieved of personal obligation for the cost of production.

It is important to distinguish between current problems of the mass magazines and continuing problems of publications like *National Review*, which have always faced financial trouble. Little magazines have been springing up and dying out for decades; the unusual publication is the solvent one. Generally, smaller magazines exist only because individuals or groups think enough of the message they disseminate—usually political or literary—to make up the deficits.

Specialized Magazines

Specialized magazines exist in bewildering variety. Some, like *Popular Mechanics*, might also be considered mass magazines if only circulation were measured. Others, like *Editor & Publisher*, struggle to reach 30,000 readers. All have a great advantage over the mass magazines: they are aimed directly at highly definable audiences, some large, some small. The readers of *Popular Mechanics* may differ strikingly in income, occupation, religion, and location, but they share an interest in mechanics and popular science. The readers of *Editor & Publisher* share an interest in the newspaper business.

Some specialized magazines, like *Popular Mechanics*, are well known, but others exist in such relative anonymity that they almost defy classification. Russell Baird and Arthur Turnbull, authors of *Industrial and Business Journalism*, have divided business publications into:

1. *Business papers*—periodicals published independently for profit that provide a particular business, industry, or profession with information essential to its practitioners.
2. *Company publications*—periodicals published by individual firms for their employees and/or dealers, customers, stockholders, and others with special company interests.
3. *Association journals*—similar to business papers, except that an association within a certain industry, business, or profession, rather than an independent publisher, is responsible for their publication.

The business publication field often seems too restrictive for many young journalists, especially if they want to retain a high degree of writing freedom. But the excitement of running a small business publication is expressed in this letter from a graduate who went straight from the campus to the editorship of a company periodical. The fourth paragraph is especially noteworthy, because it reveals both a sense of the control of management and a first-rate approach to accomplishing aims; the last sentence is an especially succinct summary of the very real value of the business publication:

> My fifteenth issue has just come out. I've written every blessed word in every magazine.
>
> The magazine has progressed, although it's awfully crammed. It's hard to cover 7,000 people, scattered all over the country and working at different jobs, in just 16 pages. There's a terrific educational job to do with it. The company grew so fast and the people were lost.
>
> I've been reading, studying, and experimenting with the magazine. Industrial journalism, if it's to be good, entails a great deal more than the basic principles. It's a wonderful challenge. The money's good—everything's good about it, I think. It takes a lot of basic psychology—well, let's just say common sense. You aren't just a reporter.
>
> I'm trying to tell the story in terms of people. If top management wants to sell them on something, I don't talk in terms of generalities; I try to find people who exemplify the idea we're trying to put across. This brings everything home and serves two purposes: informs and gives a few deserved pats on the back.
>
> I've tried to make the magazine very warm. I seem to have succeeded. The International Council of Industrial Editors gave me a very high rating on content and writing. And the people seem to put a lot of stock in the magazine—I suppose because it's their only real source of information about the company.

Chapter 1

Magazine Editors and Their Work

What do editors actually accomplish? The answer can be both simple and complicated. This chapter is divided into sections: The first briefly quotes a successful editor; the second shows how editors might establish a campus magazine, a professional magazine, and a formula for a new magazine; the third describes the duties of editors; and the last deals with reviving a once-successful magazine.

The late editor of *Harper's*, John Fischer, once described magazine editing this way:

> Somehow the indispensable ruthlessness must be combined with a genuine liking for writers, a wide acquaintanceship among them and their agents, a sympathy and respect for their work. The best editors—Frederick Lewis Allen, for example, and Maxwell Perkins—seemed to blend the two qualities effortlessly and unconsciously. They couldn't have told you how they did it because (I suspect) it was not a learned skill but a part of their character. The best editors don't try to change a novelist into a reporter, or to push a sociologist into the style of a poet; nor do they attempt to "build" a natural-born fiction editor into an economist. Instead, they seek to bring together talents of many sorts, place them into harmonious relationships with each other, and then provide the conditions under which each can flourish best. It is a slow process—but in the end it may produce a well-balanced periodical of character.*

Future editors will need to develop an instinct to tell them what people will want to read. They will also need to persuade the proper writers to produce the articles they want.

Is this a tall order? Of course it is, but journalism students cannot know their chances of becoming editors-in-chief until they have worked on the campus magazines or as assistant editors on professional magazines. They will find the job of an editor to be a delicate balance of both tough and soft. They must please the owners of the magazines, their associates and co-workers, the staff writers and free-lance writers (some of whom they must coddle, others to whom they must lay down the law unmistakably), and finally, the subscribers—so that they will talk about the magazine in such glowing terms that their ranks will continue to grow.

---

*Courtesy, Elizabeth Fischer.

The Campus Magazine

Feed/back, a quarterly publication found on the San Francisco State University campus, was begun in 1974 by an undergraduate student, David Cole; the chairman of the Journalism Department, Professor B. H. Liebes; and especially Lynn Ludlow, a part-time lecturer in journalism and a full-time reporter and assistant city editor at the *San Francisco Examiner.*

Ludlow had nourished the idea of a press review journal for many years, but just as he was making persuasive arguments to Liebes, a group of newspeople decided to launch the *San Francisco Bay Area Journalism Review.* This review stumbled along for a year and a half (eight editions) and finally succumbed to the lack of money and the inability to find someone to take control. Then, in the spring of 1974, Ludlow again tried to persuade Liebes, who responded, "The time isn't quite right." Ludlow rebutted, "There's no such thing as the right time."

During the summer of 1974, they sent announcements to Northern California newsrooms that a new journalism review was about to be born. They knew their reputations were on the line and they had no way of backing out. The first issue appeared in October with this editorial:

> The press of Northern California is free of the kind of scrutiny it's supposed to provide free of charge to public servants, corporate executives, topless dancers, school musicians, sidewalk philosophers, fire chiefs, and unclad children on hot afternoons.
>
> We will review the press of Northern California on a regular basis, but our scope is limited only by the concerns and interests of those who report and edit the news.
>
> We'll apply to ourselves the standards we expect from the working press. We'll try to be constructive, not vindictive, and we will not wear blinders.

The following paragraphs were written by then-undergraduate David Cole:

> The start of the magazine took on the aura of a Judy Garland/Mickey Rooney movie: If you build the props and do the makeup, I can sing and dance. Let's put on a show!
>
> The people who started the magazine had plenty of newspaper experience, but little magazine experience. Bud Liebes had acted as advisor to the campus news quarterly; Lynn Ludlow had written a few magazine articles, but all I knew about magazines was that you could buy them in cigar stores.

We learned quickly. The first issue had a number of flaws, but two stick out in my mind: we underpriced a year's subscription by $1; and we provided no way to mail the thing. That too seemed to be an oversight: once we printed 2,000 of them, what would we do with 'em? Finally we finagled the mailing list of the defunct *San Francisco Bay Area Journalism Review*. I remember borrowing (MORE) magazine's mailing list. This amounted to about 1,500 names and so we mailed them with wrappers that had mailing indicia. We cut the (MORE) mailing labels apart by hand and glued them onto the wrappers by hand. Oh boy. What an ordeal!

It points out that we didn't know anything about two fundamental points to making a magazine: how to handle finances and how to market.

From the outset we learned that asking people to write for free was going to be a problem. Not that you couldn't find people who would work for nothing; that was difficult, but not impossible. No, the problem was this: How do you tell a writer who you commissioned to do a free article that his piece is not up to your standards? That he must either rewrite it or the editors must kill it?

The cover story of that first issue—an interview with *Oakland Tribune* Publisher Joe Knowland and an analysis of what he had done with the paper since his father's death—ran without a byline because the *Trib* staffer who wrote the article for publication with a pen name asked to have his nom de plume pulled because he was unhappy with the editing of the story.

What we learned with that experience is that there is only one thing you can say when someone hands you a piece you asked for and it isn't up to snuff: "Thank you." This leads to an uneven editorial quality. But that's better than no editorial product at all.

Well, if you can't bend and mold stories by professional journalists to read the way you want them, what do you do? You start raiding the college newspaper for its best writers. You find kids from the frosh/soph team who aren't on the paper yet and dragoon them onto the magazine.

And you teach them everything you know about writing and stories.

Undoubtedly some of the best *feed/back* stories have been written by students. Not because the editors have tinkered with the stories so much as because everyone was relaxed: Liebes, or Ludlow, or Cole could always fix the piece in the end, if necessary.

Bryon Dobell, executive editor of *Esquire* magazine, has often said that when Tom Wolfe couldn't finish a piece on hot rods, he asked Wolfe just to type up the notes and send them to the magazine. Wolfe wrote the notes in the form of a letter to Dobell; the editor took one look, marked out the "Dear Bryon," and that was *The Kandi-Kolored-Tangerine-Flake Streamline Baby*. . . .

To be honest, it took us a while to get our editorial legs. But it took us longer to get our design legs. I'd been brought aboard as the multi-purpose flunky: production, design, headlines, with a heavy dose of etcetera. But I'd never designed a magazine before and I hadn't learned a very simple lesson: in design you borrow and steal, especially if you don't have anyone with tons of talent. So a photographer for the magazine became art director because he had a good eye and because he knew how to crib page designs.

The magazine started to look better; the editorial quality got better because of that.

But, *feed/back* was always without money. The magazine was always on the edge of financial ruin.

Out from under the direct financial control of the journalism department (Liebes, co-editor and department chair, still signed the checks) had a major impact: no longer did the magazine have to use the university's printer. We could now pick our own.

I picked a printer who owed me 1,000 favors. Five years later, he's still paying them back in a printing bill that is 75 percent to 60 percent of what the going rate for such work would be.

Ultimately, it is this low-cost printing that keeps the magazine afloat.

One thing was lacking. In 1976 we had around 750 subscribers and another 250 or 300 single-copy sales. We were busting buns and almost no one was reading us. The way to get around that was simple: promotion. It took us a few years to figure out what kind of promotion and then a few more years to learn how to do that kind of promotion.

Junk mail. Circulars. Third-class mail. Flyers. All euphemisms for direct mail promotion. But how do you use direct mail to promote a magazine that has no money? Stealth.

It is common in the magazine subscription business to loan another magazine with similar interests your mailing list and then they will loan you theirs. It's usually a 1-to-1 tradeoff. You give me 100 names, I give you 100 names. Since we had around 1,000 names (including expired subscriptions and what I so quaintly call "freebies"), I got 1,000 names from *Columbia Journalism Review*, 1,000 names from *California Journal*, or 1,000 names from *Writer's Digest*.

But what do you send these names? The S.F. State Journalism Department had once bought a duplicator offset press, which I knew how to run. We found cheap paper at close-out sales and scrounged envelopes—or did without envelopes and created a "self-mailer."

By using a third class, nonprofit mailing permit, the postage wasn't too expensive. The pieces got out.

But we weren't using the right mailing lists and our mailing pieces weren't attractive enough to garner interest.

Then in December, 1980, I decided to go whole hog: we'd been using four-color processes on our covers; I decided to use all those pretty colors in a self-mailing brochure.

Using the right mailing list, I got between a 5 percent and 6 percent return. Fantastic. It was so good and came in so fast that we ran out of Winter '81 issues to mail out to these new subscribers.

If we felt constrained, we felt little better under the auxiliary's accounting methods. In late 1979 we set up the California Journalism Foundation, Inc. to publish *feed/back*. The object was to get a federally sanctioned nonprofit corporation so that we could offer tax-deductible donations to foundations, corporations, and individuals. We still needed money.

One of the keys to our minor success has been the large number of people who have stayed with us through the years. Ludlow and I have held roughly the same jobs since the beginning. [Leonard] Sellers was brought on to replace Liebes when he took a year's leave of absence. Now Sellers and I run the day-to-day magazine, with Liebes and Ludlow giving general commentary and the four of us make policy decisions.

Mark Harden, a student, was managing editor for three years (he left to take a reporter's job in Washington state). Tim Porter, student, was art director for two years (he left to be a Sunday magazine editor in Nevada). Dan Carson left [for San Diego] after three years as associate editor. The best part is that these people still contribute. Porter is back in the Bay Area and spends his weekends doing pasteup for us. Carson writes from the southland.

It is this continuity that has helped us. Helped, hell, without it, there would be no *feed/back*.*

Because the magazine has grown steadily—now with a circulation of more than 2,000—it is considered a success. How does *feed/back* benefit the students of San Francisco State?

Almost every journalism curriculum includes at least one course that teaches students to be critical observers of press performance. One such course, "Press Analysis," is associated with *feed/back*. Instead of researching and writing for no one other than the instructor, students research and write for an audience of professional journalists. If the articles contain inaccuracies or are poorly written, it is not an instructor's angry pen writing notes in the margin that bedevils the student; instead, the comments come by phone or letter, and the remarks may be sneering or sarcastic, but always embarrassing.

Co-editor Sellers teaches "Press Analysis" with Ludlow sitting in, discussing with the students—called "staffers"—ideas for articles, the emphasis to take, research possibilities, and possible problems. Each staffer is asked to subscribe to and monitor a Northern California daily newspaper, and to read *Columbia Journalism Review, San Francisco* magazine, *California*, and A. J. Liebling's *The Press*.

When *feed/back* started, the instructors believed that about 90 percent of the articles would be written by professional journalists, the remaining 10 percent by students. Since the second year of publication, students and alumni have contributed up to about 50 percent. The articles written by students are often as capably handled and written as any by professionals. This means that a staffer might have to do two or three

---

*Courtesy, David Cole.

rewrites of an article under the guidance of the editors, but the students are made aware of the standards when they join.

When a professional agrees to write for *feed/back*, he or she often asks for help in research and interviewing. The staffers become their eyes, legs, and voices. The students are also charged with the responsibility of turning out *feed/back* fixtures: regular columns that appear in every edition or nearly every edition. The students are also given complete responsibility for designing the magazine, which includes headlines and photographs.

After each issue, a critique session is held with the Board of Directors, which is made up of professors from the university, alumni, and professional journalists. This session is a no-holds-barred, tell-it-as-it-is meeting. Occasionally, praise slips in, but the sessions are chiefly devoted to probing for and exposing weaknesses in the hope that it will lead to improvement.

The Professional Magazine

The introduction stated that about 20 of the 200 magazines begun in 1981 survived their first year. What happened? You can bet that those survivors had at least one person who knew the many ins and outs of magazine publishing. It is also a safe bet that most of the 180 magazines that died did not have wise business counseling.

For example, James Kobak, a management consultant who was responsible for helping start dozens of magazines, wrote about a business plan for beginning a new magazine in *Folio: The Magazine for Magazine Management:*

> *The concept*—State the idea for the publication as simply as possible, ideally in one sentence. Also, very briefly state who the people involved in the venture are. Keep to one page if possible.
>
> *The editorial need*—Expand in this section on the editorial idea for the publication, offering substantial evidence of this need and discussing how this need has or has not been fulfilled up to this moment. Be very specific on the types of articles and editorials.
>
> *The market*—All the facts that can be mustered about the proposed audience for the magazine. Include facts that will demonstrate why they will be interested in the proposed editorial product, and be willing to subscribe if

subscriptions are to be sold. Add facts that will demonstrate that the audience will be attractive to advertisers if advertising is going to be accepted.

The advertisers—All the specifics that can be spelled out on the types of products and services which would logically be advertised to the audience. Also clearly spell out the degree of importance advertising revenue is to the success of the venture. If the venture is projected to break even on circulation revenue with advertising revenue the key to big profits, spell it out. If success or failure is based primarily on advertising, say it.

The company—Describe in detail how the company would be organized. If products other than the magazine are envisioned, explain them.

The competition—The specifics about other magazines and other media serving the market. Give facts on their audience, rates, degrees of success, and anything else that clearly presents whom this new magazine will be competing against. If information is available regarding the shortcomings of competition, use it only if it is factual and accurate. Leave out hearsay and opinions unless those offering them are recognized authorities in the area.

The people involved—This is extremely important because a magazine is a product of people. The key individuals involved are the essential ingredient. Spell out in detail who will handle the editing, who will be the financial and business manager, who will have the overall direction of the operation, and who will be advisors. And if you already have investors, name them. Include some pertinent background (but not too much) on each principal.

Financial projections—Show for the startup period plus the first four years a forecast of cash receipts and disbursements. Indicate the basic assumptions upon which the forecasts are based (i.e., estimated circulation, percent return mailings, average ad rate, number of advertising pages, number of total pages, renewal percentages, subscription prices, etc.). Include any facts that will help the reader judge the validity of financial projections. But keep it short.*

Other magazines, of course, have been started without Kobak's planning scheme. *Reader's Digest*, for instance, began publishing in 1922 with a solid chorus of no's from many publishers and has had resounding success in 16 languages with a global circulation of 30 million. Hugh Hefner published *Playboy* for the first time in 1955 with only $11,000 and has since built a multimillion-dollar corporation. Jann Wenner began *Rolling Stone* in 1967 with only $7,000 and now has a highly successful magazine. In 1967, a group of women started *Ms.* while magazine owners and consultants said, "It will never make it." Within seven months, the staff put away their red-ink pens because they were making money.

*Courtesy, James Kobak.

Yet, in spite of these success stories, there are hundreds of other magazines that started at the same time and utterly failed. Most of all, remember: If you start your own magazine, a business person who has knowledge of magazine publishing is essential.

The Formula and Prospectus

Anyone can go to a printer and contract for the production of a magazine—but the costs are high, and outside financial backing is usually necessary. To plan the venture, the promoters should develop a *formula*, or a concept, about the magazine's personality. This conceptualization process provides answers to essential questions: What will be the title and the emphasis of the magazine? What will be its purpose? How many articles will appear in the average issue? How long will these articles be? Will there be photographs? Drawings? What about departments such as travel, business, and sports? Will there be any fiction?

Once these questions have been answered, the promoters should develop a *prospectus*, which is a brochure or flyer incorporating both the formula and the business plan. The prospectus unifies the business and editorial considerations into a promotional package that is then carried to advertisers, subscribers, and financial backers such as lending institutions and investors. A complete prospectus also includes a dummy (or suggested) cover for the first edition of the magazine so that advertisers and subscribers can get a feel for the magazine's personality.

The Duties of the Editors of Sea Frontiers

Sea Frontiers, published in Miami, is only 30 years old. Because the magazine is only one project of the International Oceanographic Foundation (IOF), most of the staff wear several hats.

The editor-in-chief and the managing editor, for example, were two of the founding members of the IOF. Together they conceived, wrote, edited, and produced the first edition of the magazine. It was two years and five more issues before they acquired an assistant. With the growth of both the Foundation and the magazine, their attention, energy, time, and expertise increasingly extended into a number of areas, projects, and activities.

The editor-in-chief, F. G. Walton Smith, is president of the IOF and director of its museum, "Planet Ocean." He is the founder and dean emeritus of the University of Miami's Rosenstiel School of Marine and Atmospheric Science. These titles do not begin to suggest all the areas in which he is involved. As his editorial title implies, however, he is also the policymaker of the magazine. His intent, philosophy, and wisdom provide direction for the magazine. He approves the content and periodically writes articles for it. While many contribute to the making of the publication, it is his word that is final.

The managing editor, F. May Smith, is vice-president and secretary, as well as membership secretary, of the IOF. In her editorial capacity, she makes major decisions concerning production by purchasing the printing and deciding on the paper. She approves the text copy and the color separations and is concerned with the "look" of the magazine. Her judgment, vigilance, and good taste set the standard for the quality of the product.

Producing each issue involves numerous tasks: planning, rounding up, and reviewing articles; circulating articles to editorial and scientific reviewers; corresponding with authors; editing, writing, and rewriting; proofing galleys; determining which illustrations are necessary and then acquiring them; making layouts; choosing typefaces; working with the typesetters and the printers; and checking color and page proofs. She ensures that review copies of books arrive, are sent to reviewers, and are reviewed on time. Copy for the gift page must be acquired and processed. Cover photographs must be chosen and information for captions gathered. Payment must be made for articles and illustrations. Complimentary copies of the issue must be sent to publishers, authors, photographers, and anyone else who has contributed toward the issue.

There are, of course, the normal office duties, also. Correspondence and phone calls must be handled from members, prospective authors, artists, photographers, and publishers wanting information, photographs, or permission to reprint. Source files of information, photographers, and publications must be maintained. Photographs must be received, acknowledged, labeled, and filed. Press releases, newsletters, newspapers, and magazines must be scanned, read, clipped, and filed.

Fortunately, there are several people to perform these tasks, but it is the duty of the executive editor, Jean Bradfisch, to keep one eye on the calendar and one finger on all of the activities listed above. It is her responsibility to take an intangible idea and see that it becomes a reality—something that will go through the mail, delight readers, inspire renewal, and bind neatly into library volumes. Much like an artist creating a collage, she puts together the magazine—collecting, polishing, reworking, patching, supplementing, arranging the pieces that others provide. She works at this full-time.

The associate editor, Faith Schaefer, wears two hats. She reviews new articles, does some editing and caption writing, and checks galleys and layouts for the magazine. But most of her time goes into the IOF newsletter, *Sea Secrets*, of which she is editor. In many ways its production is similar to that of the magazine. It has an additional dimension, however, in that it includes questions from members and provides well-researched answers. Many questions can be answered from information in the extensive information files she maintains or in the IOF library. Other questions require the expertise of outside authorities. All questions are answered, but only those of general interest are published. Members sometimes appear in person need-

MAGAZINE ORGANIZATION CHART

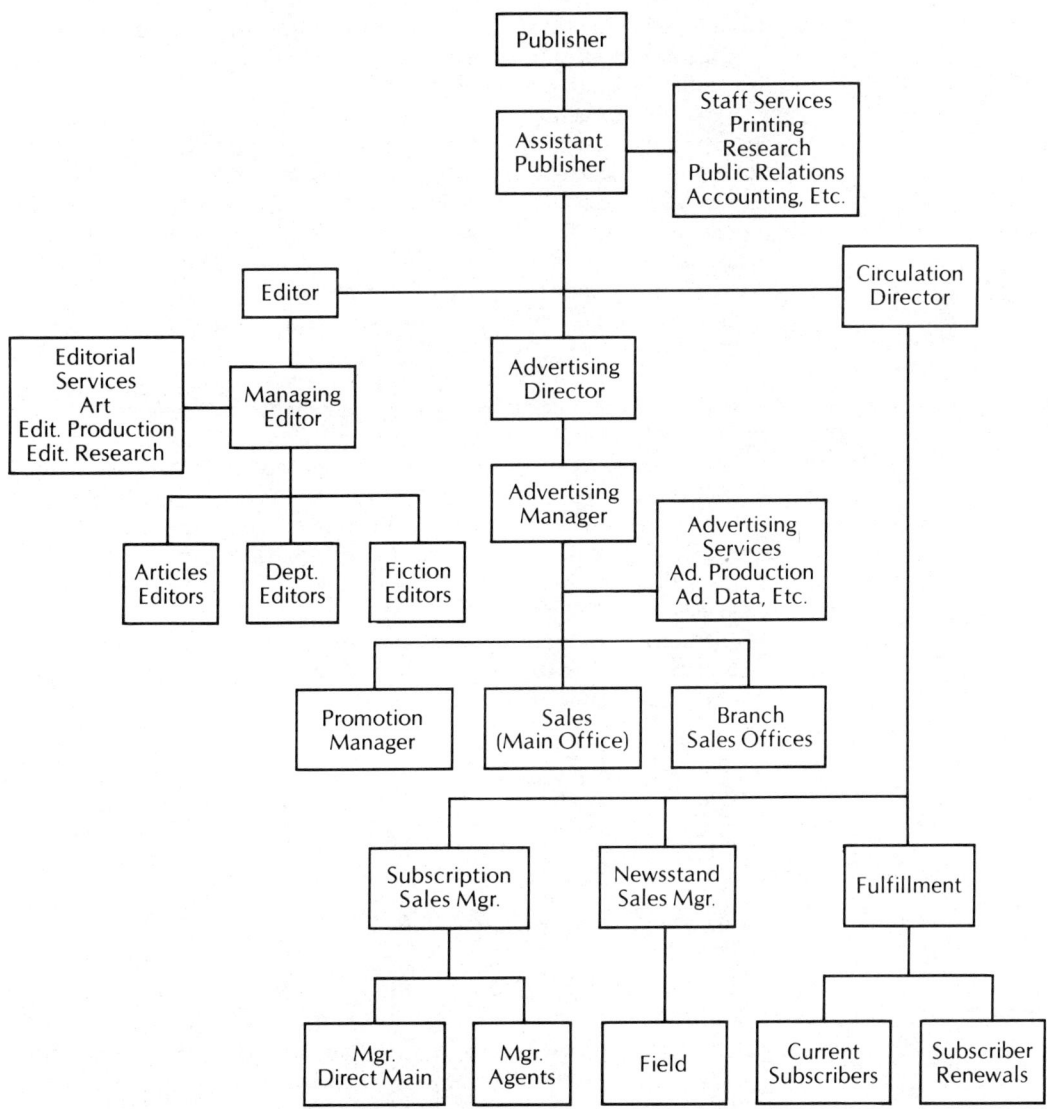

FIGURE 1-1.

ing specific information or with some beach-found curiosity in hand to be identified. There are numerous phone calls and a continuous stream of letters to be answered—few of them routine: a book author wants to check his facts about the most likely places to find fossil sharks' teeth; a child needs information for a theme on bottle-nosed dolphins; a member asks how many times submarines have collided with whales; an investor wants to know the feasibility of lobster farming on a remote Caribbean island; a coastal resident is concerned about hurricanes and beach erosion. And—always—a deadline looms. This job takes all her time.

The editorial assistant, Evelyn Aderhold, keeps track of the magazine correspondence and makes sure all articles, photographs, books, and maps (sometimes in long tubes) are logged in and acknowledged when they are received. She keeps the prodigious photo files in order and makes sure supplies are at hand. She keeps track of books out for review and checks with publishers on current prices. She writes the authors' biographies for the magazine and prepares the table of contents for typesetting. She types manuscripts. She fills in wherever needed. She, too, works in the editorial office full-time.

There are now two researchers, Susan M. Markley and Robert J. Riggio. Both are graduate students working toward their doctorates in marine science. Their knowledge is invaluable not only in helping to evaluate manuscripts submitted to the magazine, but also in answering the questions submitted to *Sea Secrets* by letter, by phone, or in person. They also help with the magazine by doing some editing and by writing captions and subheads after the layouts are made. Markley sometimes drafts maps and diagrams. They each work an average of 10 to 12 hours a week. It is never enough.

The art associate is employed full-time as director of exhibits for "Planet Ocean." Several times a year a special illustration—a painting or drawing—is needed for the magazine.*

Reviving a Once-successful Magazine

In the summer of 1978, the new editor-in-chief of *Parents*, Elizabeth Crow, was told by its new owners, "It's your ball game." She was faced with the responsibility of relaunching the magazine as a new publication. Why did Crow decide that *Parents* needed a rejuvenation? Crow explained:

*Courtesy, *Sea Frontiers*. Copyright © The International Oceanographic Foundation, Miami, Florida.

Without resuscitation, *Parents* would have died. The old *Parents* was put out by a miniscule, underpaid, exhausted, clearly demoralized staff. It was an editorial jumble—not so much designed as thrown together around ads, and it looked like it.*

Although the old *Parents* had an "inflated circulation of about a million and a half subscribers," Crow said it sold only 2,000 copies on the newsstand on a good month. Gruner & Jahr, the West German publishing conglomerate that had bought *Parents*, thought that it could be a profitable magazine. Crow recalls:

> A design consultant had been hired, but he had not been heard from since. Three staff writers had been hired, but most of the old staff had been let go. I was the only editor. There was an excellent new art director and photo researcher, but the rest of the art staff was a skeleton. There was no copy editor, no fact-checker. There was also no concept of the old staff about how to lay out a magazine. There were no layout sheets, no line-up sheets. The advertising production dummy had been used—in vain—for laying out the book for years.
>
> There's no way to express the inefficiency of the operation I inherited. The typesetting was being done in Nashville, at our printer's, and the turn-around time was one week. It was a mass of messengers who actually lost a packet of manuscripts and set us back another week. You would send something out and never expect to see it again. Just when you had forgotten all about it, it would come back—not fitting.

Although she hired new staffers and assigned articles to writers, "accessibility" was the key to the new magazine. "The magazine had to be easy to read. No one has less time to read a magazine than a busy mother," said Crow. This accessibility was to set the magazine in large, 10-point type. The "nuts-and-bolts, quick-take information" is in the front of *Parents*. The eight-part section entitled "As They Grow" that covers specific topics geared to every stage of child development is another feature. The majority of the features are self-contained, which is unheard of in most of the other women's service magazines.

What has happened since Elizabeth Crow took over as editor-in-chief? Advertising pages were up 20 percent in 1980 over 1978. Moreover, in two years, *Parents* increased from selling 2,000 newsstand copies each month to 70,000. Crow said this was the result of money: "We are very fortunate to be owned by a wealthy firm that knows what they are doing and yet has the good sense to let us do what we want to do."

---

*Courtesy, Elizabeth Crow.

Exercises

1. Create a magazine formula, giving title, suggested content, and other information outlined in this chapter. To see statements of purpose for other magazines, refer to *Standard Rate and Data's Business Publication Rates and Data*.

2. Define the market for a proposed magazine. For market information, see *Sales and Marketing Management* publications (such as the *S & MM Annual Survey of Buying Power*) and *Editor & Publisher's Annual Market Guide*. Also see Census Bureau publications such as *Statistical Abstracts of the United States*.

3. Based on the illustration on page 21, sketch an organization chart for a proposed magazine staff and write complete job descriptions for key figures in the venture. Because the duties of editors with identical titles on different magazines may vary widely, do not worry about conforming to existing patterns. Try to conceptualize thoroughly the many editorial tasks and to divide them up among staff members.

4. Name the competition for a proposed magazine and give data on the audience size and advertising and subscription rates. (See *Standard Rate and Data's Business Publication Rates and Data*.) State the purpose of each of the competitors and indicate how the purpose of the proposed magazine may differ from that of the competitors. Define the competitors' formats and personalities.

5. Summarize responses to the first four exercises in a 250-word prospectus. (Do not plan a dummy.)

6. See the next episode of "20/20," which is broadcast by ABC, or "60 Minutes," which is broadcast by CBS. You will undoubtedly see at least three stories, perhaps the longest running for 20 to 25 minutes. After seeing the broadcast, write down what you remember of it. Then read a long article in a magazine. Later on, write down what you remember of it. Finally, compare your notes on each medium.

7. Read again what Lewis Lapham said in the introduction of this book. Go to a large newsstand and list *all* of the general interest magazines. Then list the special-interest magazines, until you have doubled the number of general-interest magazines.

8. Read one issue of each of these: *Editor & Publisher,* which is written for newspaper people; *Broadcasting,* which is written for broadcasters; and *Folio*, which is written for magazine management. Which of these is the most attractive publication for you? Describe why you prefer one publication over the other two.

9. Keep in mind what John Fischer wrote at the beginning of this chapter ("Somehow, the indispensable ruthlessness must be combined with a genuine liking for writers . . ."). First, assess *yourself*. Have you ever been an editor of a high school or college newspaper or magazine? Or have you yearned to become an editor? Describe the qualities in yourself that come up to the mark he has outlined.

10. Read again the section on *feed/back*. Note especially what David Cole has written about the failings of the editors. Write what you would do if you were starting a journalism review. For example, would you call on the talents of an intelligent student in business or business administration? Would you call on an art student to direct or help with the design of the magazine?

11. As a lengthy exercise, imagine that you will take some of the advice given by James Kobak to publish a professional campus magazine. Write your concept of the magazine in one sentence; then write about the editorial needs, the market, and the advertisers. Disregard the rest of the information (which was written, of course, for professionals).

Chapter 2

*Writer-Editor
Relationships*

Student editors assume a certain amount of power. This chapter begins with a description of an editor accepting an article from a writer, including the inevitable dialogue between them. The discussion then turns to an illustration of the editor as critic and the writer-editor role reversal that occurs. Finally, the chapter explains just why editors are needed.

On any given workday, professional and amateur writers and reporters produce about 2,000 magazine articles. In any given year, they write at least one-half million articles. From this mass of manuscripts, only about 5 percent will ever be published—most written by professional writers. The other 95 percent will receive rejection slips ("Unsuited to our present needs") or, if they are lucky, notes of regret from an editor ("Sorry, this didn't quite make it"). Many of the losers assume that article writing is a closed corporation and that few editors ever read the articles that have been so coldly rejected.

The truth is that magazine editors *do* want, need, and seek new writers. Most issues are released with perhaps one excellent article, five others that are just merely good or pretty good, two or three that are competent at best, and usually one or two that got into the magazine simply because nothing better was available. To imagine an editor rejecting the work of writers solely because they are amateurs is to imagine a prospector kicking away a gold nugget because he's searching for silver.

The unfortunate truth about the failures is that 99 out of 100 rejected articles deserve rejection. The hundredth is turned back because of human errors that range from an editorial assistant placing a manuscript on the wrong stack, to an editor reading a manuscript while trying to shake a hangover. The writers of the 99 bona fide rejects fail for one of three reasons (in some cases, for all three). The first reason is that some have not learned to write clearly and provocatively. Second, others have not studied the contemporary article market and write what they want to write, not what the public wants to read. Third, still others have no concept of the amount of work that goes into a major magazine article, assuming that pieces that read so easily must have been produced easily as well.

The basic problem with nearly all writers is that they have no idea how an editor works through the many pounds of manuscripts that come in every week. If writers know how an editor works, and if they study a magazine closely, they will eventually receive encouraging letters, and later they will receive checks for their articles.

The following letter is from a magazine editor who is addressing a professional writer who had written a seven-page article about how to talk to an editor.

> "How to Talk to an Editor" has a lot going for it, but I'm afraid in its present form it's not right for us. We will gladly consider any revisions you

make on the manuscript, but the revisions would have to be submitted on speculation.

The manuscript starts out well, but I get the feeling that the article starts to lose a definite sense of direction on about page 2. After beginning with a very good anecdote, you seem to be searching for a theme to fit that anecdote, and a solid sense of direction should be established earlier than it is here.

I also get the feeling that more can be said about making a trip to New York to see editors. And more can be said about querying an editor that pertains specifically to personal visits. Some of the advice herein is a bit general, and could be applied to, for instance, query letters.

Finally, we need more anecdotes, more examples, to give the manuscript the kind of behind-the-scenes, we-are-there feel our readers like: some tales of vast success, utter failure, to illustrate the points you are making. I have also enclosed our writer's guidelines, which cover the other elements we consider vital to a story.

Let me know if you can do these revisions for us. The topic is good, and is one that will interest our readers.

The author immediately sat down and wrote seven more pages. Thanks to the editor who took the time to write such a detailed letter, the article was soon accepted for publication.

Accepting an Article

On March 27, 1980, Jean Bradfisch, executive editor of *Sea Frontiers*, received this letter from Vesta Rea-Salisbury, which was addressed to the editor, F. G. Walton Smith:*

Recently while talking to L. Anthony Leicester, a journalist friend of mine, he indicated that he was preparing an article for one of your summer issues on the Columbus landfalls at San Salvador, Bahamas. In our discussion a story idea developed on information I had on the island residents at the time of the Columbus arrival. I thought perhaps you might be interested in what I have to offer.

Columbus' Arawaks—The Virtuous Savage

The Arawaks were a "bright colored," attractive, gentle tribe who came into the Bahamas around AD 850 through a steady migration from South

*Courtesy, *Sea Frontiers*. Copyright © The International Oceanographic Foundation, Miami, Florida.

America, the Orinoco Valley, down the Venezuelan coast and into the West Indies by way of the Greater Antilles. They kept moving northward because they were the principal delicacy of the bloodthirsty, cannibalistic Caribs of the Caribbean. Their extinction would finally come in the outer islands of the Bahamas, but not before Columbus had met them in 1492 on San Salvador—the Admiral's first landfall.

The article I wish to propose will cover the final period (AD 850–1492) of the Arawaks in the Bahama Islands, and primarily how they lived during the time of the Columbus visit on San Salvador. Customs and idol worship will be elaborated on, as well as the archaeological sites of discovery on the island. Illustrations will be color transparencies and B/W photos.

In the upper margin of Rea-Salisbury's letter, Bradfisch handwrote this to the editor: "Dr. Smith: Good idea, wrong publication. What do you think? JB 1 April 1980." Dr. Smith responded, "Might be interesting change of pace—with pix," and Bradfisch wrote in the right margin this handwritten message as a guide for a reply letter that the editorial assistant sent out: "Would be interested in seeing her article, but suggest she remember that our magazine has to do with the sea, with emphasis on the marine sciences. Does her idea tie in with this? Send guidelines [to Rea-Salisbury]." The letter from Bradfisch carried this message:

Thank you for your letter of 27 March with a query about an article on the Arawaks in the Bahama Islands at the time of Columbus. We would be interested in seeing your article for possible publication in *Sea Frontiers*. We must point out, however, that our magazine has to do with the sea, with emphasis on the marine sciences. Does your idea tie in with this?

For your information we are enclosing our guidelines for authors and photographers.

We appreciate your interest and will look forward to hearing from you again.

Rea-Salisbury wrote to Bradfisch saying:

I am pleased with your continued interest in the article.

Yes, I believe I can easily tie the Arawaks of San Salvador into your sea format.

You can expect the article by May 19th; illustrated with both color and B/W.

Three weeks later, Rea-Salisbury wrote this letter to Bradfisch accompanying the article:

As promised, enclosed is an article on the Arawaks and how they lived from the sea during the time of Columbus' landfall.

You will find the story tied in with respects with Mr. Leicester. I thought you might be planning to publish both articles in the same issue, since they deal with the events on San Salvador in 1492.

If you have any questions, or if I can be of further service, please do not hesitate to contact me.

The article opened like this:

<u>Columbus' Arawaks</u>

<u>The Sea and the Virtuous Savage</u>

by

Vesta Rea-Salisbury

Rodrigo de Triana stood in the forecastle of the <u>Pinta</u> and watched Jupiter rising in the east. He leaned against the foremast with the warm semi-tropical winds blowing across his tanned face and wondered when this mad-man, this Italian, this "Admiral of the Ocean Sea"--Cristoforo Colombo-- would turn his floatilla around and head back to Spain. After all, they had been on this voyage to find a "new world" for over a month. Rodrigo glanced outward over the water. The ocean was still heaving and the wind was brisk. His eyes moved across the watery expanse of space and on to the horizon. Instantly, something gleaming white in the west appeared into view. His eyes locked in

on the object. He felt excitement start to mount.
Inside his stomach butterflies...

--MORE--*

Bradfisch explained to the author of this book that "As a general rule, articles are sent to one or more authorities for their comments—even though the author is knowledgeable in the subject." She went on to say: "If you were to study the original materials, you would find that the markings are in as many as six colors, for we are color-coded here—each of us uses our own color so that we don't have to initial every mark, and so that anyone with a question about an editing mark knows whom to ask."

Next, Bradfisch wrote this remark on a prepared form: "We encouraged her on this and I think it would work in SF [*Sea Frontiers*]." On the same form, Walton Smith, the editor, wrote this: "Needs editing down—too long to hold attention. WS." As a guide for composing the letter to follow, Bradfisch wrote: "(To be cut and edited somewhat.)" Bradfisch's letter to Rea-Salisbury read:

> We like your article "Columbus' Arawaks—The Sea and the Virtuous Savage" and want to use it in *Sea Frontiers*. It has not been scheduled as yet and will be cut and edited somewhat. Payment will be made upon publication. As you may know, we buy all rights to a manuscript. (If the author requests them, we will reassign those rights to the author after publication.)
>
> We have your biography for our authors' section of the magazine, but hope you will also send photo to be included.
>
> When an author's article appears in the magazine, we send him 10 complimentary copies of that issue; however, authors may purchase additional copies for only 50¢ each.
>
> We think your article will make interesting reading for our members and we will look forward to publishing it.

Rea-Salisbury wrote in return the following letter to Bradfisch:

> I received your letter of June 20th, and was pleased that you plan to use the Arawak article. As to the B/W author photo—I should have it to you in a month or so.
>
> I now wish to query you about a second idea. Come September, I will be in the San Blas Islands off the coast of Panama. The 300 islets sit in the

---

*Courtesy, *Sea Frontiers*. Copyright © The International Oceanographic Foundation, Miami, Florida.

back-waters of the Caribbean—a sea that seldom drops below 200 feet with no appreciable ocean current. These conditions with the assistance of the hot tropical sun create an evaporation pool leaving behind water that is noticeably more saline in content. This salinity, coupled with an abundance of nutrients washed into the island area by many jungle rivers and streams from the mainland of Panama and Colombia, supports a hugh plankton population. It is believed that these enriched waters feed an extensive coral growth and a large population of marine invertebrates—particularly the bristleworms, featherduster worms, plus dozens of species of anthozoa. Black coral forests are prevalent and found in depths of 30 to 40 feet. Crustaceans such as the spotted lobster and spiny lobster are absolutely everywhere and reef fish of every type have no fear of the diver. It is virgin diving in a virgin area.

The story will deal with the area's abundance of unique sea life, as well as the Indians that make the islands their home—the Cunas—who are indigenous to Panama and date back to 1513 when Balboa crossed the Isthmus. I believe the article should provide interesting reading for *Sea Frontiers*.

Let me hear from you.

Bradfisch responded with this letter:

Thank you for your query letter of 30 June concerning an article on the San Blas Islands. Our editorial board has decided that we will pass on this one.

We appreciate your sending the photo for the authors' section of our September–October issue and are looking forward to seeing your Arawak article in print.

Thanks for thinking of us again.

The following is the edited version of the beginning of Rea-Salisbury's article:

<u>Rodrigo de Triana</u> stood in the forecastle of <u>Pinta</u> and watched Jupiter rising in the east. He leaned against the foremast ~~with the warm semi-tropical winds blowing across his tanned face~~ and wondered when this mad man, this Italian, Cristoforo Colombo, would turn his flotilla around and head back to Spain. After all, they had been on this western voyage ~~to find a "new world"~~ for over a month.

¶ Rodrigo glanced outward over the water. The ocean was still heaving, and the warm semitropical wind was brisk. His eyes moved across the watery expanse of space and on to the horizon. Instantly, something gleaming white in the west appeared into view. His eyes locked in on the object. He felt excitement start to mount. ~~Inside his stomach butterflies~~

The following letter accompanied it to Rea-Salisbury:

> Enclosed is a xerox of the edited version of your manuscript on the Arawaks (Lucayans) of San Salvador. We have edited it some to bring it more into our style and cut parts of it to make it tighter and thereby focus on the marine aspects. Please read it over to make sure you agree with the changes. If you have any suggestions, please let us know. We want to make sure that it meets with your approval.
>
> We do have several questions. The Arawaks on San Salvador called themselves Lucayans and we have tried to focus on them. There are some places where we weren't sure if this could be done and still be accurate, however. We have marked the questioned areas on the manuscript.
>
> We also are puzzled about the canoes on page 3. If they were made of log—especially the 75-foot one mentioned—we wondered from what tree? Do any grow that large in the Bahamas? Or did Columbus see the canoes in the Bahamas? Were the Indians he saw Lucayans?
>
> Also see the question about the fishing methods and the reef fishes on the bottom of page 3. Something should be said that clarifies this.
>
> It is an interesting article and we are sure our readers will enjoy it. We hope to use it in the September–October issue (Columbus Day) along with Mr. Leicester's. This issue is now being typeset, so we would appreciate hearing from you within the next day or two. If you wish, you may mark directly on the manuscript, or—better still—call me collect. Hope to hear from you very soon.

Following a long telephone conversation, Rea-Salisbury responded with the following letter:

> It was a pleasure working with you over the phone today, and I do hope all your questions were answered.
>
> If I can assist you in any manner please do not hesitate to contact me again.

Editor-Writer Disagreements

A young man who regularly writes for a magazine on sailing finally became incensed after the editors had made many small changes in his articles and published them without consulting him. He sent a long letter to the editor-in-chief, complaining:

> The manuscript of "Instructive Mistakes" begins: "Experience," said Oscar Wilde, "is the name everyone gives to their mistakes." The printed article begins: "Experience," said Oscar Wilde, ". . . is merely the name men give to their mistakes."
>
> First, how can a professional editor possibly change a direct quotation taken from the works of an author as famous as Oscar Wilde? The quotation is taken from Wilde's *Lady Windermere's Fan*, Act III. Second, the published quotation is punctuated incorrectly. Ellipses are correct only if some part of the quotation has been left out; Wilde's complete sentence is in my manuscript. Third, the meaning has been subtly changed; and fourth, the new quote is flatter than Wilde's original.
>
> For a second example, in my June article on the Class Racing Committee, the manuscript paragraph on Bill Winters began: "Bill Winters, gold medal crew for John Benson at the Olympics last summer, will be . . ." Someone changed that sentence to: "Bill Winters gold medal Soling crew for John Benson in the Olympics last summer and in FDs in 1976, will be . . ." The structure of that sentence isn't parallel and is therefore confusing. The most obvious interpretation of the sentence is that Benson also won a gold medal in 1976, which is not correct.

This letter illustrates a fairly typical problem in writer-editor relations. After citing these changes, the writer mentioned another that disturbed him, then added: "I won't bother you with further examples of this sort, but there have been about half a dozen similar changes that alter the thrust of what I am trying to say." Many writers send letters reciting in paralyzing detail how their works have been "butchered." At least a few fail to add, as this writer did, "I'm not saying that my writing doesn't need any editing." Many *do* doubt that their writing needs editing.

This particular author had reason to complain: his arguments are valid. And he is also correct about another change in the article entitled "Instructive Mistakes." The original sentence read, "But if you will make the right kind of mistakes, and lots of them, you will gain valuable experience which will sharpen your racing skills." An editor had changed it to: "But if you make the 'right' kind of mistakes, you will gain valuable experience which will sharpen your racing skills." The quotation marks around "right" surely seemed to some readers pretentious; it is condescending to point out to them that "right" should not be defined in its usual sense.

The editor's worst error was failing to clear these changes with the writer before publication. The American Society of Journalists and Authors states:

> Editors may correct or delete copy for purposes of style, grammar, conciseness, or arrangement, but may not change the intent or sense without the writer's permission.

Defending the Editor

All editing, bad as it can be at times, is based on certain practices, some laudable, others indefensible.

First, consider the Oscar Wilde quotation. The writer was correct in arguing that the exact quotation should have been left as he had written it, but the editor who made the change had followed a laudable practice: checking on the writer to make certain that the quotation is accurate. Unfortunately, like many other writers, Wilde often used an adage in one form in one piece of writing and in a slightly different form in another. The writer quoted from one of Wilde's works; the editor quoted from another. Praise to the editor for taking the trouble to check—damnation to him for checking the wrong source!

Next, the editor added information to the sentence about Bill Winters. While this is sometimes a good practice (depending on the length of the sentence and the amount of information it already includes), it was wrong in this instance for the reasons noted in the writer's letter.

Third, the editor was trying to clarify meaning when he put quotation marks around "right"—trying to make certain that readers would not misunderstand or be confused. Possibly the editor was correct; surely no reader could misunderstand "right" in quotation marks. However, in this case the writer was again correct; the condescending tone in those quotation marks made clarity for every reader too expensive.

As for the editor's failure to check changes with the writer, many editors argue that they seldom have time to check small corrections with writers who live some distance away—especially because so many writers miss deadlines. Besides, some editors feel that most writers are far too possessive about every word they wrote, every bit of punctuation, and become defensive about *any* change. Telling them about minor changes often leads to endless arguments over small incidents. This time, however, the writer was indeed correct once again; he was not unreasonable about most changes that the editor made.

Article Rejections

Both to demonstrate that writers are not always right and to show other functions of magazine editors, let us examine an instance in which an editor encouraged a talented young free-lancer, Michael Pollock, to write an article. Pollock had sent the editor a query, a short article proposal submitted to discern whether or not a subject that a writer wants to undertake might fit an editor's needs; it is a common and useful practice. Queries save time for both writer and editor. If the writer's queries in a subject fail to interest any editor, the writer can drop the project without wasting further work. An editor who is flooded with manuscripts can decide quickly from a well-written query whether or not the subject might be worthwhile. That is the theory; sometimes it backfires.

In this example, although the editor did not promise to buy and publish the article (editors are usually careful not to make such promises), he replied that he would like to consider it. Pollock did his research and wrote the article carefully—no doubt counting the cash in his imagination while he worked—and mailed it. The editor rejected it.

There are scores of reasons to respond positively to a query and then to reject the article. This time, the editor was attracted by the query, which began:

> A young woman is reading from a hand-scrawled paragraph to others sitting around a table:
> "I'm walking on a beach and I see the wreckage of a car or something . . . twisted metal and a mangled body inside. Then I see two other people standing by the wreck, and they're laughing at the body."
> The woman is a participant in a Jungian dream workshop. . . .

The letter went on to provide a brief description of the workshop, which is led by a social worker who lives in the city where the magazine is published. The writer made it clear that the workshop leader was not a psychologist or psychiatrist—and that some of the 500 area residents who had taken the course were not convinced that it works. The writer pointed out that many participants have gone on to more advanced workshops and into psychiatric treatment. The writer also suggested that some of the pictures drawn by workshop participants to describe their dreams might be published with the article.

So far, it sounds interesting. But the article the editor received began:

> "I've spent more than half a century investigating natural symbols, and I've concluded that dreams are not stupid and meaningless. On the contrary, they provide the most interesting information for those who take the trouble to understand their symbols."

These are the words of Swiss psychologist Carl G. Jung. When he died in 1961, he bequeathed to the world a method of delving into the unconscious mind through dream analysis.

But until a few years ago, few nonprofessionals cared. Now things have changed, perhaps for the same reasons which fostered movements such as . . .

The contrast between the beginning of the query and the beginning of the article suggests one reason for the rejection: The query is more readable than the article. Although magazine articles can begin at a more leisurely pace than newspaper features, those written for city magazines should not begin with a general statement that only gradually comes to the point or the local angle.

The lead could have been changed, but the writer could not change another aspect of the story that he had mentioned in the query but that seemed like a real problematic area: Some participants had considered the dream-analysis workshop a failure. If the social worker were a recognized authority, the article might have been worth publishing nonetheless; he was, however, an amateur.

Often editors think and hope that a writer *may* be able to revise an article successfully. But what if the revision does not work? If the editor promises to pay the writer a "kill fee"—a guaranteed sum whether the article is eventually used or not—it may strain the editorial budget. If he does not promise to pay anything, how much additional work can he ask the writer to do on speculation? In either instance, continuing to work with a writer who may not satisfactorily complete an article will eat into the time that the editor might devote to more promising articles. *All editors complain that hours and days are too short for everything they have to do, and wasting time can only result in strained relations.*

Critiquing Articles

In some cases, an editor considering a manuscript will offer a critique. The balance between harsh and delicate criticism is, of course, an important one.

Many magazines are produced by one person. On some, the copy editor is the *only* editor—or vice versa. One editor of a fraternity magazine wrote most of the issues herself, including a special issue published the following spring. She frequently asked for contributions from fraternity members, and her reflections on working with amateur writers is instructive:

This being the first time that I had done this, I was not explicit enough in my directions about what to write—people do want tight guidelines and need them or else you end up with an article that may have 20 different subjects, a lot of beginnings and no ends, i.e., the result is a lot of rambling thoughts. . . .

All of the people were amateur writers, flattered beyond belief that they were asked to write an article. For this reason, I had to be careful with my editing, since most of them had worked for months on their articles and thought they were perfect. When they handed in their pieces, they did so with 101 excuses for why they were so poor, knowing full well that I had better think that they were masterpieces. For the most part, I ran them as they were, with minor construction and grammatical changes. I was careful not to change the tone of each, since that was "the sign of the author." Of course, after the magazine came out, they all wanted to know the reactions to their articles.*

On most other publications, the editor is more caustic. The following is from the late John Fischer, a veteran editor, commenting on the editor's necessary ruthlessness:

Happy is he who is born cruel, for if not he will have to school himself in cruelty. Without it, he is unfit for his job; because the kindly editor soon finds his columns filled with junk.

"I know too many people," Harold Ross once remarked—and every editor knows just what he meant. Hardly ever does an editor go to a dinner party without acquiring a manuscript, thrust into his hands by some sweet old lady who was always sure she could write—"I feel it *here*!"—if only someone would give her a little encouragement. It happens on the street, too. A London cab driver once produced 400 pages of a novel from under his seat the moment I asked him to drive me to the office of a well-known publisher. And just last summer I came away from a college commencement with three manuscripts, slipped to me by a pretty undergraduate, a professor, and a parent. All are nice people, and only a brute could refuse to publish their work.

In addition to such windfalls, a typical magazine office will get through the mail at least 20,000 manuscripts a year. It can publish perhaps one percent of them. . . .

But in the end, at least 19,800 of the year's inflow will have to be rejected heartlessly, regardless of broken friendships, crushed ambitions, and the tears of charming poetesses just out of Vassar. This is the hardest lesson of all, and one I have not yet mastered. I still waste far too much time salving bruised egos and writing what I hope are comforting notes explaining why this piece won't quite do. But I'm learning: I get meaner every day.**

*Courtesy, Patricia Newport.
**Courtesy, Elizabeth Fisher.

To fill the next issue editors must first have ideas for articles (or choose among those submitted by free-lancers and staff writers). They then assign articles to writers who can do the research and write at least competently, although they always hope the articles will be written brilliantly. When an article is finally in hand, the editor must police it while keeping in mind the fragile sensibilities of the writer who invested more time, energy, and talent in it than even the best newspaper or broadcast journalist invests in day-to-day reporting. Magazine writers put so much of themselves into their prose, but editors must remain firm, and the tension can lead to strained relationships.

An Editor-Writer Reversal

To reverse the editor-writer relationship, consider the situation at *Fortune* magazine. Some of the editors at *Fortune*, like many other editors, prefer to be staff writers, even though they make less money, because most staff writers must turn in only four or five articles a year. During the rest of the time, they can free-lance. One basic problem emerges: staff writers must face the story editor after they submit their articles. Several years ago, the managing editor of *Fortune* decided to step down to become a staff writer. Although he was an excellent writer, *he had to rewrite his own articles.* As with most writers—good or bad—the succeeding drafts were better than the originals he had submitted.

For 20 years, Ken Purdy was an editor and a writer. He worked as a reporter for three newspapers and an editor of one; an associate editor of *Look* magazine and two other magazines; managing editor of one magazine; an editorial consultant to two magazines; and as an editor-in-chief of four magazines. During these years, he was also a free-lancer who sold short stories and articles to 20-odd magazines, and he published two books. Because he had extensive experience as a writer and as an editor, he said the following:

> The relationship between editor and writer is, now and then, a happy one. Now and then, indeed. A warm, pleasant, long-standing relationship between an editor and a writer is a rarity. By the very nature of things, it must be. These two people, the editor and the writer, do not begin to understand each other.

Why Magazines Need Editors

Editors best serve their writers when they represent the reader, so the best editors try to ask questions the readers might ask: Why is this point made at the beginning of this paragraph when it might better round off the paragraph by ending with it? Why isn't it explained where Taiwan is? Why is all this garble included about black English when most readers—including the blacks—don't understand what it's about? When all this historical stuff is put together, it becomes so tedious that the reader will stop reading; why not change it by breaking it *here*, then end with the rest of the historical stuff, plus a better ending?

Editors must have an engineer's eye for the structure of an article. They will often have to read an article many times to understand what the writer is attempting to write. When an editor sees what a writer is trying for, the editor should explain to the writer how to reassemble the article. In some cases, the editor should actually write—not try to explain in words—how to reassemble the article.

Henry R. Grunwald, the editor-in-chief of Time, Inc., said in a speech in 1981:

> In a sense, I began my editing career at *Time* many years ago when I was an office boy. I used to read copy while delivering it, and from there it was only a step to try to improve it. I took to rewriting cover stories to show my elders and betters how I thought it should be done. This practice of mine was not uniformly popular. Once, according to *Time* legend, I was standing in a writer's office peering over his shoulder as he sat at his typewriter. I was somewhat startled to find that the words he was typing were as follows: "Kid, if you don't cut this out, I'll break every bone in your body." It is said, though I personally don't remember it, that I left the office in a hurry but muttering as I walked out: "Cliché."
>
> I was a *Time* writer for many years before I was made an editor, and for a long time after that I wasn't sure that I didn't prefer writing. But I distinctly remember the moment when I might have settled down contentedly to being an editor. I happened to be sick at the time. I was at home and had some copy sent to me from the office. I recall reading one short piece that was so perfect that I jumped out of bed and started walking around the room in high excitement. Maybe it was my temperature. But I felt happy—as happy as if I had written it myself.*

The moral of Grunwald's story is that editors must be self-effacing. They must also remember this: Editors exist to help journalists.

*Courtesy, Henry Grunwald.

Many writers are convinced that copy editors exist only to make the writer's life difficult and his or her prose unreadable. Yet the perceptive editor will grasp the essence of an article and improve it. One news magazine editor encountered this line in an article: "Winston Churchill, half British, half American . . ." He demonstrated his understanding of the enigma of Churchill with a few strokes of his pencil, so that the line read, "Winston Churchill, wholly British, half American . . ."

It is also true that the copy editor, whose value rests in the fresh eye given to an article, is crippled when he or she attacks flabby writing. Cutting heavily into several ballooning sentences almost invariably halts the flow of the writing and makes sentences too choppy or too decisive. The editor may recognize the failing, but will simply be powerless to do much about it. After all, the *writer* has all the information; the *editor* (who in this circumstance has become a rewrite person) seldom knows enough about the subject to add the fact-filled clauses and phrases that make writing rhythmic. Correcting this failing usually requires the editor and writer to work together.

Exercises

1. Create a list of six possible stories in your community that might capture a national audience and therefore be suitable for publication in a general-interest magazine. Write one or two sentences of description for each story; then match it with a magazine that publishes the same type of article. *Writer's Market* may help you select suitable publications.

2. Write sample queries of three of the ideas you created for Exercise 1. They should take the form of business letters addressed to the editors of each of the magazines you thought suitable for your articles. Present your ideas in a lively, readable fashion, and indicate the lengths of the proposed articles. Make suggestions for possible illustrations, if warranted. Naturally, the queries should be neatly typed, succinct, and free of grammatical errors.

3. Now don the other hat: Select *at random* a query written by a classmate and assume you are the magazine editor to whom the query has been addressed. After carefully weighing the publication's purpose against the writer's proposal, construct a thoughtful response. Write a formal business letter of about 200 words explaining why the proposal is, or is not, acceptable. Include suggestions for improvement.

4. Find an "offbeat" publication—a house organ or trade magazine, for example—and read it carefully, looking for the *worst* article. Ignoring grammatical and spelling errors, critique the article on the basis of structure. Ask yourself these questions: Is the article focused? Does it hang together? Does it flow? Is it labored, dull, or hackneyed? Are persons properly identified? Count the number of words. Is the piece too long, making it drag, or too short, lacking full development? What about illustrations? Did they enhance the piece, or detract from it because of poor quality? (If there were no illustrations, indicate whether or not there should have been any.) Write a 500-word summary of your critique, including specific examples of problems cited, and attach it to a copy of the proposed article.

5. Because this chapter describes situations involving the writer vs. the editor, discuss in writing the differences between the writer's goals and the editor's goals. Remember, all writers are writing for themselves. On the other hand, the editors must keep in mind that they are not just working for themselves; the magazine must be first in their minds.

6. Read the following piece. Then write a 500-word critique addressing the following:

- In general, is the piece any good? Why or why not? How could it be improved? Who might read this article? What kind of publication would buy it?
- Is the writer good? If you were an editor, how much would you be willing to pay the author for his or her effort? Make a guess about how long it took to write the piece.
- Regarding the mechanics of the piece, is it well constructed? Why or why not? What about the length? Is it focused?
- Assuming that no photos have been taken for the piece, do you feel there is a need for some? (Remember, photos will markedly increase the price the publication will pay to purchase the piece.) If photos are needed, make a list of suggested shots, but *be specific*. If photos are used, can the length be cut? Where would you make the cuts?

HOW TO TALK TO AN EDITOR

During the early years of *The New Yorker,* Editor Harold Ross heard of the "editorial tea" that was a regular ceremony of the British magazine *Punch*. As Ross understood it, the editors of *Punch* would invite contributors to the weekly tea and allow those who had had one article accepted to stay for a short period, those who could boast two or three acceptances to stay slightly longer, and so on.

As the American magazine editor who believed more strongly than any other in friendly, idea-stimulating contacts between free-lance writers and editors, Ross was intrigued by the *Punch* ritual and the purpose it served. He decided something like it would help *The New Yorker.*

To provide a warm, Prohibition-period atmosphere for contributors, Harold Ross established the only private speakeasy under magazine sponsorship in the United States.

"*The New Yorker* speak" was only moderately successful as a literary stimulus, but it was shut down for another reason. The way the story goes, an editor unlocked the door early one morning and found two friends of the "conference" of the night before—a man and a woman—sound asleep together.

At any rate, free-lancer–editor talks, despite their informality, have become highly institutionalized. The professional article writer who lives in the hinterlands and doesn't travel to New York on "idea trips" once a year is becoming a rarity. The New York–based writer who doesn't talk to editors regularly is, like James Thurber's "Unicorn in the Garden," a mythical beast.

The result of this, for beginners, is despair. Most neophytes see a vast conspiracy of favoritism and friendship among established writers and editors shutting out those who have not arrived. One beginner who had knocked unsuccessfully on editorial doors summed it up: "I couldn't get a single assignment. It's a closed corporation." Writers *prefer* to think of their work in terms of the heaven-sent muse and divine inspiration and God-given talent, but the successful article writer is also a salesman.

Two Salesmen

For example, a writer who lived, not in New York City, but in Portland, Oregon, learned in a short time that in the magazine world there is nothing so important as a good idea for an article. Editors welcomed his articles, but not because he was a richly talented writer. More often than not, his phrases were somewhat matter-of-fact, and his sentences did not sing. The editors often had to rework long sections of his articles (and sometimes the articles themselves) to put them in shape for publication. But the writer had interesting ideas for articles—such as "They Never Go Back to Pocatello" and "The Decay of the State Legislature"—and techniques for developing them, and he supported both with careful and wide-ranging research.

The late Frank J. Taylor—who was lauded by *Time* magazine as "The Most Successful Free-lancer"—said that his once-a-year trips to New York from California were absolutely necessary. He learned too much on these "apple-peddling expeditions" to forego them. Taylor acquired insights into what the magazine may want for months ahead. When he had lunch with three editors of a single magazine, an idea struck a spark with one even though it did not interest the others.

Here is what Taylor said to me about his traveling campaigns: "Before taking off on an expedition, I always sifted through my ideas and jotted down enough facts to talk about each story intelligently. If I didn't have enough facts to talk up the story, I got on the phone or did some in-person interviewing to case the story idea. I also checked *Reader's Guide to Periodical Literature* to make certain that the magazine had not recently run an article that I was proposing.

"My pocket notebook intrigued my editors," Taylor continued. "Before we had downed the first cocktail at lunch, one of them would say, 'Get out your little notebook, and let's see what's in it.' Some topics would win a go-ahead right away. The editor might want more information on others. That was my cue to say, 'How would you like to have me case the idea and send you a report?' The answer usually was, 'Okay, we'll protect you on the story until you can give us an outline.' Often, editors offered to pay my expenses while I was casing a story, and sometimes they would pay for my work even if they eventually decided against giving me a go-ahead.

"As soon as I return from these expeditions, I write to the editors to thank them for their time and to outline the story ideas they want me to turn into manuscripts and those I am to case. This firms up the assignments and guards against misunderstandings,'' Taylor concluded.

Like Taylor, the great majority of article writers recognize that they have merchandise for sale, so they set about selling it. Most of them do at least part of their merchandising through correspondence—and they give as much attention to query letters as any hardwareman devotes to direct mail promotion.

More often, however, the writers who can manage it are making a ritual of presenting their ideas face-to-face. *Time* magazine, surveying free-lancers, learned that even the most successful writers sell only one of five ideas they suggest, which indicates that the large, cozy world of favoritism and friendship conjured by the beginner on the outside is imaginary. One successful free-lancer has told of the time he suggested 10 ideas in a row to an editor and received a firm "No" in every case.

But the beginner continues to believe that if he or she could only get in to see an editor—not an assistant, one of the top editors—the beginner would live happily ever after on large checks.

Rules of Thumb

Here's an unhappy rule of thumb for the rank beginner who's planning that first trip to New York hoping to come back with first-level assignments: *Don't go.*

You'll not only be wasting an editor's time, if you're lucky enough to see an editor, you'd have a better time of it yourself atop the Empire State Building. After all, the writer who has never published is not necessarily a writer at all from the magazine editor's point of view. The editor can't even know whether the neophyte can master a simple, declarative sentence. The editor would have a better view of the beginner's style and ability from a letter.

The *general* rule holds: Outsiders should have something to show their abilities besides an aptitude for building themselves up. Saying you can write won't get you an audience with the article editor, who's much too busy talking to writers who have proved themselves.

A *larger* group of relative beginners—writers who have sold a few pieces to national publications—also think that a trip to New York might be the "open sesame" to full-time careers. It could happen, but the process isn't cut-and-dried.

The most important single step for the relative beginner to take before he sets up appointments, makes the trip, and proposes ideas is: Know your magazine.

It may be that *Writer's Digest* has printed that phrase more often than any other, but I suggest something more than the words usually mean. It's necessary for a writer who is to talk to the editor of a magazine to learn the publication in depth, to develop an understanding of the magazine's subtleties.

The late Wilson Hicks, the executive editor of *Life*, considered this phase the most important in developing ideas for magazines.

Hicks suggested: "Don't just read a few issues of a magazine to determine exactly what has been published, then suggest similar pieces. You should read a magazine to discover its approach, its 'formula,' its policy.

"The editor doesn't want what he has *had*. Instead, he will look with more favor upon the writer who tries to understand the background of the publication's larger ideas, its attitude toward people, public questions, and events. Anyone who hopes to be a successful free-lancer should read a magazine regularly to see what its editors are trying to do."

And it won't do to judge from a general reading of a magazine "what its editors are trying to do." The editor may not even be able to say in a few sentences what the mission of the magazine is, but the editor knows. Most important: Any competent editor can tell from your suggestions whether you really know the magazine.

As for building yourself up beyond your record as a free-lancer: Don't try it. Hicks, who dealt with some of the leading American writers but placed a great deal of stress on giving newcomers a chance, says emphatically: "Don't think you can fool an editor about your experience and ability. The editor becomes very adept at uncovering phonies, even on the phone."

Seven Suggestions

Here are some tips:

1. Write to an editor, and receive an answer from him or her, before making the trip.
2. Say in your letter when you will be in New York, but don't try to set a specific day or a specific hour. Some days are reserved for staff conferences, etc., and most magazines set up specific hours for seeing contributors.
3. Let the editor, in his or her reply, suggest a luncheon appointment, if there is to be one. The lunch hour in New York is part of the business day.
4. Don't write to *the* editor unless the staff is small. It's better to write to the managing editor, best to write to one of the article editors. On nearly all magazines, editorial positions are listed on the masthead.
5. Mention, explicitly, what you've written. Don't say "I've done a lot of writing for national magazines." Instead: "I had a piece in the March *Esquire* and another in the August *Ms*." Don't make a production of listing your publications—the editor talks every day to people who have been publishing for years—but don't slight them. The

fact that you were managing editor of your college paper isn't a recommendation (unless you're proposing an article on college publications).
6. Don't plan a trip if you have only one idea. The changes are good that you'll mention it, the editor will say, "We've got something like that coming out next month," and that will be all.
7. Never collar editors in a hotel lobby or pull them aside at a party to suggest ideas. The unknowns who force themselves on an editor could gain from their brashness, but they'll probably lose.

This list is so heavy with "don'ts" that I hasten to stress the positive points:
1. Be informed about your subjects.
2. Be prepared to furnish an angle, or theme, for each of the articles you suggest.
3. Be natural.

The first point simply means that you need more than a vague idea for an article; you should also be able to supply a great many subsidiary facts to support your idea.

The second point suggests that an idea for an article is not enough, that the piece must be approached from a particular point of view. One editor makes writers conscious of this need by saying, "What's the theme?" It doesn't matter whether you consider theme and idea the same; the important matter is that you'd better have both.

I've included naturalness because so many editors have mentioned that they detest talking to a writer who puts up a front. "Some of them come in here and try to make me believe, usually by over-using magazine language, that they're old hands," a regional editor told me. "They talk about 'the book' and 'running it through the typewriter' and 'he-she stories' and 'dummy, positive blue' and a lot of other terms I never heard of and they cram them all in one sentence. I'm against them from the start. I try not to let it bother me or influence me, but it does. I don't care if they don't know what a by-line is if they'll just give me some acceptable ideas. But the thing is, they give you all this talk and think they ought to get a commission on an article—no speculation for them. I don't even want to talk to them."

Multiplying Assignments

If talking to an editor has drawn you an assignment, sometimes one article will lead to another article if you are observant enough to notice the path. Shelley Smolkin, the co-author of the third edition of a book, *Free-Lancer and Staff Writer*, published in 1981, was covering a ski race for *Women's Sports* magazine. She met a contestant in the race who she felt would be a good subject for a *Women's Sports* profile. She sold the idea to an editor and traveled to a freestyle skiing training camp in order to interview the skier. Smolkin wrote the article and then decided that a piece on freestyle training camps would be suitable for another magazine, *Sportswoman*. The editor accepted the idea, and Smolkin went to one of the country's top freestyle training camps to do some interviews. While there, she met another skier, a young girl whose coach claimed that she could already do tricks that no other woman on the freestyle circuit was able to do. Not one to miss an opportunity, Smolkin interviewed the girl, took her picture, and sold both to *Women's Sports*.

The ultimate example of how a writer can exploit a subject was described by Bruce Bliven, Jr., in an article entitled "My Table-Tennis Racket" that appeared in *The Atlantic*. Bliven talked to the articles editor of *Life* and extracted an assignment to write a story about the ping-pong champion. *Life* bought the article for $1,000 but never published it. Bliven sent the article to *Look* and was rewarded with a check for $500. *Look* ran only a one-page photo of the champion with a 200-word caption. Bliven then sold the article to *Esquire* for $400. In this case, the entire piece was printed. Several years later, he suggested another story on the ping-pong champion, who had managed to retain his title, to *Sports Illustrated*. The editor bought the article and printed it. At the time Bliven wrote *The Atlantic* story, the champion had finally retired, but the intrepid author still hoped for one more comeback.

If I've given the impression that editors are to be approached in fear and trembling, the picture has been overdrawn. There is more informality than I've been able to indicate, and talking to editors can be a stimulating experience.

To quote one professional writer: "Everything's buying and selling; all the rest is scenery."

Chapter 3

Magazine Copy Editing

What can magazine copy editors do to stay on good terms with the writer of a first-draft article that needs monumental work? One editor's relationship with a friend is illustrated by this letter to the author-friend, who had written about college athletes:

> There are three main problems with the piece as it stands: (1) it isn't focused enough; (2) it is top-heavy with general quotations instead of specific cases; and (3) it is a bit too involuted, and hence a little dull.
>
> 1. If I read you right, your thesis is as follows: College athletes have their existence on campus defined for them as *athlete* and nothing else. For the man who *wants* to be an athlete and nothing else, that's fine; but for the man who considers himself a student or a person as well, it leads to tensions and frustrations. . . .
>
> This is essentially a simple enough thesis. It can be expressed in a syllogism pretty easily: (a) athletes are more and more like other students; (b) athletes are under great pressure to keep to themselves; (c) therefore, athletes are increasingly unhappy with their lot. Despite the fact that this is clearly a thesis article, you have written it more like a rambling exploration of the college athlete—it is never clear to the reader if you know what you are trying to prove. . . .
>
> 2. Your conclusions about college athletes are neither difficult to understand nor difficult to accept. There is little reason, therefore, for extensive quotations reexplaining and reasserting the same points. Some of your paragraphs seem to have the following structure: "A is true. X says A is true. Y says A is true. Therefore, A is true." This is more or less justifiable to the extent that A is a complicated and arguable statement. X, Y, and Z are certified experts, and what they say is unusually well expressed. Often, however, A is a simple, well-accepted proposition; X, Y, and Z are unknowns; and their prose is unimpressively identical with each other and with your own. Such paragraphs become incredibly tedious.
>
> What you need, I think, are fewer quotations and more examples—specific anecdotes, in your words or the words of athletes who experienced them. Especially desirable would be one *long* anecdote which exemplifies as much of your hypothesis as possible.
>
> 3. I think the problem of too complex, involuted, academic, and dull a style will be very much minimized when the structure is clearer and some of the quotes have been replaced with anecdotes. Still, you should try to change it a bit yourself. What you want is a bit less wordiness, and a little more colorful vocabulary, a few less weasel words and explanatory clauses, and a bit simpler sentence structure.

Critiques are seldom written in such detail (the actual letter covered seven pages), unless the editor likes the article and expects his or her magazine to publish a revision. In this particular case, the writer went back to work, revised his article almost wholly, and the revision was purchased.

Many writers have complained bitterly that, given detailed directions, they could bring their first drafts up to the publishable level. This may be true in a few cases. More often, though, the editor decides quite accurately that, although the subject may be timely and provocative and all the information may be in hand, *this writer* is probably incapable of fashioning an acceptable piece. Without thinking in such terms, the editor is actually making a distinction between writing as craft and writing as art. In effect, he or she is saying: "I could devote several hours to typing a critique that would suggest how this writer can use anecdote, example, illustration—all techniques of appealing prose—and improve this article markedly. And the writer could probably follow my directions. But even though he'd get the *craft* right, something would be missing. He wouldn't have the flair and style of the artist."

Newspaper vs. Magazine Copy Editing

The similarities in newspaper and magazine copy editing are emphasized by the fact that one of the greatest American magazines, *The New Yorker*, often hires newspaper copy editors. As newspapers publish longer stories, the similarities become more obvious. But the trouble with a magazine hiring newspaper copy editors is that the editors will work much faster and much more sketchily than they need to do on a magazine. For example, if the editors had worked on small to medium-sized dailies, they would be accustomed to editing 20 or more stories a day. Because magazines ordinarily cover a subject much more fully than most newspapers can, the magazine copy editor must emphasize more strongly the devices for organizing a piece of writing, especially transitions. And because a magazine is published less frequently than a daily newspaper, the editor has more time to work over copy, shape it, and refine it.

Becoming a Magazine Copy Editor

If a prospective editor is not a good writer, he or she can still be a good editor. In fact, very few good writers are also good editors.

First of all, editors must know the English language well and also be interested in it. Being finicky about English grammar and usage is the first step—but *only* a step. Jacques Barzun, a former provost of Columbia University, commented on magazine copy editors this way:

> The effort to be safe first misdirects attention, then corrupts judgment. This is illustrated by the verifying which goes on in editorial and publishing offices. Trivialities are set right and large errors of logic and sense pass by unseen. This is deplorable even in journalism; at every higher stage of intellect this bias spoils more and more important elements. As Judge Cardoza observed many years ago, "There is an accuracy that defeats itself by the overemphasis of details."

Prospective editors should study a wide range of information in almost every field so that, if their memories are sharp, they can continue to edit stories of many kinds over many years.

Editors must learn to recheck every bit of copy. For example, consider what happened to John Ciardi, the poetry editor of *Saturday Review*. He was cabled in London to write a summary of the career of Edna St. Vincent Millay:

> The cable reached me late on Friday afternoon and copy had to be off by air mail on Monday morning. I began to make notes that Friday night, but I had few books with me and none of Miss Millay's poetry. My head was still full of her lines, however, and I quoted from memory as I went. I spent most of Saturday prowling London bookstores for copies of her books in which I might check my quotations and re-read her poems, but though I tried for eight full hours, I could not turn up a single copy.
>
> I turned to my desk to scribble and revise (still quoting from memory), scribbled and revised again all Sunday morning and afternoon, and finally two-fingered the piece through the typewriter on Sunday night. Monday morning I was at the American Embassy Library when the doors opened. There I found two volumes of the poems and managed to check three or four of my quotations. And then time was up. I added a note to the editor explaining the state of the quotations and underlined the need to check all but the three or four I had marked with an asterisk.
>
> We were in Paris when the article appeared. I did not see it nor did I know the quotations had not been checked.*

Later he learned that his errors had been printed and that angry letters had come to the magazine. When articles are published containing errors that could have and should have been checked, the reputation of the magazine suffers. Such sloppiness is intolerable.

---

*Courtesy, John Ciardi.

Functions of a Copy Editor

The first function is correctness. Editors must be fanatics about the use of English. Here is a simplified form of 17 punctuation marks.

Punctuation Marks	Signals to the Reader
Period .	Stop at a period.
Exclamation point !	Stop in astonishment or surprise at an exclamation mark.
Question mark ?	Stop because the writer is asking a question.
Comma ,	Pause at a comma.
Brackets [ ]	Correct, add, delete, or modify information. Brackets are also used to place parenthetical elements already found within parentheses.
Apostrophe '	Part of a contracted word (such as "won't") is left out. An apostrophe is also used to form some plurals and to show possession.
Ellipsis . . .	Ellipsis (three spaced periods) indicate an omitted part of a quotation.
Ellipsis (2)	Ellipsis (three spaced periods) indicate an omitted part of a quotation. When four periods come at the end of a sentence, the first period indicates the conclusion of the sentence and the following three periods indicate the omission.
Semicolon ;	Semicolons divide two independent phrases or sentences.
Colon :	The words before a colon introduce the words that follow.
Dashes —XXX XXXX—	Dashes momentarily interrupt the sentence to insert the words between the dashes.
Dash —XXX XXX XXXXX.	Pause at a dash, then read emphasis into the following words.
Hyphen XX-XXXX	A hyphen makes two words read as though they were one.
Quotation marks "XXXXXXX"	Quotation marks indicate verbatim quotation of spoken or written language.
Parentheses (XXXXX)	Words in parentheses are usually less important than others in the sentence.
Quotation marks, commas, and periods ," and ."	Commas and periods should fall within quotation marks.
Quotation marks, semicolons, and colons "; and ":	Semicolons and colons should *not* fall within quotation marks.

Readers intuitively understand the meanings of most punctuation marks. But copy editors need to understand precisely when and why to use a period, an exclamation point, a question mark, or any other mark of punctuation.

Editors must also use accurate spelling. If you are even a marginal speller, study the following rules:

1. Remember this old jingle:

   Write *i* before *e*
   Except after *c*
   Or when sounded like *a*
   As in neighbor or weigh.

i before *e*	except after *c*	or when sounded as *a*
achieve	ceiling	freight
believe	deceive	obeisance
piece	perceive	reign
yield	receive	vein

   Some exceptions:
   height
   seize
   weird

2. A *prefix* is one or more letters that can be attached before a word to make a new word.

   a. Use the hyphen with prefixes such as *great-, all-, pro-, self-,* and *ex-:*

      Her *great-uncle* was here yesterday.

      That kind of term is an *all-purpose* word.

      I was *pro-British* from the beginning.

      Frank is becoming a *self-made* man.

      He's an *ex-mayor* now.

   b. To avoid ambiguity and awkward phrases, use hyphens to make certain that the reader won't confuse words:

      Hunting is good recreation, but it doesn't compare to the re-creation of a room.

      I'll have to resort to buying a new carburetor instead of re-sorting all the parts.

c. Retain all the letters of a word when the last letter of a prefix is the same as the first letter in the word:

mis plus *spell* = misspell

un plus *noticeable* = unnoticeable

3. A *suffix* is one or more syllables attached to the end of a word that makes a new word.
    a. Usually, delete the final e before a suffix beginning with a vowel:

    come   coming

    ride   riding

    value   valuable

    locate   location

    Most exceptions are made when it's necessary to keep c or g soft before *a* or *o*:

    notice plus *able* = noticeable

    peace plus *able* = peaceable

    Also:

    dyeing (to prevent confusion with dying)

    practicable (c sounds like k)

    b. Usually, retain the final e when the suffix begins with a consonant:

    entire plus *ly* = entirely

    hate plus *ful* = hateful

    Some exceptions:

    due plus *ly* = duly

    judge plus *ment* = judgment

4. When the suffix is added, the final y is usually changed to *i*:

    happy plus *ness* = happiness

    forty plus *eth* = fortieth

funny plus *er* = funnier

rectify plus *er* = rectifier

5. a. Add *s* to the singular to form the plurals of most nouns:

   chair plus *s* = chairs

   lock plus *s* = locks

   shovelful plus *s* = shovelfuls

   set plus *s* = sets

   b. To form the plurals of most singular nouns ending in *s, ch, sh,* or *x,* add *es*:

   boss plus *es* = bosses

   box plus *es* = boxes

   bush plus *es* = bushes

   porch plus *es* = porches

   Exception: monarchs

   c. To form the plurals of words ending in *y* preceded by a consonant, add *es* after changing the *y* to *i*:

   country plus *es* = countries

   theory plus *es* = theories

   cry plus *es* = cries

6. a. Informal writing is usually characterized by using the apostrophe, which shows that one or more letters have been omitted:

   It'll be there. (It will be there.)

   We're going. (We are going.)

   They're here. (They are here.)

   I'm late. (I am late.)

   b. The apostrophe is used often in place of *not*:

He *doesn't* think. (He does not think.)

I *can't* go there. (I cannot go there.)

She *isn't* going. (She is not going.)

He *wouldn't* go. (He would not go.)

I *won't* listen. (I will not listen.)

He *hasn't* any money. (He has not any money.)

I *haven't* heard you. (I have not heard you.)

7. a. Use the apostrophe in editing the possessives of nouns. Add an apostrophe and an *s* to the plain form of a noun to produce a possessive:

    John *Jackson's* glove is here.

    A *student's* book is expensive.

    My *brother's* car isn't functioning.

    His *roommate's* coat is ragged.

   b. When editing, be sure to use either the singular or the plural. If it's plural, add only an apostrophe at the end:

    Two *years'* pay is meager.

    Four *hours'* drive is too long.

    The *Americans'* daughters are beautiful.

    Exceptions:

    The *men's* locker rooms are bare.

    The *women's* necklaces are expensive.

   c. No apostrophe should be used when you're editing the possessive forms of personal pronouns:

    His football is lost.

    Hers isn't there.

    Its owner isn't known.

    The dress is *yours*.

    The baseballs are *theirs*.

To make certain about matters of grammar, refer to Henry Fowler's *Modern English Usage*, or to a freshman English textbook such as:

Random House Handbook by Frederick Crewes (Random House),

Writing with a Purpose by James McCrimmon (Houghton Mifflin), or

The Complete Stylist and Handbook by Sheridan Baker (Harper & Row).

Style. The way each writer expresses himself or herself is his or her literary style. A copy editor must think of *style* in another sense: Conventions of writing that all writers follow on a magazine are covered in the stylebook. (A sample stylebook is printed at the end of this text as Appendix D.)

Headings. Copy editorial work on a small or medium-sized magazine entails knowing how to write headings. Some magazines imitate newspapers and write headings as though they were headlines. Most magazines, however, prefer to head their articles with titles.

Technical Excellence. Copy editors must do more than make the writing clear, concise, and readable. They must also be certain of its factual accuracy. At *Time* magazine, at least five editors work on each story, while a researcher puts a red dot above each word in the copy that is from a primary source and a black dot above each from a secondary source.

The following paragraph from James Thurber's *The Years with Ross* describes what it was like to work with Harold Ross, the longtime editor of *The New Yorker* magazine:

> Having a manuscript under Ross' scrutiny was like putting your car in the hands of a skilled mechanic, not an automotive engineer with a bachelor of science degree, but a guy who knows what makes a motor go, and sputter, and wheeze, and sometimes come to a dead stop; a man with an ear for the faintest body squeak as well as the loudest engine rattle. When you first gazed, appalled, upon an uncorrected proof of one of your articles, each margin had a thicket of queries and complaints—one writer got a hundred and forty-four on one profile. It was as though you beheld the works of your car spread all over the garage floor, and the job of getting the thing together again and making it work seemed impossible. Then you realized that Ross was trying to make your Model T or old Stutz Bearcat into a Cadillac or Rolls-Royce. He was at work with the tools of his unflagging perfectionism and, after an exchange of growls or snarls, you set to work to join him in his enterprise.

Marking Copy

Nearly all magazines, like most newspapers, use these symbols to edit copy:

Spell out or abbreviate	(77) (New Jersey) (Ga.)
Insert space	and⎮the or and⎮the
Delete word or words	six ~~new~~ freshmen
Delete letter	judg*e*ment
Close up space	maga⌒zine
Insert letter or word	bas^eball she likes^this college
Insert several words	speaking^(on writing) to the audience.
Insert comma	⌃,
Insert quotes or single quote	⌄" ⌄' ⌄'
Insert period	⊙ or ⊗
Change to lowercase	Jack Schutz, /Dean
Change to capital letter	s̲c̲hutz
Small capital letters	the university
Make italic	Gainesville Sun
Make boldface	Hi-Jinks
Transpose	univer⁀sity the ⎣slender⎮three⎦ women
Indicate new paragraph	⎣Dean Schutz said or said Schutz. ¶ "But
Hyphen	by=line
Dash	all right⌢that is
End of story	(#) or (30)
Correct your mistake	Forget ~~this~~ (stet) editing ("stet" means that you have made a mistake in editing)
Mark centering like this	]Atmosphere of Doubt[
Left justify	⎣ But the witness for the prosecution indicated that ...

62 CHAPTER 3

    Right justify $222.06
                                      3,300.15
                                      1,718.00
                                      4,650.50

    Symbol for continuing   You should run it in, ~~even if you don't like it~~ with a connecting line.

Preparing Copy   Writers should follow some simple instructions, noted in Figure 3-1, before submitting copy to an editor.

Marking All-cap Articles   On some magazines, you must learn to mark the articles that are in all-capital letters. The convention is that you must mark it as though it were in small letters. Every word that is capitalized is marked, and all other capitals will be set lowercase. Observe the following all-capital letters of a paragraph that are marked:

JULIAN HARVEY WAS TELLING THE COAST GUARD IN MIAMI OF A FATAL ACCIDENT ABOARD HIS KETCH WHEN WORD ARRIVED THAT 11-YEAR-OLD TERRY JO DUPPERAULT HAD BEEN FOUND ALIVE IN THE CARIBBEAN AFTER 82 HOURS ADRIFT ON A RAFT. HARVEY, WHO HAD TOLD ~~MOST OF~~ (stet) THE INVESTIGATORS THAT ALL THOSE, INCLUDING HIS WIFE, ABOARD HIS 60-FOOT KETCH BLUEBELL--ON THE FIFTH DAY OF A SEVEN-DAY CRUISE--HAD DIED AFTER A FIERCE SQUALL AND

Your name

Your address

                Title of Article

                Your By-line

    The title is typed about one-fifth down the page to leave room at the top for the editor's instructions to the printer. The manuscript should be double-spaced to facilitate easy reading and to leave room for editing marks between lines.

    The second and all succeeding pages should carry the writer's name in the upper left corner; the page numbers should be at the center or right corner. All pages after the first should start in the conventional place, a few spaces down from the top, and a margin of about one inch should be left on all sides.

    A pica or elite typewriter should be used (never script or other unconventional type). Black type on white paper is preferred, and only one side of the paper should be used.

    Where possible, a page should end at the end of a paragraph. This has several advantages, among them the fact that in writing memos to other editors or to the writer, an editor can refer to "the last paragraph on 5" rather than to "the paragraph that begins on 5 and ends on 6."

FIGURE 3–1.

A FIRE AND HE ALONE HAD SURVIVED, SHOULD HAVE BEEN DELIGHTED BY THE NEWS. INSTEAD͟ THE ͟B͟AHAMAS CHARTER CAPTAIN HURRIED FROM THE HEARING ROOM. H͟IS BODY WAS FOUND IN HIS MOTEL ROOM THE NEXT DAY.

Inserting New Material

Most good copy editors make insertions in the articles they edit. On most magazines, it is *not* acceptable to circle a sentence and note that it should appear on another page. Also, it is *not* recommended that you clip or staple a strip of inserted material on a manuscript; it may be torn off and lost.

When a sentence or a paragraph must be retyped, use a full-width piece of paper as an insert. The page where you place the insert should then be cut and the insert pasted in. If the insert is lengthy, use it as a separate insert. The material should be typed on a full sheet and marked with appropriate symbols. Write "Insert A" on the insert itself; then, at the appropriate place in the copy, write "Insert A" and circle it.

Finally, if entire pages are placed in the article, or if pages must be renumbered, be certain that the pagination is clear and accurate. Mark the numbers in the upper right corner. Use one of two methods: If a new page comes between pages 7 and 8, mark it 7a; or simply renumber the entire article.

Remember, printers are paid to "follow the copy out the window." The copy editor must make instructions entirely clear. The printer may be stupid or brilliant, but it doesn't matter; you are the boss.

Examples of Professional Editors' Work

Here is how James Arntz, a veteran editor, edited the first long paragraph of an article about the Washington correspondents who cover the Supreme Court:

Arntz's Editing

Just before the dedication of the new Supreme Court's building in 1935, one of the justices quipped about that grandiose marble mausoleum: "What are we supposed to do, ride in on nine elephants?" Anyone who visits a session of the Supreme Court for the first time will find that the Court's procedures are also rather more Byzantine than one would expect of an American governmental institution in the late twentieth century. For the neophyte reporter who is attempting to cover the Supreme Court, this formal, anachronistic style can be unnerving and confusing. But even the experienced correspondent, who has learned the jargon and become accustomed to the ritual, finds the imperial aloofness and silence of the justices a bewildering and frustrating phenomenon of contemporary government. The justices of the Supreme Court *never* speak publicly or critically either of one another or of the cases before them.

Original Version

When the construction of the Supreme Court's new building was completed in 1935, one of the justices asked about that cold, marble mausoleum: "What are we supposed to do, ride in on nine elephants?" Anyone who visits a session of the Supreme Court for the first time will find that the Court is conducted much as it was in the last century. Although the justices no longer wear wigs, their bodies are encased in long black robes. All nine justices may loathe another justice—or all of them—but they never speak critically of another in public. When an attorney is presenting a case to the Supreme Court, he'll speak of "my brother"—who turns out to be, not a relative, but the opposing attorney. All of this may confuse beginning correspondents who are attempting to cover the Supreme Court.

The most important editing Arntz has done here is to keep the paragraph to its subject. Although the writer probably congratulated himself for the paragraph he had written, it is badly organized. Note that the paragraph starts with the nine justices, then wanders aimlessly into describing the manner of an attorney. Knowing that the paragraph will appeal to almost anyone who is interested in the Supreme Court, Arntz rewrote that paragraph to end on a high note. Moreover, observe how adroitly Arntz has rewritten the paragraph. Each sentence seems to spring from the preceding sentence until, by the end of the paragraph, you have read a well-wrought beginning of the article.

Arntz, like many copy editors, has his own style of editing that works best for him. He has described his technique in the following essay. Note especially how long it takes to skim an article, to find a central thread, and so on.

> I proceed through the manuscript, page by page, challenging and improving the logic, the coherence, the economy, and the style and readability of the writing. I seldom read through the whole article before I begin the actual line-by-line editing. I always skim the material to get a sense of what the writer has to say and how well he or she writes (badly means that I will give more attention to the reading and point of view of the piece; good writing

will tell me that I can focus more on style and polish). During the skimming process, I also begin to attune my ear to the voice and rhythms of the writer, so that (if the writing is decent) I can edit unobtrusively.

The line-by-line editing usually involves blocks of material, hopefully paragraphs. I try to follow the writer's thinking; decide whether that block of material is, indeed, of use to his or her article; and if I think it is of value, I then try to shape it, clarify it, polish it. Once I've found a line—a thread—to the writer's work, I try to maintain that focus and will cut away or reorganize blocks of material for the sake of cogency and coherence. If the writer has dropped the thread, I figure out how to restore it by reading ahead until I find the theme again (or until I realize, in the case of very bad writing, that there is no thread, and that, therefore, I will have to create one for the writer). Until I run into a serious problem, though, I rarely read ahead in a manuscript, at least with any sort of depth. I try to deal with one idea, one paragraph, at a time.

After a largish section of paragraphs is completed, I will then go back to check my work and to get an overall grasp of the piece. If the piece has been heavily edited, I usually like to have the material retyped so that I can read the new version with ease.

Also, if I'm dealing with a writer who is not accustomed to my work, and if I do a good bit of work on the writing, I will write explanatory notes along the way, telling him or her why I've made major changes and suggesting where he or she might do some additional writing to strengthen the work. I also take care of the mechanical matters—punctuation, spelling—almost by rote; and by raising questions about the accuracy of information if something strikes me oddly.

The process of improving the logic and the cogency of a piece is more or less internal—a matter of my thinking about what the writer is trying to say and why it isn't being said more clearly. The matter of economy and style is more verbal and ear—I frequently read the material aloud to catch the rhythms and connections.

The major difference between editing a book and an article is in the first reading. With an article, I simply skim and give little attention to structure other than, perhaps, paying a bit of extra attention to the writer's headings, if any. Once I have an idea of how the writer writes and what he or she wants to say, I simply begin with sentence one, paragraph one.*

Here is another example of how a magazine editor alters an article. This is from the middle of an article in which the writer is reporting on how ABC–TV Washington correspondents work.

```
    No reporter assigned to events on Capitol Hill

has reported into the bureau yet today.  Like many
```

---

*Courtesy, James Arntz.

Washington reporters in the other media, the ABC reporters focus their work on the story of the day while covering all their regular contacts. They will return to the bureau when the reporting is done for the day, but there's literally no need for them to check into the office before their work is done. On the one hand, the reporters are covering something specific, a hearing or a controversy, a press conference or a junket. On the other, they are looking ahead for the future issues in their areas of expertise. At the simplest level this means taking an early morning glance at the United Press International's "daybook," which relays notices of the scheduled important events in Washington and New York. But virtually every Washington reporter has developed a personal system for keeping on top of a beat.

Note that the first paragraph was written in three sentences, which traced the paths of the reporters from the beginning of the day until the end. The editor then started another paragraph because the first one seemed complete. Because the editor had a fresh (and intelligent) eye, he saw that he could extend that first paragraph to the end of the second simply by cutting the first sentence of the second paragraph and putting the end sentence of the first paragraph at the end of the second paragraph. Because it was then complete, he marked ⊏ to indicate that these two paragraphs are actually one.

Read two more sentences written by the writer:

> The exterior of ABC News' Washington Bureau looks stark, pristine among the other buildings along Connecticut Avenue. Its facade is perfectly flat and marble white.

Now read what the editor has done with these two sentences:

> The facade of ABC's Washington Bureau, perfectly flat and marble white, seemed modest, stark, orderly among the sumptuous hotels and office buildings along Connecticut Avenue.

As you can see, the writer described the building in an average-long sentence, then found that he could describe it better with another short sentence. The editor saw those two sentences and wondered why the writer didn't use words to describe the building in one captivating sentence. If you again read the writer's and the editor's sentences, you will probably prefer the editor's single-sentence description.

Computerized Magazine Editing

Few magazines actually use computers in editorial work, but journalism graduates should know the rudiments of computerized magazine editing anyway. When *Time* introduced its computer system in 1978, the editors sent correspondents explicit instructions. The following pages show the initial instructions and format, plus the final comments after the system had been used for several months. Notice how important small details, such as placement of periods and colons or specific combinations of letters, are in keeping a computerized newsroom free from chaos.

STANDARD HEADING FORMAT, INCOMING TO NEW YORK

```
STM: _____(1)_____      MSG: _____(2)_____      _____(3)_____
TO:  _____(4)_____      FOR: _____(5)_____
FROM: _____(6)_____      BY:  _____(7)_____      IN: _____(8)_____
SLUG: _____(9)_____      CLOSE: _____(10)_____      TK: _____(11)_____
```

(text of message)

ETX:
(13)

EXPLANATION OF
STANDARD HEADING FORMAT, INCOMING TO NEW YORK

The numbers in parentheses on the attached form are guides to these notes, and not part of the normal heading. Similarly, there is obviously no underlining in messages. That's just to indicate, on this form, where your information goes.

All key words and codes to the various elements must be followed by a colon (:). For instance: "FROM:" or "ETX:" The colon must be used with ETX even though no information follows it.

First, the heading always starts with STM:. "Start TIME Message." Always.

(1) STM: is immediately followed by the wire room message code, containing the bureau abbreviation, a sequence number, and date. For instance: BO/4 NYK Dec 3 77. This is the form used now by the wire rooms.

MSG: is followed by (2) the message type. This is the most complicated element in the heading (and it is not very hard). All types of messages are reduced to three-letter abbreviations, such as "FIL" for file, "ADV" for advisory, "PLA" for playback, "SKQ" for scheduling query, "CAC" for comments and corrections, etc. A complete guide to the message types is written on the bottom of your sample format sheets. I strongly suggest you commit them to memory.

After the message type is (3), a space for a code identifying a special "class" of messages. This is optional, and should be filled out only if the message is of a special class. Such as "RUSH" for rush. "CON" for confidential. "RED" for red tag. "PRIV" for private messages. Confidential messages will be given tightly controlled distribution. "PRIV" messages will go into a separately coded part of the computer memory which will not be available to just anyone with access to a CRT. Access will be only for desk personnel (who see such traffic now) and to the addressee.

(4) The name of the section to which you are filing. If you are sending your message to an individual not in a section, this should be "news desk."

(5) Optional. The name of the person whom you are addressing.

Elements (4) and (5) combine, for example, to read "To: Time World For: Spence Davidson," or "To: Time News Desk For: Gart."

(6) The originating point, or home bureau of the correspondent or stringer.

(7) The name of the author of the message (occasionally optional if the bureau is the originator, as in a story list).

(8) (Optional) The physical location of the author.

Elements (6) (7) and (8) might combine to read: FROM: Washington BY: SIDEY IN: Plains GA.

(9) SLUG: You all know what a slug is. But now it really matters. Only a live News Desk person knows that "Death of the Silver Bullet" is the same story as "Japanese Train." If you fail to follow the slug *on the scheduling query* (not necessarily on your suggestion), the computer will be confused, and so may your file. Slugs may be no more than 20 characters, including spaces.

(10) The month and day on which the story closes, as taken from the scheduling query. Use numbers separated by a slash (/).

(11) The take number of your file. Use a number, not a word or Roman numerals.

(12) EOH: must go here on all messages. It's simple enough; it tells the computer that this is the End of Heading. The text of the message follows. After the text of the entire message is complete, it must end with element (13) which is ETX:. <u>Do not omit ETX: at the end of your message.</u> It tells the computer to stop reading, and if you forget it, your files may be augmented by messages to Money Ad Sales. ETX: Must go on a separate line at the very bottom of the message after the operator's time-off.

SAMPLE FILE USING NEW COMPUTER FORMAT

STM: WASH/21 NYK NOV 29 77   MSG: FIL, RUSH

TO: TIME NATION

FROM: WASHINGTON   BY: JOHN STACKS   IN: PHILADELPHIA

SLUG: CONGRESS DEBATE   CLOSE: 11/3   TK: 2   EOH:

    text text text text text text text text text text text text text text text text text text text text text text text text text text text text text text text text text text text text text text text text text text text text etc. etc. etc. More tk.

CA 1045

ETX:

SAMPLE ADVISORY USING NEW COMPUTER FORMAT

STM: BEVE WESTEDIT/ 3NYK   SANF   DEC 5 77   MSG: ADV

TO: TIME SHOWBIZ   FOR: MARTHA DUFFY

FROM: WESTEDIT   BY: JIM WILLWERTH

SLUG: STAR WARS   CLOSE: 12/24   EOH:

    text text text text text text text text text text text text text text text text text text text text text text text text text text text text text text text text text text text text text text text text text text text text text text text text text text text text text text text text text text text End it.

CA 1146

ETX:

STN:NYK25/WESTEDIT /RP/ MAR 17 78   MSG: ADM

TO: WASHINGTON, ATLANTA, BOSTON, MIDWEST, WESTEDIT

FROM: NEWSDESK   BY: BILL STEWART

SLUG: COMPUTER EOH

TO ALL BUREAUS:

FIRST, MANY THANKS FOR YOUR PATIENCE AND COOPERATION DURING THE FIRST FEW WEEKS OF WORKING WITH THE COMPUTERS. LARGELY AS A RESULT OF YOUR EFFORTS, WE HAVE A SMALLER NUMBER OF CORRECTIVE POINTS THAN WE ANTICIPATED. THE ONES WE DO HAVE MAY SOUND MINOR, EVEN NITPICKING, BUT IF THE EXACT FORMS ARE NOT FOLLOWED, YOUR MESSAGES END UP IN THE COMPUTER'S HOLDING PATTERN AND DELIVERY IS UNNECESSARILY DELAYED. OUR POINTS:

1) DO NOT USE THE WORD ''BUREAU'' IN YOUR HEADING, AS IN ''FROM: PARIS BUREAU.'' ALWAYS USE ''FROM: PARIS.''

2) ALWAYS SPELL OUT FROM:, NEVER USE FM:

3) USE THE NEW PICTURE FORM FOR ALL PIX MESSAGES AS WELL AS ALL PACKET MESSAGES. MESSAGE TYPE SHOULD BE ''PIX'' FOR BOTH. PLEASE INCLUDE SLUG WHERE APPLICABLE. THE CLOSING DATE ON PIX MESSAGES IS NOT NECESSARY.

4) THE NEW AMERICAN SCENE SECTION WILL BE CALLED, AS FAR AS THE COMPUTER IS CONCERNED, ''TIMESCENE.'' PLEASE ADDRESS YOUR MESSAGES TO TIMESCENE WITH APPROPRIATE SLUGS.

5) PLEASE AVOID WHEREVER POSSIBLE USING THE MESSAGE TYPE ''ADV'' EXCEPT ON A QUERIED STORY.

PLEASE USE MESSAGE TYPE ''SUG.'' THE COMPUTER ONLY RECOGNIZES 'ADV' ON SCHEDULED STORIES. HOWEVER, IT MAY BE USED WHEN ADDRESSING MESSAGES TO THE NEWS DESK.

6) KEEP SLUGS EXACT. THAT INCLUDES USE OF COLONS, SPACES, APOSTROPHES, ETC.

7) MOST IMPORTANT -- MESSAGES MUST START WITH ''STN:'' THE HEADING MUST END WITH ''EOH:'' AND THE MESSAGE MUST END WITH ''ETX:'' AND IT MUST BE EXACT. AN STN: OR AN EOH WITHOUT THE COLON IS ENOUGH TO THROW THE ENTIRE FILE INTO THE GARBAGE PILE.

8) WHEN ADDRESSING MESSAGES TO INDIVIDUALS, PLEASE INCLUDE SECTION. FOR EXAMPLE, TO: WORLD FOR: ELSON OR TO: NEWS DESK FOR: ELSON -- NEVER TO: ELSON.

THE EXCEPTION IS MURRAY GART. ALL MESSAGES TO GART SHOULD BE ADDRESSED SIMPLY TO: GART.

AGAIN, MANY THANKS.

RT/DN/10:22P

Editorial Research

Editors must always be alert to discrepancies in copy, obvious errors, and illogical statements of ideas. Much of the skill in checking facts is in knowing when and what to doubt. The most frequent errors in stories are in names, dates, locations, and descriptions of past events.

When the copy editor is in doubt or has a question about a story, there are four courses open to him or her:

1. If it can be cleared up by using a reference book, it can be checked easily.
2. If the writer is available, it can be referred to him or her.
3. If it is a question of policy, taste, or consistency, the copy editor should know the answer. If the copy editor doesn't know, he or she must consult the chief copy editor.
4. If the fact is not vital, and if it cannot be readily checked, it can be deleted from the story. This, of course, is the last resort, not merely an easy way out of a difficulty. Statements that are absurd or dangerous are always deleted without question. A fact that is essential to the story must be checked at all costs, but a fact that can be deleted without serious harm to the story should be taken out when the time is short and the means for verification are not readily available.

Here are a few of the reference books that should be on hand (publishers are noted in parentheses):

Bartlett's Familiar Quotations (Little, Brown). This famous source lists sayings and writings from 2000 B.C. to the present and is a valuable reference tool.

Book Review Digest (Wilson). This publication condenses published reviews of books.

City and county directories and official publications of the city and county.

Columbia Encyclopedia (Columbia University Press). This one-volume edition is an excellent research tool and contains a wide range of information. It is far from a replacement for the *Encyclopedia Britannica* or the 30-volume *Encyclopedia Americana*, but its most recent fifth edition is an excellent handbook.

Congressional Directory (Government Printing Office). This is the best source for biographical information on members of Congress and their committee assignments.

Congressional Record (Government Printing Office). The daily *Record* is set into type a few hours after the House and Senate complete the legislative day and is available the next morning.

Contemporary Authors (Gale Research). Restricted to living authors, it includes those who have written relatively little and also those who have written in obscure fields.

Current Biography (Wilson). Prominent persons in the news of the day are sketched in informal word portraits and published monthly.

Editor & Publisher International Yearbook (Editor & Publisher). This book lists daily newspapers in the United States and Canada and provides basic information about them.

Encyclopedia of American History (Harper & Row). This book has been organized both chronologically and topically, so that influential persons and notable dates, achievements, and events stand out, but the whole can be read as a narrative.

Facts on File (Facts on File, Inc.). Published weekly, this is a valuable encyclopedia that culls the news of the day from metropolitan newspapers.

Statistical Abstract of the United States (Government Printing Office). This is a digest of data collected by all the statistical agencies of the United States (and some private agencies).

Television News Index and Abstracts (Vanderbilt University). Published since 1972, this monthly volume is a summary of the evening news broadcasts of the three major television networks.

The Guinness Book of World Records (Guinness Superlatives). This book is the final authority on who has the world record in almost any undertaking.

The New York Times Index (New York Times). This is a valuable index to the daily *Times*.

The Times Atlas of World History (London: Hammond). This fresh and instructive approach to world history from the origins of man to the present is presented visually and cartographically.

Webster's Third New International Dictionary of the English Language (G. C. Merriam). This book offers excellent definitions, careful editing, and the largest number of word entries among American dictionaries.

Who's Who in America (Marquis). This biennial is considered the standard source on notable living Americans. It consists of brief, fact-packed biographies and current addresses.

Names are almost always an important part of any story. Any time a name is used in connection with a crime, accident, tragedy, or in any other undesirable circumstance, the name *must* be checked. To verify a name, you must check with an appropriate source, such as a reference book or directory, the reporter who wrote the story, the person named, or the person's family. A name should *not* be checked in old newspaper clippings, a police report, or the guess of another person. Tricky names such as Clark (Clarke), Fisher (Fischer), Olsen (Olson), and Smith (Smythe) should always be checked, even in the most routine stories.

Exercises

1. Insert punctuation where needed.

   a. Dr Elton B Smith Jr former communications director for the FBI asked about the administrations policy toward the TV fairness doctrine

   b. The young man approached two elderly women and asked Who started the riot One of the women she wore a print dress turned to the other and said Did he ask who started the riot Yes the other replied he certainly did

   c. Dashes are used for the following 1 to mark breaks 2 to set off summaries and 3 to set off parenthetical elements

2. Fill in the blanks with either *ei* or *ie*.

s___ve	bes___ge	pr___st
conc___ve	dec___t	s___ne
f___nd	r___gned	th___f
h___r	c___ling	y___ld

3. Examine the list for misspelled words and make corrections.

absense	vengance	independance
heros	sargeant	vacum
hypocracy	changeable	synonamous
reminisce	gramatically	sophmore
equiptment	lengthning	roommate
guaranteed	height	bookeeper
shepherd	psychoanalysis	breadth
compatable	decieve	co-relate
clothes	accompaniemant	adolescent
advise	annualy	altogether

4. Combine the following roots and suffixes.

   Example: bride + -al = bridal

care	+	-ful	=
fame	+	-ous	=
entire	+	-ly	=
precede	+	-ence	=
peruse	+	-al	=
love	+	-ly	=
arrange	+	-ment	=
prime	+	-ary	=
rude	+	-ness	=
plume	+	-age	=
like	+	-able	=
like	+	-ly	=
like	+	-lihood	=
like	+	-ness	=
like	+	-ing	=

5. Edit with copy editing symbols:

LIKE A COUPLE STARING AT DIVORCE OR A BUSINESS ON THE BRINK OF BANKRUPTCY, THE TOWN OF GREENWICH HAS RECENTLY SPENT MANY PAINFUL HOURS PONERING THE QUESTION: "WHERE DID WE GO WRONG?"

FOR THIS PARTICULAR CONNETICUT COMMUNITY, RUMMAG-ING THROUGH THE PAST FOR X REASONS HAS A SPECIAL

IRONY. THIS IS A PLACE WHERE HARD QUESTIONS ABOUT ABOUT FAILURE SEEM EXPECIALLY INAPPROPRIATE. HISTORICALLY GREENWICH HAS BEEN ONE OF THE MOST REASSURING TOWN'S IN THE REPUBLIC-A WELL SODDED 48 SQ. MILES OF ROLLING HILLS JUST TWENTY-EIGHT MILES N.E. OF MANHATTAN. THE ANNOUNCEMENTS OF AFFLUENCE MADE BY IT'S IMPOSING HOUSES, DRIVEWAYS ZND WROUGHTIRON GATES THAT OPEN DRAMATICALLY MORE CERTAIN STATEMENTS OF SUCCESS THAN MOST YOU'RE LIKELY TO DISCOVER IN THE NATIONS NORTHEAST CORNER.

6. Check the following for factual errors and make the necessary corrections.

   a. The only flying mammals are bats.

   b. The world's northernmost capital is Rekjavik, Iceland, at latitude 64° 06′ S.

   c. Dr. Daniel D. Boorstin, librarian of Congress, won a Pulitzer Prize for his fictional trilogy *The Americans*.

   d. The folding of the Washington *Star* left the United States with only 1,763 daily newspapers.

   e. "Hooch," slang for illegal liquor, is short for Hoochinoo, an Alaskan Indian tribe known for its own brand of firewater.

   f. Although the English Parliament in 1766 repealed the Stamp Act for the American colonies, it kept a similar tax for publications at home.

   g. Over long distances, the runner may burn up to 100 calories per mile.

   h. "Good fences make good neighbors," according to American poet Robert Frost, who was a native of San Francisco.

   i. Napoleon signed his abdication at Fontainebleau on April 20, 1814.

   j. The heaviest of the alkali elements is francium.

7. Finding facts is the first job of the journalist. For each of the following items, find the appropriate facts. Type them in complete sentences as though they were part of a story. *Following the answer to each item, list all the sources you used and tell approximately how much time you spent finding the answer.* (If you ask *anyone* to help you, you'll defeat the purpose of this exercise.)

   a. Where can one find a review of Margaret Mitchell's *Gone With the Wind*? Use this information as though it is part of a story you are writing. Name your sources.

   b. What was Johannes Brahms's education and music training? Write two sentences about this question as though you're writing a story. Name your sources.

   c. Where and how does one find the difference between the atomic bomb and the hydrogen bomb? Write your answer simply as though you're writing a story. Name your sources.

   d. Where would one find a biographical sketch of the senior senator from Colorado if you don't know his name? Write this information as though you're writing a story. Name your sources.

   e. What is the origin of the phrase "fifth columnist"? Use this information to write a short paragraph as though you're writing a story. Name your sources.

8. Interview an editor of a magazine or a newspaper and ask exactly what he or she does. Take notes. Type what the editor said and then compare it to what James Arntz does.

Chapter 4

Correcting Words, Sentences, and Paragraphs

The following sentence is awkward and convoluted:

> Surroundings and materials which facilitate the initiating and development of a unit with people should be arranged as effectively as possible.

It could easily be restated more clearly:

> Put the furniture in the right places.

Winston Churchill, prime minister of Great Britain during World War II, restated the following sentence:

> The information obtained from our sources in France of the general picture there indicates that the situation is deteriorating.

He stated it this way instead:

> The news from France is bad.

Simplicity in writing is one goal of good editing. The "Dick-and-Jane" type of simplicity should, of course, be avoided, in which sentences longer than 15 words are reduced to 9 or 10 words. Try to remember Ridge Warren, the Theodore White character in *The Fortieth Floor*. Warren, president of a publishing firm, was the conglomeration of the many editors White had worked for on *Collier's, The Reporter, Time,* and other magazines. At one point in the novel, Ridge Warren says:

> It was the first time anybody except the President of the United States had to sit in his office and think about this whole damned country all at once. Some editor had to think not just what the local people in Chicago, or New York, or Charleston, or San Francisco might want to read, but what would hold this audience together across the whole land, from coast to coast.

Students should think of themselves as Ridge Warren, then edit as though working for a popular magazine. This will be one important step toward simplicity.

Editing Words

Redundancy. One important job of the editor is to eliminate redundancy. The words at the left and the single word at the right say the same thing:

the city of Los Angeles	Los Angeles
the sum of $7.50	$7.50
past history	history
a rectangular shape	rectangle
entirely decapitated	decapitated
completely unique	unique
in a dying state	dying
the year of 1978	1978
old traditions of the past	traditions
canary bird	canary
old adage	adage
lift up	lift
entire monopoly	monopoly
the hour of noon	noon
in the meantime	meantime
made out of iron	iron
the subject of charity	charity
present incumbent	incumbent
new recruit	recruit
actual fact	fact

The phrase "actual fact" is an exception and can be used for emphasis to single out the one factual item of information among several that had been supposed at an earlier time to be facts.

Repetition. Variety of expression is important, too. When editing an article about one narrow topic, the writer often repeats the same words and phrases again and again. Some repetition, of course, is necessary and perfectly acceptable. The writer cannot refer to the topic of his or her article once in the opening paragraph and then refer to it as "it" for the next three pages. The reader needs the handle of a specific topical reference to understand the focus of the writer's thought from sentence to sentence and paragraph to paragraph.

On the other hand, the repetition of the same word, sentence after sentence, would make the reading (and the writing) of an article very monotonous. Consider these sentences:

> The situation was characterized by the heightened sensitivity to darkness.
> Due to this heightened sensitivity, he was almost always afraid.

In this case, the writer repeats words in a monotonous way. Instead, the idea might be stated this way:

The situation was characterized by the heightened sensitivity to dark. He was almost always afraid.

Using and Not Using "Say." When editing an article containing many quotations, check the words that introduce or follow the quotations. The editor should substitute a synonym of "say" that is appropriate to the tone and the meaning of the remark that is quoted. This list contains most of the synonyms of "say" and their meanings:

say	express in words
remark	express casually
mention	express in pausing
comment	express with interpretation
declare	express in a formal or public way
state	express clearly and definitely
aver	express with confidence
maintain	express with conviction

The following verbs should be used in place of "say" when the intention parallels meanings with the right column.

assert	express boldly on the basis of personal authority or conviction
allege	assert without proof
affirm	declare as true
charge	accuse formally
claim	demand as a right
explain	make known something not known or clearly understood
relate	give account of something experienced
report	give a public account
announce	declare for the first time
reveal	uncover as if drawing away a veil
disclose	make known what has been secret or private
divulge	disclose an impropriety or surprising fact
point out	refer to an undisputed fact

Clichés and Jargon. A cliché is not merely a descriptive phrase that has become familiar over the years. The phrase "the narrow street," for example, has been written billions of times by millions of writers, but this word combination is just as useful and acceptable now as it was the first time it was written. The same is true of most descriptive phrases: they merely give information; they do not constitute clichés.

A cliché is a familiar descriptive phrase that *calls attention to itself*, either because of its vivid but ancient imagery ("light as a feather," "chip off the old block") or because of its overuse and predictability in describing a type of person, object, or situation (the criminal who is a "loner," "the glittering first-night audience"). The cliché provides information, but it does so with a familiarity and predictability that makes the reader cringe. Moreover, because the phrase has been borrowed so often by so many writers, it has lost its effectiveness as meaningful description. The reader thinks more about the obviousness of the cliché than the idea the writer was trying to express.

The fact that clichés come so readily to the mind of the writer demonstrates our reliance on visual and memorable language. Instead of chastising the writer who uses a cliché, consider the usage positively; the writer, after all, was trying to be expressive. So the instinct was right, but the writer's reach was too short.

Editors who work with copy loaded with clichés can either revise the cliché into plain, unselfconscious English, or can compose an original descriptive phrase. To do this, the editor uses the structure of the cliché and then substitutes a new, fresher image. Students assigned to create new imagery for some of our hoariest clichés came up with many delightful phrases, among them:

Cliché: as smooth as silk

Student creation: as smooth as a salesman's smile

Cliché: as comfortable as a couch

Student creation: as comfortable as a bachelor changing a diaper

If an editor runs into problems trying to create original imagery, the safer road—simply revising the cliché into plain English—is available.

Her skin was as smooth as silk.

Her skin was strikingly smooth and luminescent.

Jargon is another form of cliché—an exclusive vocabulary of overused terms and phrases adopted by a specialized group (an academic discipline, a profession, a religious or political sect) to express the ideas and technical information that feature the group's special interest. The term "jargon" generally implies unintelligibility, especially for those outside the group. The term also connotes a feeling of self-importance among the jargonists, who are demonstrating that they are members of an in-group and that their field of interest is so specialized that it cannot be discussed in ordinary language.

Jargon is especially rampant in education, as illustrated by the following excerpt from a letter to parents by the principal of a high school in Houston:

> Our school's cross-graded, multi-ethnic, individualized learning program is designed to enhance the concept of an open-ended learning program with emphasis on a continuum of multi-ethnic, academically enriched learning using the identified intellectually gifted child as the agent or director of his own learning. Major emphasis is on cross-graded, multi-ethnic learning with the main objective being to learn respect for the uniqueness of a person.

One parent responded to the principal with: "I have a college degree, speak two foreign languages and four Indian dialects, have been to a number of county fairs and three goat ropings, but I haven't the faintest idea as to what the hell you're talking about. Do you?"

The response is well put. The principal could have said exactly the same thing—more clearly and succinctly—in everyday language:

> Our school makes bright children responsible for their own learning. We emphasize respect for all people as unique, regardless of their race or background.

We tend to resort to the empty phrases of jargon in our writing because of our constant exposure to them, just as we tend to think first of the old chestnuts when we are searching for an apt descriptive phrase. If editors adhere to the principles of plain writing when they edit, they will come to recognize jargon for what it is—semantic spinach.

Editing Sentences

This advice is from E. B. White, the famous essayist of *The New Yorker*:

> Do not overwrite.
> Do not construct awkward adverbs.

Avoid fancy words.

Be clear.

Prefer the standard to the offbeat.

Now read an edited sentence (the unnecessary words are marked with italics):

> The moral of such examples is that all intelligent criticism *of any instance* of language *in use* must begin with understanding *of* the motives *and purposes* of the speaker *in that situation.*

After reading this sentence twice—first with all the words, then without the italicized words—it should become clear why the edited sentence is better.

After struggling through an article written by a student who had a penchant for long, complex sentences, the instructor turned to her typewriter, inserted the backside of the student's final page, and typed period after period until the page was almost filled. Then she added this message at the bottom of the page: "These interesting objects, which apparently you have never encountered, are known as periods. You will find them most helpful, and I urge you to use them—often."

The problem of interminable and overly complex sentences is a common one. Even the newspapers, which pride themselves on their short, readable sentences, are sometimes guilty of overloading their sentences:

> The records show that the recruiter made calls from his Austin, Texas, office to the police department and the Angelina County district attorney's office in Lufkin, Texas, November 12, 1979, according to the Marines, who also say a third call was made to the county sheriff's office but there was no telephone receipt to prove it.

The difficulty of this sentence is not so much due to its length—very long sentences, if they are carefully written, can be perfectly direct and clear. The problem in this example is the amount of information crowded into a single sentence. The reader cannot possibly understand or retain all of this information in one reading and must stop and start over several times to comprehend the intended meaning.

R. J. Cappon, general news editor of the Associated Press, has described some of the major causes for the problem of unwieldy sentences. First, there is the failure to limit a sentence to a single idea. If writers cram one or more ideas into a sentence, they overcomplicate their writing with *who, that,* and *which* clauses: "The King of Spain, *who* had been a favorite of the Falangist Party *which* had ruled Spain for the 30-odd years *that* intervened between the Spanish Civil War and his coronation, told the President of France, *who* . . ." This kind of sentence is a linguistic traffic jam. Similar problems, Cappon notes, result from a reckless use of conjunctions like "and" or "but." Cappon's example:

> The amendment, sponsored by Rep. John Dingell, closely follows the recommendations of the Environmental Protection Agency and is regarded as a compromise between the five-year freeze and the even tighter standards currently.

This sentence is far more understandable if a period is placed after "Agency," if "and" is deleted, and if the next sentence starts with, "It is . . ."

Cappon's bad example is not that seriously flawed. Compare his sentence with the following sentences composed by inexperienced writers who apparently were unfamiliar with those "interesting objects known as periods":

> The reaction was not a common one and it was undoubtedly well justified because Deputy Chief Engineer, John Kozack of the Toll Bridge Authority committee had announced that the bridge construction could begin within a month, consultation and research at the local level had been practically ignored, and the community was quick to respond with suits.

> The union is betting on the regent's cooperation in order to substantiate legislative proposals which would in turn tax the growers and their machines which displace workers, and not the taxpayers who foot most of the bill for unemployment and welfare in addition to the bulk of the university mechanization research.

These sentences seem like they'll never stop, and are typical of those writers who never learned the importance of limiting a sentence either to *one* idea or to the simplest possible declaration of two or more closely related ideas. Overburdened sentences seldom occur in speech; even the most flagrant motor-mouths naturally inject frequent pauses (the equivalent of a comma or period) to give their listeners a chance to absorb the information they've imparted. Yet writers of all sorts are equally guilty of mounting idea upon idea until the so-called sentence is a chaotic, unreadable jumble.

The point is that good plain writing should follow the simple pattern of speech. The editor must group and relate the writer's ideas thoughtfully. Precision may require that a single sentence includes a relative ("who," "which," "that") clause, or the connection of several related ideas. But the editor should not make the mistake of thinking that writing is unworthy unless it is more long-winded and complex than everyday speech.

Editing Paragraphs

More than 50 years ago, Henry W. Fowler published a writing handbook, *Modern English Usage*, which is still highly respected as a reference work for both professional and student writers. In defining a paragraph, Fowler wrote:

> The purpose of a paragraph is to give the reader a rest. . . . The writer is saying to [the reader]: "Have you got that? If so, I'll go on to the next point." There can be no general rule about the most suitable length for a paragraph; a succession of very short ones is as irritating as very long ones are wearisome. The paragraph is essentially a unit of thought, not of length. . . .

"A unit of thought"—that's the key to the proper formation of paragraphs. Consider the following student-written example:

> Advertising offers a writer a broad and diversified market. There is virtually nothing these days that does not rely on some form of advertising. Our sensibilities are bombarded from every direction with ads on everything from hamburgers to church services.
> Breaking into advertising copywriting is . . .

The three sentences in the first paragraph make up one unit of thought—a unit which considers the broad range of advertising writing. The next paragraph begins a new thought: how to break into advertising. These are appropriate paragraphs. They are based on units of thought and provide a momentary rest for the reader between thoughts. The paragraph break gives the reader a chance to digest the ideas of the previous paragraph and to prepare to apply these ideas to the next.

As Fowler suggests, it is irritating to the reader to contend with a succession of very short paragraphs that all deal with the same basic unit of thought. Look at this example from a student writer's review of a John Denver special:

> After ABC pumped in about 15 seconds of laughter and hand-clapping, Denver launched into his first song.

> The song was a mediocre tune that began like many other cheap pop country hits: "I'm just a poor country boy...."
>
> The only difference was that Denver had an orchestra backing him up, and the orchestra couldn't keep time.

This is newspaper style, and it works well in that format of very small print and narrow columns. A single sentence can fill several lines in a newspaper column, so the reader's eye requires more frequent stops. Lengthy, multisentence paragraphs would turn the newspaper page into an uninviting and unreadable blur of gray.

A magazine editor must think carefully, not of newspaper writing, but of magazine writing. Magazine writers generally do not have to contend with the spatial and visual restrictions of the newspaper column; their major concern in paragraphing can be the organizational pattern of the ideas. Still, writers must also give some attention to the visual pattern of paragraphs.

Fowler accounts for the visual aspect of paragraphing as well. A paragraph should be a unit of thought—but, Fowler adds:

> Paragraphing is also a matter of the eye. A reader will address himself more readily to his task if he sees from the start that he will have breathing-spaces from time to time than if what is before him looks like a marathon course.

Consider the following very long paragraph from a scholarly article written for historians:

> This observation indicates the essential difference between the layman and the professional historian. Although a layman may develop either a personal or a professional interest in some aspect of the past—and may then study it thoroughly and become an authority—the historian's work consists entirely of analyzing the past. Because the past can be examined only through its traces, the historian devotes himself to them: coins, stamps, art objects, buildings, and especially documents. How the historian examines the past is indicated in part by the sketch of Professor Anderson's work. We can discover that a particular detail in a document is false by comparing that detail to facts established in other studies. Those facts, in turn, were first examined to determine whether they corresponded to other facts that had previously been established by careful examination. It is not oversimplifying to say that the writing of history is based on correspondences—on the degree to which purported fact corresponds to established fact. Essentially, historians assert *probabilities*, although many are so little in doubt that their factual basis is unquestioned. We cannot *know* in the sense of experience and observation, for example, that the members of the Continental Congress signed the Declaration of Independence on the second of August, but the other facts that make this probable are so well established that it is not to be doubted....

This paragraph is, indeed, a marathon course; in fact, this excerpt is merely a portion of the complete paragraph, which rambled on for another 26 lines. Because the article was written for a scholarly audience, perhaps the great length and density of its paragraphs are not inappropriate. Still, scholars are human, too; they would surely have appreciated an occasional break in order to digest the author's ideas.

Although this paragraph can be considered a single unit of thought, it could also have been broken logically into briefer, more attractive and attainable units. A second paragraph could have been formed, for example, with the fourth sentence, "How the historian examines . . ." And still another paragraph could have begun with, "It is thus not oversimplifying . . ." With these breaks, the author's thought pattern would remain intact, but it would also be clearer and easier for the reader to grasp. As for the visual pattern of the article, these breaks would make it more inviting.

In most article writing, a paragraph length of three to six sentences is both attractively brief yet long enough to express fully a unit of thought. When you see a chance to edit a long paragraph of lengthy sentences, take it! It is also important that the visual pattern of paragraphs be fairly uniform. A choppy pattern of very long and very short paragraphs can be disconcerting to the reader, in that it interferes with the pace and rhythm of easy reading.

A Student Example

Can a paragraph ever be as short as one sentence? Yes, but only to achieve a special effect. Consider these opening paragraphs from a student article:

> It hurts.
> Stretching, bending, and leaping to music hurts. In your ribs. In your calf muscles. Even your head hurts from thinking so hard. The patterns and tempo become more complex. And that woman. She demands perfection. After an hour you have sympathy for students at the Bolshoi School of Ballet. You have a sweaty, if not spiritual, affinity with Rudolf Nureyev. And when people see you dance, they murmur, "What grace! What style!"

The student writer of this article had a specific purpose in beginning her article with a one-sentence paragraph—and a two-word sentence at that! She was writing a "style piece," a descriptive article on her experiences in ballet class, and she wanted her readers to share the hard work, the pain, and the joy of achievement which she had experienced as a dance student. She therefore chose to begin with short sentences and sentence fragments which would evoke the halting, breathless exercises at the ballet *barre*. The opening sentence and paragraph cleverly sums it all up, sets the proper mood for the article, and intrigues the reader with its unconventionality.

One- or two-sentence paragraphs can be used either to hook the reader or to summarize and dramatize a point. But because this device is unconventional and dramatic, it should be used very sparingly. It should also suit the mood and tone of the article as a whole. And finally, as in the example above, it should relate rhythmically to the next (or the preceding) paragraph. One would not be well advised, for example, to begin a serious and rather lengthy article with a clipped, one-sentence paragraph. That would probably strike the readers as unsuitably coy or flippant. On the other hand, a one-sentence paragraph—if it were a provocative summary idea—might make an interesting and thoughtful *ending* to a serious article. For example, a student who was writing an article about the yellow jackets that were attacking students wrote this as the last paragraph:

Happily, the yellow jackets soon will have called a truce for the winter.

When judging the length of the writer's paragraphs, the structure of thought in the article is most important. Every paragraph should be self-contained in its development of a single idea. The paragraph break allows the reader to rest, to think about the ideas of the preceding paragraph, and to prepare to apply those ideas to the next paragraph. Beyond this thought pattern, the article writer should be further concerned with brevity and with the visual and aural impact of the paragraphing. The paragraphs should be as brief as possible, and the appearance and tone of the paragraphs should be reasonably well balanced and consistent throughout the article. In this way, an editor can present the writer's work in an open, fairly uniform, attractive, and inviting page of text.

The writing of dialogue is an exception. Because of the necessity for distinguishing the speakers in a dialogue, each paragraph should be checked as an exchange between two or more speakers:

"Including all its services, the union could break even by the end of the school year," Durham said. He was leaning forward in his chair, thinking intensely. His eyes seemed to bore into his interviewer.

"But that seems impossible," she said.

"We have received a mandate from the university budgetary group to break even by June," Durham rejoined.

Professional Writing of a Paragraph

In June 1940, most American college students gathered around dormitory radios early one evening to listen to a speech by Winston Churchill. He had just been appointed prime minister and was faced with the responsibility of reassuring a frightened and demoralized British people. France was about to fall to the Nazis, and it seemed certain that a German invasion of England would soon follow. Here is a paragraph from the Churchill speech:

> Even though large tracts of Europe and many old and famous states have fallen or may fall into the grip of the Gestapo and all the odious apparatus of Nazi rule, we shall not flag or fail. We shall go on to the end. We shall fight in France, we shall fight on the sea and oceans, we shall fight with growing strength in the air, we shall defend our island, whatever the cost may be. We shall fight on the beaches, we shall fight on the landing grounds, we shall fight in the fields and in the streets, we shall fight in the hills. We shall never surrender.

Among the many examples of fine writing in this passage, Churchill's use of the phrase "we shall fight . . ., we shall fight . . ., we shall fight . . .," demonstrates his mastery of a very tricky writing technique—repetition. An inept or careless writer will use repetition and produce sheer monotony. A superb craftsman like Churchill, however, used repetition to produce the effect of hammer blows.

Even more important to the impact of the writing is Churchill's brilliant combination of the "we shall fight" phrase with the carefully thought-out progression of battlefields, on which he promises to resist the Nazi invaders. Note that he begins with France, where the British troops were then engaging the Germans; then moves to the "seas and oceans" (still at a distance from English soil); then to the air, the beaches, the fields, the streets. And, finally, he ends the series with a retreat into the hills—implying that, rather than surrender, the British would carry on a guerrilla warfare against the German armies.

Churchill's goal in writing this speech was to rally the British to fight, and no one then or now could deny that his writing was perfectly matched to his purpose. When he ended the speech with the simple, climactic declaration "We shall never surrender!" the American students, the British citizens, the whole nonfascist world were thrilled and inspired.

Churchill must have begun writing this by thinking about the *theme*—the idea or point of the paragraph. His thoughts might have been along these lines:

> I must inspire my people to resist, to remain determined and courageous, even though Hitler now seems invincible. We must fight; we must never surrender to this evil force. If the Nazis invade, we must continue to fight in every city and town, and, finally, in the fields and hills of Scotland and Wales.

Expert writer that he was, Churchill undoubtedly reflected on this theme and then summarized it in a sentence that would identify the purpose of the paragraph and provide a starting point. He probably began, for instance, by writing:

> Even though Hitler seems invincible, and even if the evil Nazi forces invade our island, we shall fight—we shall never surrender.

With this topic sentence, he could proceed to construct the paragraph which would explain and expand on his theme. He might have continued with some of the sentences that ended up in the final version of his speech:

> We shall go on to the end. We shall fight in France. We shall fight on the beaches. We shall fight in the streets and fields. We shall fight in the hills.

These words could have given him the idea to list the geographical progression of battlefields to dramatize the danger faced by his country and the courage and determination needed by his people. Pleased with this idea, Churchill probably went back over the paragraph, revising the topic sentence to make it more subtle and interesting, adding several new potential battlegrounds, and rearranging the sentences so that they could fit into the geography.

Knowing Churchill's love of the language, it's certain that he revised the paragraph several more times to choose more precise and evocative words and phrases that would help him incite and inspire the British people. For example, he chose to use many alliterative words—words that repeat a similar consonant sound—because he knew that this writing device, when used carefully and sparingly, has a pleasing and exciting effect to the ear. Note all of the alliteration in the first sentence:

> *f*amous *s*tates have *f*allen
> *g*rip of the *G*estapo
> *od*ious *ap*para*tus*
> *f*lag or *f*ail

He also chose to use the technique of repetition—the "we shall fight" sentences—because he meant this speech to be a call to arms, and repetition is at the core of every battle cry. But Churchill was aware that repetition can become monotonous and counterproductive; thus, he separated the long series of "we shall fight" sentences with a summary statement: "We shall defend our island." Note also how he varied the *rhythm* of this series in order to build the drama of his words and focus attention on the ideas and images he was expressing.

Lastly, Churchill chose words and phrases that were carefully calculated to brace his people for the possibility of an invasion. He offered them some hope by reminding them of the remarkable successes of the outnumbered Royal Air Force (". . . with growing confidence and growing strength in the air"). But he also emphasized the danger, using fear to convince his listeners that they must resist an invasion. Note that he didn't say that "large tracts of Europe" had fallen to the "German armies" or to the "German government." He chose instead to name only the Gestapo and to refer as well to "all the odious apparatus of Nazi rule."

By this use of the most fearful words and images relating to government, Churchill meant to make clear to his people that this was not a traditional war in which one government wins and one loses, and then the two simply negotiate a settlement of lands. He was warning, indirectly but not so subtly, that if Great Britain surrendered to Hitler, the British people could be subjected to all of the cruelties of Nazi rule.

Why the lengthy analysis of a single paragraph in a speech written in 1940? Because you should understand what a writer is trying to accomplish in one paragraph. The following paragraph was written by Ernest Gowers:

> Use no more words than are necessary to express your meaning, for if you use more you are likely to obscure it and to tire your reader. In particular do not use superfluous adjectives and adverbs and do not use roundabout phrases where single words would serve.

Exercises

1. Some of the following sentences may stand as they are, but slang and clichés should be edited from the others. Use copy editing symbols to make the necessary changes.

   a. He said to cut it out or he'd break every bone in my body.

   b. If we'd of known you was comin', we'd of baked a cake.

   c. James Beard really knows how to dish up the chow.

   d. One of President Richard Nixon's favorite metaphors was "the light at the end of the tunnel."

   e. "Everyone who comes to camp usually gets so enthused that they want to come back next year," a female camp counselor said.

   f. Yesterday he gets Crawford to do just one teensy-weensy little job: he shook out the front doormat.

   g. A man sporting a porkpie hat and Topsiders knocked loudly at the front door. His skin was sort of dry.

   h. I've only got one thing to say and that is I don't give a hoot if Howard Ruff wants to call me a dumb jackass, a fat Mussolini or even Adolph as long as he gives my correct address: I'll take all the publicity I can get.

   i. We suspicioned his heritage because of his many corny expressions, such as "How'd you like them apples?"

   j. The dean wouldn't have made all that hullabaloo if he hadn't been plenty peeved.

2. Where possible, get rid of wordiness, redundancy, and unnecessary complexity in the following sentences. Use copy editing symbols to make the necessary changes.

   a. There are many people in this area who are planning to go to the meeting which is scheduled for next Tuesday.

   b. As for this book, it will have served a major purpose if it demonstrates the great potential for the use of communication statistics and if it stimulates efforts to improve our qualitative knowledge about how our communication industries operate in this day and age.

   c. Bob wrote little, because of the fact that his childhood had been an uneventful one.

d. When a film attempts to soar into the oneiric, it is like   be grounded by the critics.

e. A young girl of high-school age often shows a desire to read, but the girl's parents always ignore this desire.

f. In 1975, William F. Buckley Jr. wrote that Nelson Rockefeller's opsimathy should be welcomed.

g. The proposition "Either some ants are parasitic or none are" is an analytic proposition, for one need not resort to observation to discover that there either are or are not ants which are parasitic. If one knows what is the function of the words "either," "or," and "not," then one can see that any proposition of the form "Either p is true or p is not true" is valid, independently of experience.

h. The House Ways and Means Committee already has filed most of its reports, so the only report to be reported out today will concern the taxation of racetrack concessions.

i. The development of the downtown area has been placed under the supervision of a committee. It will be a bipartisan committee politically. The cost of the development project will be about $20 million.

j. In saying that there are still May Queens in England, and that the existence of May Queens is a relic of tree-worship, I have already asserted the existence in England of a relic of tree-worship.

3. The following paragraphs were published in widely circulated publications. Rewrite them unless you believe they can stand as they are.

> PORTLAND—While Tacoma was busy clinching the Pacific Coast League Northern Division second-half pennant Tuesday with a double-header sweep of Edmonton, there was little else for the bridesmaid Portland Beavers to do but relax, take a 6–1 win from Vancouver and talk about the .500 season they clinched.
>
> And the 2,247 who turned out got a chance to see a young man Beaver Manager Pete Ward calls potentially as good a pro prospect as there is in the league.

> Maybe those figures will convince you widows, orphans, and poverty stricken businessmen that you'll go broke in a hand basket listening to the "expert" advice of those saintly God fearing gentlemen who run off at the mouth like a Louisiana hound that has treed a coon at all of the financial seminars proclaiming you'll get filthy rich if you'll only buy their great sure fire newsletter or book. In my humble opinion, if they lost their golden pens

and golden tongues, they would be hard pressed to be even used car salesmen. Nuff said.

There may be two films more dissimilar than "Condorman" and "Baby Snakes," but they will do for an example of virtually complete opposites. Nevertheless, this is double header day at the old reviewing shop, and those are the two under consideration.

SEATTLE—If Don James could have Vince Coby back the way he remembers him best, the time he spends worrying about how his Washington football team is going to move the ball on the ground would be manageable.
Washington could use him in the worst way.

4. Although this chapter cites 20 words that can be used for "say," you can add many other synonyms. Add at least 10 different synonyms for "say" with their meanings.

5. After reading the Winston Churchill paragraph near the end of this chapter, read it again, then attempt to write the same paragraph while the book is closed. After writing that paragraph, open the book and match your paragraph to Churchill's. If you read both paragraphs thoughtfully, you can probably begin to understand the difference.

6. The following paragraphs, left and right, have been written about the same story. Choose the better story and write at least 100 words about the following: (a.) Which is more unified (with paragraphs growing out of another paragraph), and (b.) Thinking of chronology, which of these is written like a fictional short story?

Palo Alto Ambulance Service chief Jack Balcon admits that "Stanford's a big problem" for his service because of its complicated street patterns. Balcon adds that "the Stanford police and fire departments can do a lot of things we can't" in reaching an injured or ill person quickly.

Stanford Fire Chief Frank Jurian says that he doesn't "think the ambulance service to the University community has been that good for years." He adds that it is "frustrating for the Fire Department for us to arrive at the scene and then just sit

Palo Alto Ambulance Service chief Jack Balcon admits that "Stanford's a big problem" for his service because of its complicated street patterns. Balcon adds that the Stanford police and fire departments can do a lot of things we can't in reaching an injured or ill person quickly.

Stanford Fire Chief Frank Jurian says that it is "frustrating for the Fire Department for us to arrive at the scene and then just sit there and wait (for an ambulance), knowing that the Hospital is just a half mile away. He comments that the Ambulance there and wait (for an ambulance), knowing that the Hospital is just a half mile away."

Jurian says that the Ambulance Service's "familiarity with streets and buildings" on campus is not as good as it ought to be. He comments that the Ambulance Service would need "a tremendous staff" to keep track of which streets have been cut off by construction or by the jump posts which dot the campus.

Asst. Prof. of Surgery Ernest Kaplan, who supervises the Stanford Hospital's Emergency Room, believes that current ambulances are "not designed for resuscitation and care for the patient." Kaplan says that such ill-equipped ambulances are often little better than "hearses with resuscitators."

A major factor in the poor quality of ambulance service here is the high rate of turnover among drivers and attendants. Balcon cites other time commitments such as school, undesirable working conditions and "bad publicity" as major reasons for the turnover rate.

Balcon also complains that his Service's performance is hurt by the inadequate directions given to his drivers by the Santa Clara County ambulance dispatcher.

Jurian explains that the "long hours and the rate of pay (attendants start at $128.80 a week) dictate that the men are not stable with the (ambulance) company. They don't stay there." Like Balcon, Jurian feels that "the channel of communications" to the Ambulance Service can cause delays and mistaken directions.

Kaplan says that the average ambulance driver or attendant stays on for only nine months. He adds that this is not long enough for them to become adequately familiar with Stanford, in addition to the other communities covered by the Service (Palo Alto, Los Altos Hills, Menlo Park and Atherton).

Jurian believes that "we could do our job better if we had an ambulance in our department."

Service would need "a tremendous staff" to keep track of which streets have been cut off by construction or by the jump posts which dot the campus.

Nonetheless, Jurian says that the Ambulance Service's "familiarity with streets and buildings" on campus is not as good as it ought to be" and that he doesn't "think the ambulance service to the University community has been that good for years."

Balcon complains that his service's performance is hurt by the inadequate directions given his drivers by the Santa Clara County ambulance dispatcher. Jurian agrees that "the channel of communications" to the Ambulance Service can cause delays and mistaken directions.

A major factor in the poor quality of ambulance service here is the high rate of turnover among ambulance drivers and attendants. Balcon cites other time commitments such as school, undesirable working conditions, and "bad publicity" as major reasons for the turn-over rate.

Jurian explains that the "long hours and the rate of pay (attendants start at $128.80 a week) dictate that the men are not stable with the (ambulance) company. They don't stay there."

Asst. Prof. of Surgery Ernest Kaplan, who supervises the Stanford Hospital's Emergency Room, says that the average ambulance driver attendant stays on for only nine months. He adds that this is not long enough for them to become adequately familiar with Stanford, in addition to the other communities covered by the Service (Palo Alto, Los Altos Hills, Menlo Park and Atherton).

Kaplan also holds that the ambulances are "not designed for resuscitation and care for the patient." He says that such ill-equipped ambulances are often little better than "hearses with resuscitators."

Jurian believes that "we could do our job better if we had an ambulance in our department."

Chapter 5

Writing Headlines and Titles

Magazines use both headlines and titles, and the term *headings* covers both. Properly, though, a headline summarizes an article. It is a complete sentence that omits articles and most conjunctions. It also capsulizes the news and uses or implies the present tense. For example:

**PRESIDENT ATTACKS
FOES IN BUREAUCRACY**

On the other hand, the title merely hints at the gist of the article it surmounts and may omit verbs or subjects altogether. For example:

THE EXECUTIVES AND THE BUREAUCRACY (No Verb)
or
REVITALIZING THE DOWNTOWN SCENE (No Subject)

Magazine Headlines

Magazines like *Harper's* and *California* ordinarily use only titles for their articles:

BANKER'S CASINO *(Harper's)*
THE GREAT BLACK HOPE *(California)*

Having to guess what each article is about should intrigue the reader. The *Harper's* article is actually about multinational banks and bunco artists that are subject to two fatal threats. Also, the *California* article is about coal, which has long been touted as the answer to our energy needs.

Contrast those titles with these headlines used in *Editor & Publisher*, the weekly magazine of the newspaper business:

**WOMEN WILL GET
⅓ OF EDITORIAL
JOBS AT NEWSWEEK**

**ABA GAVEL AWARDS
GIVEN TO NEWSPAPERS**

Each of these headlines is written from information in the lead of the article. Readers can learn from the headline itself whether they're interested in the article.

Although most magazines use titles rather than headlines, headlines are common in the specialized magazines. For example, some magazines, like *Business Week*, use this type of headline over stories that have a strong news element:

ENERGY
GARBAGE POWER PAYS OFF

INDUSTRIAL PRODUCTION
A POWDER METAL BOOM PRODUCES A SHORTAGE

But *Business Week* also uses titles:

INSIDE IBM'S MANAGEMENT

THE CURE FOR A CHEMICAL GIANT

The practice at *Business Week* reflects fairly well the distinction made by some magazines: headlines over news articles, titles over feature articles. Most magazines, however, use titles.

Counting Headlines

When attempting to count a headline, remember that some letters are wider than others. The basic letter width is called a *unit*. The following count system works with most typefaces:

Lowercase
    Small letters (except *f, i, j, l, m, t,* and *w*)   1 unit
    Small *f, i, j, l,* and *t*   ½ unit
    Small *m* and *w*   1½ units

Uppercase
    Capital letters (except *I, J, M,* and *W*)   1½ units
    Capital *I* and *J*   1 unit
    Capital *M* and *W*   2 units

Space
    Space between words   ½ unit

Numbers and Symbols
    All figures except 1   1 unit
    $ % ? " and #   1 unit
    1 and . , : ; ! ' (and)   ½ unit

When counting a headline, go straight through a line and add units. The illustration below is counted.

1½	1½	1	½	2	1	1	½	1½	½	1	1½	=	13½ units
T	w	o		M	e	n		V	i	e	w		

1½	1	1	½	1	1	½	½	1	1	1	=	10 units
A	u	s	t	r	a	l	i	a	n	s		

The first line will only fit a column where the count can go as long as 13½ units. Also, note that in the number of letters in each line, the second will seem longer to the unpracticed eye because it uses 11 letters to the 10 letters in the first line. But the width of the letters differs markedly.

Ordinarily, most magazines give headline counts in two ways. First, the magazine states a range for a line, 10 to 15 units. This means that each line will be acceptable if it measures at least 10, but no more than 15, units. Second, a magazine can give its staff members a maximum number of units. For example, the count may be stated as 16. Thus, each line must not go over 16 units.

Writing Headlines

Writing a headline is a special type of news lead. In newswriting, the leads explain the five W's and the H: *who, what, where, when, why,* and *how.* The headline may use any of the W's, but it ordinarily answers *who* and *what.*

Because it must convey a maximum of information with a minimum of language symbols, the headline should be constructed of language that the readers can easily understand—for immediacy is the purpose of the headline. Large letters are used for easy reading, so that the readers can see at a glance what the article is about. For example, a news lead reads:

Live perch rain from the sky during a waterspout at Bourdeaux.

The headline writer converted those words into a one-line headline:

FISH RAIN FROM SKY AT BOURDEAUX

The words used in the lead of any story are used to convey information of an event. If the key words of the lead have headline utility, they should be used; if they don't, discard them as quickly as any other word would be discarded.

There is always a tendency to hang onto a headline idea, even if it is not working. Editors become so attached to a line that fits that even if unable to find a second line to work with the first, they are unable to give up the idea. It is always best to see the headline as a whole, and most good editors work on a headline as a unit rather than as a group of separate lines.

Observe how an editor of *The Quill*, a magazine for journalists, uses the lead of a story to create a headline:

The U.S. Supreme Court has agreed to rule whether the public can have access to the transcripts of Henry Kissinger's telephone conversations while he was secretary of state and White House national security adviser.

The editor reads this lead thoughtfully. Of course, the "U.S. Supreme Court," "Henry Kissinger," "whether the public can have access to the transcripts," and so on cannot possibly fit into the limited space of a headline. So, after trying several synonyms, the editor came out with this:

THE HIGH COURT WILL RULE ON KISSINGER'S TRANSCRIPTS

The construction of headlines is one of the most challenging jobs of an editor. It is no simple task to assemble the key facts of a complex story and arrange them in a limited space to summarize them accurately and to catch the reader's eye. Good headlines cannot be constructed from a list of rules, but these rules of thumb should help.

1. Use nouns to make the headline as specific as possible: *NATO* is better than *International Body*. A prominent person would ordinarily be named in a headline, but in many cases it would be better to use a label, such as *Princeton Dean* or *Russian Leader*, if readers will not readily recognize the name.
2. Use strong verbs. In most cases, use active verbs. Forms of *to be* and *to have* should ordinarily be avoided.
3. Try to avoid adjectives and adverbs in headlines. Some of the most overused words in headlines are "first," "new," and "last." They are used too often and with too little meaning in the cramped space of a headline.
4. Punctuation rules are much the same in writing headlines as in writing articles. Periods are not normally used in headlines; semicolons are used to separate two complete thoughts, just as a period would. A comma has the special use of substituting for the word "and." A dash is used to substitute for the word "says" near the end of a headline. For example:

JUDICIAL REFORM NEEDED NOW—MARTINEZ

A quotation mark is used as it is in sentences, except that it is general practice to use single quotation marks instead of double quotation marks. In some instances, quotation marks will be used to give a word a double meaning or to show that things are not what they appear to be. For example:

'DEAD' PILOT APPEARS AT OWN WAKE

A colon is used like a dash for attribution when it comes at the beginning of the headline. For example:

POLSKY: NEW HOSPITAL NEEDED

As a general rule, avoid abbreviations in headlines, except those commonly used in ordinary writing.

Headline Grammar

Verbs. Headlines are distinguished by the fact that they make statements instead of merely labels. The key to this distinction is the presence of a verb. The headline verb may be either explicit or implied, and the use of the verb often determines whether the headline has punch or is dull. For this reason, the verb should be placed in the first line of the headline to get the action started early. The present tense is customarily used to describe both past and present action. It puts the readers on the scene and makes them participants in the action. It also brings the event into immediacy.

The headline without a subject is known as a *verb head*. It seems to make a command. Unfortunately, the subject, which has been deleted, is what gives meaning to the action in the news. Avoid verb heads if possible.

Capitalization. Headline capitalization, like other styles, is a matter of choice. There are two basic styles of capitalization—*upstyle* and *downstyle*—and dozens of modifications of each. In downstyle, *only the first letter of each unit* of the headline (and the proper nouns) are capitalized. Its advantages are that it is easier to read, provides for a fatter headline count—more characters per line—and requires fewer keyboard functions for the typesetter. In upstyle, each word of the headline except articles, conjunctions, and the "to" of the infinitive (when used within the line) begins with a capital letter. In both of these styles, both parts of hyphenated words are capitalized if the first word is capitalized.

Omission of Words. Articles are usually, but not always, dropped from headlines. The headline attempts to approximate ordinary speech as closely as possible; thus, articles may be used without hesitancy when they are needed for clarity. The verbs "is" and "are" are allowed, but only on occasion.

Padding. To pad the headline means to find ways of filling space with words other than additional facts. Padding should be avoided because it is distracting, often obvious, and can destroy an otherwise good headline. Some of the common means of padding are substituting space-consuming words for shorter ones, making lengthy identification when a short one will do, and switching to space-devouring forms of words or phrases.

Headlines to Avoid

Never repeat words in a deck or an entire headline. Repetition in a headline irritates the reader's mental ear.

Never strain for humor. The effort to be funny too often sounds as if the editor had struggled for wit. For example, read the following headline published in a magazine:

**CONGRESSMAN CONDEMNS
PARAPLEGIC PRESIDENCY**

Never split grammatical units between lines, because it makes the headline confusing or hard to read. For example, here are two such splits:

**EXAMINING TEAM TO   VISITS TO SIX LAW
COVER SIX COLLEGES   SCHOOLS ARE SLATED**

Avoid headlines in which the minimum number of units allowed (such as 12) is in one line, and the maximum number of units (such as 16) is in the next line. Almost invariably you'll be writing a ragged headline, like this:

**EXAMINING COMMITTEE
TO COME HERE**

Magazine Titles

These headings over *Newsweek* stories are clearly titles, not headlines:

**THE FBI:
FINDING DICK TRACY**

**WEST POINT:
THE SILENCING**

COMPUTERIZING A MESS

GOO-GOO AND CUCKOO

Unlike headlines, most titles try to capture readers by hinting at the gist of the story—sometimes so cryptically that readers will be led to complete the story if only to resolve their puzzlement. "Computerizing a Mess" and "Goo-goo and Cuckoo" suggest this kind of appeal. Most titles are not at all like sentences!

Writing a title is both easier and harder than writing a headline. First, it is easier because a title need not summarize. Second, white space around a title is usually attractive, so an editor can write a short title without worrying about capturing the lead of an article, or about filling space exactly.

The difficulty is in capturing the essence of an article and then extracting a point that can be expressed in a few words. A good title need not be awe-provoking; in fact, some straightforward titles seem just right, so deft that no other phrasing would seem as good. For example, an article on the boom in Florida land sales to northerners seeking sunshine was aptly entitled

PARADISE ON THE INSTALLMENT PLAN

An article on the dismissal of an associate professor of English who professed to follow Mao Tse-Tung was entitled

ASSOCIATE PROFESSOR OF MAOISM

At the beginning, the editor has an article written by one of the magazine's staff who has put a title on it. The editor may want to change the title to something better, and must also choose a typeface and style that will suit the layout of the article. Eventually the editor will probably have to adjust words or try different combinations of words in the title.

One journalist, who was a staff writer for *The Reporter* gave an article he had written the following title: "The Wooing of John J. Rooney." (Rooney was a powerful congressman.) Because *The Reporter* had a high status with its sophisticated readers, one of the editors changed the title to "The Foreign Policy of John J. Rooney." On reflection, the writer agreed with the editor.

Almost all magazines have title schedules to establish the minimum and maximum units for use in writing article titles. Most magazines leave much white space, so the maximum title length does not account for all space in a line. For example, thumb through *Harper's, California, Cosmopolitan,* or *Playboy.* In most cases, white space is generous.

Writing Good Titles

To write good titles, the editor must be exact, concrete, and concise. A good title is often fresh and unusual. For example, read the following title:

**FAMILIES, HAPPILY,
ARE ALL ALIKE**

The article was arranged like this, including all the white space:

**FAMILIES, HAPPILY,
ARE ALL ALIKE**

A composition   by Suzanne Mantell

Another title:

Skeptic   by Howard Junker

**A PLEA FOR RESTORATION
203 YEARS LATER**

One editor wrote the following about titles:

Being devious, cryptic, or otherwise playing tricks on the readers is bad. Puns deter reading.
    Use of dramatic, emotionally charged words tends to increase reader interest in a piece.
    The well-known device of using *you, I,* or *how to* is good in titling.
    Readers express a preference for having the title above the subtitle. If the subtitle is placed above for variety, readers like to have it read into the title.

Writing Subtitles

A secondary headline is known as a "deck." If a magazine uses titles, and most do, the secondary title is called a *subtitle*. (A subtitle is *not* a *subhead;* a subhead is a line of small headings in the body of an article.) The subtitle ordinarily is printed in much smaller type than the title. It almost always is printed after the title and uses many words, like this:

(Title)   **A CORAL REEF GIVES UP SOME SECRETS—
AS SCIENTISTS BUILD A REEF OF THEIR OWN**

(Subtitle in
small type)

Smithsonian divers explore one undersea world in Central America, and create another in the National Museum of Natural History

Another title and subtitle:

CALIFORNIA JOURNAL / FRANK O'DONNELL

**GIVE ME THAT
OLD-TIME RELIGION**

". . . No abductions of high school cheerleaders or perpetration of horrors unspeakable. These Druids promote good clean Dionysian fun. . . ."

Almost anything is acceptable in a title, provided it works. Reader surveys suggest that many don't read the subtitles, and some of them do. However, as Ludeke has found, "Our research came up with the conclusion that it is better to use subtitles than not to use them."

*Subheads,
Page Heads,
Jump Heads,
and Blurbs*

Subheads. The *subhead* is a device for breaking up long, gray stretches of text. For example, read the following paragraph from an article in *The Quill*, then the subhead, then the next paragraph:

For days there was no response from the government. Erwin Knoll, editor of *The Progressive*, consulted the magazine's lawyer. The lawyer, telling Knoll of the vague and severe criminal provisions of the Atomic Energy Act, advised him to send the entire article to the Department of Energy in order to permit the placement of the government-held portion in the whole context. It was a serious mistake for a publication that believed it was exercising its First Amendment rights. (Knoll now says he has serious reservations about the wisdom of his move.)

Energy's message to *The Progressive*

The Department of Energy informed The Progressive that it had

> three choices: 1. don't publish the article; 2. let the Department of Energy rewrite the entire article (the government said it could not inform the editor which portions were sensitive because that information itself is sensitive); or 3. publish the article and face prosecution. The magazine informed the government that it intended to publish the article as it stood, and the government obtained a restraining order to prevent publication.

The editor included the boldface subhead above almost as though it is a headline for the paragraph that follows it.

Here is a different kind of subhead:

> This genius rating is enthusiastically seconded by Robert Masters, codirector with his wife, Jean Houston, of the Foundation for Mind Research in Pomona, New York. Masters has been for years both a student and teacher of many of the world's body-mind systems, ancient and modern, Oriental and Occidental, from F. M. Alexander to Zen. "Feldenkrais is the man who has gone further than anyone else, past or present," says Masters. "Employing his methods, even I can do some amazing things for people. And the potential applications of it have scarcely begun to be realized—they are clearly useful throughout life, from early childhood to advanced old age."
>
> *Learning to walk with grace*
>
> The first time I met Moshe in his cramped New York hotel room, he was giving a lesson to Sarah Rosinsky, a young woman with cerebral palsy whom he had "taught" previously in San Francisco. When she heard he was back in the country, but not coming West this time, she had flown in to have a few sessions. Moshe, she related months later, had not only taught her to talk and breathe more freely but also to walk with grace and balance, something which helped her go through a pregnancy in comfort and without falling.

The editor wrote this subhead as a short headline and has paid no attention to the white space he has left.

Because the primary reason for subheads is to relieve the tedium of reading paragraph after paragraph after paragraph, many editors have created different kinds of devices. For example:

- Large capital letters are used on some paragraphs with white space above caps.
- The first word or two in some paragraphs are marked in capital letters, small capital letters, or boldface, and spaces are left before the paragraphs.
- Included are 12 or 18 points of white space with no device of any kind.

Readers of *The New Yorker* may think that single paragraphs seem to go on and on for column after column. Although this magazine is designed for discriminating readers, it also employs a device to break up the copy:

> respects to everybody's parents and grandparents and maiden aunts in the provinces. Mme. Gonçalves, my concierge, left for Portugal.
>
> •
>
> A FEW weeks ago, I was in Portugal. The country seemed sleepy again, almost the way it had before April 25, 1974—which was the day

Page Heads. Most magazines put page heads on the second, third, and following pages of the article for as long as it continues. In some of the newer magazines, this kind of page head can be seen on the second page of an article:

> *"I have never been a 'hatchet man,' and I would never be, and the President would never ask me to be."*

Within reasonable limits, the page head can be as long as the available space permits. The above page head was placed across the entire page.

The following page head was over one column of an article in a magazine, because the other column was filled with an advertisement:

> **Critics say the Energy Commission is trying to repeal the Industrial Revolution. Barry Keene and some utilities are trying to repeal the CEC.**

Jump Heads. Few articles are continued near the end of the magazine, but occasionally they must be. For example, the title of an article in *Playboy*, on page 131, is this:

**CRONKITE'S
LAST STAND**

The editor used the same title for the jump head, but in smaller type, on page 202, with this "(continued from page 131)."

Another editor used this title on page 4:

**BETTY BOOP,
JIM RUDDLE
AND I**

He used the same typeface in his one-line jump head on page 14 like this:

BETTY BOOP
from page 4

Although jump heads are available, many editors have decided not to publish articles except as one continuing unit.

Blurbs. A *blurb* is a few lines describing the background and qualifications of the author of the article. Here is an example of a blurb, printed under a rule (a thin line) in *The New Republic*:

> Carl L. Proffer is professor of Slavic languages and literature at the University of Michigan. He is co-editor of *Russian Literature Triquarterly*.

A blurb can be placed under any column if the article continues onto other pages.

In *Playboy*, all blurbs are placed together on one page near the beginning of the magazine. For example, in the February 1981 issue of *Playboy*, one blurb went:

> We like a touch of humor in our mystery fiction, and if you're of like mind, you have a treat in store. Donald E. Westlake has resurrected his lovable thief Dortmunder for a nifty caper entitled *Ask a Silly Question*.

Specifications for the Printer

To ensure that the headline or title appears in the desired typeface and column widths, they must be marked with clear instructions for the printer. All printers have a *head schedule*, which is an array of heads in different faces and sizes. Editors mark specifications for heads with various names, like this:

Students / Students to Study
#A / Various Disciplines

(The headline is typed or handwritten, and an appropriate slug and head number are marked at the upper left. A circle can also be used instead of the diagonal slash.) If the head is to be printed on a separate page or at the top of the article, it should be clarified and noted by the editor-in-chief or the printer.

Exercises

1. Classify the following as labels or headings, and as upstyle or downstyle.
   a. Carbohydrates have gotten a bad press
   b. Oman: Guardian of the Gulf
   c. A Pilot Tries for Takeoff
   d. What Can Your Film Really Do?
   e. HOUSING'S STORM: The squeeze on builders, lenders, and buyers
   f. Males and Females and what you may not know about them
   g. Nitrosamines: Reason enough to give up bacon?
   h. BADLANDS OIL BOOM
   i. TROUBLED KIDS HIT THE TRAIL
   j. Irwin Shaw: The Conflict Between Big Bucks and Good Books

2. Do counts of the following titles.

   Example: 2 1 1 1   ½   1½ ½ 1 1 1   ½   2 ½ 1 1 1 1½ = 18 units
   W o o d   S t o v e   W i s d o m

   a. The Forgotten Fleet
   b. The Arts in Chicago
   c. The Power of the Empty Pill
   d. 8 solar add-ons that will help heat your home
   e. Surefire Way to Field Dress Your Deer
   f. The Making of a Blockbuster Exhibit
   g. Great Places to Fish This Month
   h. '82 Cars: Detroit shifts gears
   i. As Others See Us
   j. DNA: New Clues to the Ultimate Secret

3. Following the instructions at the end of each excerpt, write titles for each of these feature articles.

Remember when the Hardy Boys and Nancy Drew novels were the favorite reading matter of teen-agers, and the good guys always outwitted the bad guys, thanks to their knack for unraveling mysteries detective-style?

Well, times change. Today, millions of teen-agers are reading about the Dollanganger family, who have a knack for something else: incest. One Dollanganger marries her half uncle. A Dollanganger daughter seduces her mother's second husband. And a Dollanganger brother falls passionately in love with his Dollanganger sister.

All this happens in three current best-selling paperbacks—"Flowers in the Attic," "Petals on the Wind" and "If There Be Thorns"—the work of never-before-published author Virginia C. Andrews. Last month Miss Andrews's three books, all issued within the last 18 months, appeared simultaneously on the Top 10 Mass Market Best Sellers list compiled by the B. Dalton bookstore chain—the first time an author has scored such a bookish "hat trick" since John Jakes's Kent Family Chronicles in 1975. "Thorns," the latest, released in June, already has sold 3.7 million copies and is in its ninth printing, making it the fastest seller ever for Gulf & Western Industries Inc.'s Pocket Books unit. (3 lines, 16–20 units each line)

Bob Blakestad wriggles his lanky frame over a pile of orange and yellow rocks at the entrance to an abandoned mine tunnel in the Sierra Nevada, then turns to caution his companion: "We'll go slow right here. It's a good place for rattlesnakes."

Kicking the rocks with a heavy boot, he satisfies himself that no rattlers are around. Then he inches forward out of the hot afternoon sun into the tunnel's cool, black mouth. Stooping and squatting through tight spots, he picks his way over rotted, collapsed timbers. The patch of daylight at his back grows smaller and disappears, and the inky black ahead is pushed back only by the light atop his hard hat.

Now and then he chips the tunnel wall with a rock hammer. At one spot he shines his light on loose rocks overhead and warns: "We call those widow makers. Don't hit those." At another spot he examines a sample and exclaims: "Wow! That's just dynamite-looking rock. I don't understand why it hasn't been mined."

A modern-day prospector, 34-year-old Robert B. Blakestad is searching for gold, although not on his own account. He is one of the top exploration geologists for Homestake Mining Co. of San Francisco, the nation's largest gold producer. A growing number of natural-resource concerns like Homestake are stepping up their hunt for gold—despite recent sharp price declines—and prospectors like Mr. Blakestad are their lifeblood. (3 lines, 16–20 units each line)

Ever since it bought Wescom Inc. last year, Rockwell International Corp. has gloated over its instant expansion in the telecommunications business. At

$38 million, the acquisition "was a bargain," Rockwell said in a press release last June, "because overnight Rockwell became a much bigger factor in the business telephone systems market."

But according to insiders, when Rockwell took over Wescom it also took on a lot of problems. The firm's customer relations were poor, its telephone-switching technology needed development, and competitors were cutting into its share of the market. For awhile, executives, whom Rockwell installed at Wescom, made things seem better than they were by minimizing losses and by churning out sanguine forecasts.

But last June, just as Rockwell was speaking of "euphoria at the Downers Grove, Ill., headquarters" of Wescom, officials at Wescom were sending the bad news to Rockwell headquarters in Pittsburgh: The fiscal 1981 loss, previously estimated at $2 million, would be closer to $16 million. (2 lines, 26–30 units each line)

Back when James Current ran Shell Oil Co.'s West Coast oil and gas producing operations, he never dreamed he'd someday be worrying about Mediterranean fruit flies.

Now that Mr. Current also heads Shell's recently acquired farming division, the fly and its appetite are only the latest of the uncertainties he has had to deal with. Last year he agonized over $1 million loss in carrots when prices plunged. "I kept wondering if we should get out of carrots, but I couldn't decide because I knew next to nothing about them," he recalls.

Mr. Current's frustrations are typical of those felt by companies that have diversified into agriculture. Lured a decade ago by rising crop prices and dire predictions of a world food shortage, many corporations saw fruit and vegetable farming as a quick and easy return on their investment. There was a scramble to get in on the "glamour" of food, prompting outcries that the multinationals were taking over American agriculture.

The clamor was premature. Most companies failed miserably, largely because they were ill-prepared for the vagaries of agriculture. They couldn't cope with uncertainties created by drought, pestilence, and a highly charged labor movement. A U.S. Department of Agriculture economist estimates there are only seven publicly traded non-agriculture corporations involved in farming today, in contrast to 25 a decade ago. (2 lines, 26–30 units each line)

At the beginning of this year, Ford Motor Co. was sitting on $340 million in tax credits that it couldn't use. CSX Corp., which owns the Chessie railroad system, was holding $200 million of unusable credits, and Bethlehem Steel Corp. had nearly $150 million.

The companies couldn't use the tax breaks because they didn't owe enough taxes against which to apply the benefits. But starting with tax credits that the concerns accumulate this year, all that has changed.

Thanks to Congress and the Reagan administration, these companies and thousands like them can cash in on the generous corporate-tax reductions in the recently passed Economic Recovery Tax Act even if they don't owe any taxes. Essentially, they can sell their depreciation deductions and investment tax credits to well-heeled companies wanting to reduce their own taxes. (2 lines, 26–30 units each line)

4. Following instructions at the end of each lead, write headings for the following news stories.

BEIRUT, LEBANON—A powerful bomb explosion ripped through the prime ministry in Tehran Sunday, killing Iran's president and prime minister, Tehran Radio announced Monday.

Five other persons were killed in the explosion, and 13 others were wounded, the official Iranian news agency Pars reported. (1 line, 40 units)

NEW YORK—The National Football League has been conducting an investigation for several weeks into Houston Oilers quarterback Ken Stabler's associations with a known gambler, NFL Executive Director Don Weiss said Sunday night. (1 line, 30 units)

The Reagan administration's budget policies amount to a "rape of the future" whose true costs have yet to be felt, the vice chairwoman of the Democratic National Committee charged Sunday.

Lynn Cutler said plans to funnel federal funds to the states through a few large "block grants" rather than through individual programs sound better than they are. (3 lines, 8–10 units each line)

SALEM, ORE.—An Oregon State Penitentiary inmate was found dead in his cell early Sunday in what officials termed an apparent suicide.

State Human Resources Department spokesman David Fiskum said Gregory Osborn, 23, apparently hanged himself with a bedsheet. Osborn was serving a five-year sentence for a Clatsop County burglary conviction. (2 lines, 12–14 units each line)

5. Choose an issue of the magazine in which you are most interested and read five of the titles or headlines. In each case, read all of each article, then change each printed title or headline to a title or headline that you think is better.

6. Scan three magazines that use headlines and three other magazines that use titles. As you know, many magazines do not use headlines primarily because all the 1,760 daily newspapers use headlines. After scanning or reading the six magazines, write as many reasons as you can why you prefer the titles to headlines, or vice versa.

7. Time yourself while writing headlines on four articles; then time yourself again while writing four titles. Which should you do faster? The answer depends on *you*, because you may be a natural headline writer or a natural title writer.

Chapter 6

Graphic Arts

Most magazine manufacturing is done by commercial printers. Although it is not uncommon for a magazine to operate its own typesetting, or *composition*, department, magazine publishers generally do not own heavier printing equipment such as graphic arts cameras, platemaking machines, presses, and bindery equipment. Magazine *production*—that is, the mechanical processes that convert the publication from paper and ink to a slick consumer product—actually begins when the copy and artwork leave the editorial department and head for the printing plant. Magazine production, with the possible exception of typesetting and paste-up, is therefore in the hands of the printer rather than the editor. Editors' knowledge of printing processes need not be extensive, but sufficient enough to communicate with the printer.

In magazine production, three basic printing processes prevail: letterpress, gravure, and lithography (or *offset*). In America, the overwhelming majority of magazines are printed on lithographic presses, but letterpress and gravure also have their place. Before turning to a detailed discussion of the three main printing processes, the major steps in the production process should be reviewed. These are editing, layout and design, composition and paste-up, camera work, stripping, platemaking, presswork, and binding.

Editing, of course, is the process of revising copy to correct errors of fact and effect improvements in style and usage. (Chapters 1–5 described editing in much greater detail.)

On small publications, *layout and design* also fall within the province of the editor. This is the process of writing titles, copyfitting (making sure that the text is long or short enough to fall within the allotted space), and scaling and cropping photos and artwork. (Layout and design will be discussed in Chapter 8.)

Composition is the process of setting type. In the day of the letterpress, type was set by *hot metal* compositors working at Linotype, Intertype, and Ludlow machines, which cast *slugs*, or lines of type, from a molten lead alloy (hence, "hot metal"). Modern composition systems employ computer-driven lenses and strobe lights that project actinic images onto photosensitive paper. *Paste-up* is the process of cutting and pasting these images onto opaque paper or poster board in preparation for camera work. Hot wax is the preferred adhesive, but rubber cement is also used.

Camera work is the process of making negatives of the paste-ups. This is done in a giant *process camera*, which commonly uses sheets of high-contrast *lith film* (or *ortho film*) bigger than newspaper pages. The most versatile tool in the printing plant, the process camera is used also for "shooting" halftones (converting continuous-tone glossy photos to thousands of dots of different sizes) and for color separations (also discussed in Chapter 8).

Stripping, sometimes called *negative assembly*, is the process of aligning all negatives required for each plate and masking out unwanted areas. The completed assembly is called a *flat*.

Platemaking is the process of laying down the flat on a photosensitive metal surface and subjecting it to intense ultraviolet light in a *plateburner*. Depending on the composition of the plate emulsion, any of a large number of chemicals, including water, may be employed in developing the plate.

Presswork begins when all the plates are ready for the press run. One page of a magazine with four colors on it will require at least four plates and, on a one-color press, four passes through the machine.

Binding begins after the sheets have been printed and given a few hours for the ink to *set*, or dry. The sheets are collated, folded, *stitched* (or stapled), and cut on a large paper cutter. The magazines are also wrapped, packaged, and sometimes even mailed from the bindery.

The Printing Processes

Depending on how they are classified, there either are a few or many printing processes. *Flexography*, for example, is much like letterpress, but the plates are rubber instead of lead, and the inks are quite fluid instead of stiff and tacky. *Electrostatic printing*, also called *xerography* after its chief promoter, Xerox Corporation, is a somewhat different printing process. *Silkscreen printing*, sometimes called a *screen process*, is the oldest known printing process, and it still plays a major role in the production of billboards, point-of-purchase displays, bumper stickers, printed fabrics, decals, and computer circuit boards. *Ink jet* printing is considered the printing process of the future because it eliminates film, plates, and even presses.

As far as the capital investment and quality of reproduction, letterpress, lithography, and gravure are the mainstays of the publishing industry.

Letterpress. The letterpress works in a similar way as a rubber stamp: the type is in *relief*, and it is a mirror image of what is to be reproduced. Ink is applied to the surface of the plate, and the plate is pressed against paper with a small amount of pressure (over a large area, of course, the pressure is substantial). As an art form, letterpress finds expression as woodcuts and linoleum block prints.

Although printing from relief images was done before him, Johann Gutenberg (circa 1397–1468) is often credited with the invention of letterpress printing as we know it today. Because letterpress was the only printing process until well after the start of the Industrial Revolution (1760), it experienced a high degree of mechanization and, in turn, capital investment. The rapid expansion of the American penny press in the second half of the 19th century witnessed the birth of letterpress printing plants worth more than $1 million. These capital-intense industries, coupled with a highly organized work force, effectively blocked the development of lithography for more than a century. By the 1930s, technological innovations had made letterpress the highest quality medium for the production of America's leading consumer magazines.

The greater flexibility, lower costs, and higher quality of lithography, however, eventually forced commercial printers to scrap their letterpresses for the new lithographic equipment. The heyday of letterpresses ended in the late 1950s, but even now there are huge printing plants with letterpress equipment—primarily newspaper plants—because the cost of replacing the presses runs into millions of dollars.

Where it exists today, letterpress is a curious blend of lithographic and letterpress technologies; lightweight plastic plates with photosensitive surfaces have replaced the 40-pound stereotypes of former days, and some letterpresses have been converted to take a lithographic plate that prints directly on the sheet rather than being *offset*, as is done on a normal lithographic press.

The role that letterpress plays today in magazine publishing is in the production of medium-sized, low-quality, one-color publications. Occasionally it is used for *specialty work*: embossing, hot-foil stamping, scoring, creasing, perforating, and die-cutting.

Lithography. Aloysius Senefelder (1771–1834), the inventor of lithography, was an erstwhile Bavarian playwright and composer in search of an inexpensive method of reproducing his own musical scores. At that time, letterpress was altogether unsuitable—the process had been invented for straight text, not musical scores—and the usual method for printing music, which employed hand-engraved copper plates, was very expensive. After years of experimentation, Senefelder discovered that Bavarian limestone served as a suitable plate—hence "lithography," which is a combination of the Greek words for stone and writing. His process, still practiced by modern artists, is as follows:

- A slab of limestone is carefully smoothed down.
- A reverse (mirror) image is hand-sketched in grease pencil on the stone.
- Weak acid and gum solutions are brushed onto the stone to "desensitize" nonimage areas. This makes the blank areas nonreceptive to ink, and being watery solutions, they do not adhere to the greasy image.
- Turpentine is rubbed over the greasy areas, exposing the dry, porous stone underneath.
- A soft, rubber water roller is run over the surface to apply a thin film of water, which stands on the gum but is quickly absorbed by the porous image areas.
- A soft ink roller is run over the surface, and it leaves ink only where the original image had been.
- And paper is pressed against the surface by means of a heavy press.

The expression "original lithograph" is sometimes used to denote a work of art produced by the above process, but modern lithography is no art form. Modern lithography is based on the same principle—namely, that ink and water do not mix—but zinc and aluminum plates have replaced the limestone, and photographic images have replaced the hand-sketched images of the 19th century. When zinc plates came into use in the late 1890s, it was quickly discovered that they could be wrapped around a cylinder on a high-speed rotary press. It was learned also that a sharper reproduction was obtained when the image was first *offset* onto rubber before printing onto paper—giving rise to the process of *offset lithography*.

Lithography goes by other names as well: *planography*, because the plate surface is flat rather than relief or etched; and *photolithography*, because of the extensive use of photographic images. The process sometimes also is called *photo-offset* and even *chemical printing*.

The modern offset press has many more rollers than does a letterpress. A gum arabic solution is applied in the platemaking department, but on the press, a special set of rollers carries a weak acid solution to the plate before it encounters the inking rollers, depositing water everywhere on the plate except on the image areas. The inking rollers that next encounter the plate will not deposit ink anywhere but on the image areas, because greasy ink and water are mutually repellent. After inking, the plate encounters a rubber *blanket* cylinder after which the impression is made.

Intense research and development of photographic methods in the 20th century, coupled with the rise of powerful industrial organizations such as the National Association of Printers and Lithographers, have made lithography the dominant commercial process in the United States. Until recently, lithography was considered suitable only for runs of more than 10,000 and less than 100,000, but plate development has spawned short-run, low-cost plates for jobs of less than 1,000; and multimetal plates have pushed plate life well beyond the 100,000 mark, making lithography competitive even with gravure.

Once press runs exceed 1 million impressions, however, gravure becomes a viable alternative.

Gravure. The word derives from the same root as does *engrave,* and gravure is based on the same principle as engraving: shallow recesses are etched into an otherwise smooth plate, a fluid ink is liberally applied to the surface, the excess ink is squeegeed off with a *doctor blade,* and paper is then pressed against the plate surface. The paper must be relatively absorbent, because the ink must seep into the fibers. The plate itself is made of copper, chrome, stainless steel, or any of a number of other metals and alloys. The generic term for the process is *intaglio,* and the art forms, aside from engravings, are etchings and aquatints.

Modern gravure does not employ flat plates but cylindrical ones, mounted on rotary presses—hence the expression *rotogravure.* The images on these cylinders are not composed of etched lines, but consist of thousands of tiny dots created with a screen. Examination of a gravure product with a magnifying glass will reveal a regular sawtooth pattern along the edges of all type characters—a fact that makes it a low-quality process for editors concerned with fine typography. Proponents of gravure insist that color reproduction is superior, however, because of the ink's tendency to be absorbed by the stock. This minimizes the so-called *rosette pattern* characteristic of color reproduction on lithographic and letterpress equipment. Gravure is most commonly used in the production of newspaper supplements, catalogues, calendars, wallpaper, vinyl flooring, packaging materials, and similar products.

A gravure plate is very expensive because the image is etched directly onto the printing cylinder, which may weigh hundreds or even thousands of pounds. The etching is done with either acids or a computer-driven diamond stylus. Once the image has worn away, the plate surface is ground off on a metal lathe, and the entire cylinder is recoated in an electroplating process.

Although the cost of a gravure plate is very high, the plate has exceedingly long run life—a million impressions is commonplace—so the cost per printed item eventually comes down as the number of impressions increases.

Typography

We all recognize typefaces we like and those we don't like—even though we may not know why certain ones appeal to us. This section discusses two important criteria: type measurement and type classification.

Type Measurement

Type has its own system of measurement, quite unlike anything laypeople encounter. Just as feet and inches are the basic units of measurement, so picas and points are the basic units in the printer's system of measurement.

A *pica* is about ⅙ inch, and a *point* is about 1/72 inch. We say "about" because six picas do not equal *exactly* one inch; just for the record, one pica equals .1660184043 inch.

For practical purposes, this is not a useful figure. We usually say that six picas are slightly less than an inch—about .996 inch, actually. It is important to know the *exact* length of a pica because, when measuring the width of a magazine centerfold in picas and making a conversion to inches, the measurement could be off as much as 1/16 inch because magazines are so wide when opened up. (A sixteenth of an inch is a large error.)

Within the system itself, the conversions are easier to make because a pica is equal exactly to 12 points. When typefaces are measured, points are generally used; and when larger things such as the widths of columns and photos are measured, picas are used.

Typefaces themselves have traditionally been manufactured in standard sizes that are still used today, such as 10-point and 12-point type. A complete series would include at least the following sizes: 8, 9, 10, 11, 12, 14, 18, 24, 30, 36, 48, 60, and 72.

Sizes below 14 points are called *text* or *body* types, and sizes of 14 points or larger are called *display* types. The text of a magazine is set in body type—in fact, most magazines use 10-point body type—and the titles of articles are set in display type. A 48-point head is probably big enough for most titles of magazine articles, or *pieces*, as they are usually called.

This leads us to a sticky subject: the formulation of rules about the sizes of titles of magazine pieces. In a typical magazine, 24-, 30-, 36-, and 48-point types serve the reader well in "indexing" the content of each piece in the publication.

But what is type "size"? For our purposes, it is sufficient to define the size of a type to be the distance from the top of the *ascender* (the long upstroke over b, d, h, l, etc.) to the bottom of the *descender* (the long downstroke under j, p, q, y, etc.). The term x-height is used to refer to the size of the characters without ascenders or descenders.

$$\text{x height} \quad \textbf{original} \quad \text{type size}$$

Type, of course, is two dimensional; its width also warrants discussion. In the printing business, the width of a typeface is referred to as its *set width*.

In a normal typeface, the width of a capital *M* is equal to the type size. This is such a universal concept for all typefaces and all type sizes that printers developed the concept of an *em*—often defined as the square of the type size. The em is therefore a variable measure: an 18-point em is 18 points wide and 18 points high; it is bigger than a 14-point em, which is 14 points wide and 14 points high. In body type, one em is a typical paragraph indention.

If each character of the alphabet were squeezed slightly, it would reduce the set width of the alphabet and thereby create what is called a *condensed* face. Also, we could make each character fatter, and thereby create an *extended* or *expanded* face. If a typographer says, for example, that a given face is 12-point, 11½-set, she means that it is slightly condensed. Both the examples below are 24-point Trade Gothic, but the bottom one is condensed.

fashion in art is
fashion in art is a necessity

A complete inventory of display types on any magazine should include some condensed and some extended faces—not only for contrast but also for those unhappy situations in which the "perfect" word will not fit in the available space.

Although most of the discussion so far has been in reference to display types, the same considerations apply across the board to body types: we can, for example, pack more words into our magazine by using a condensed body type, but this makes for a "gray" page. In fact, of all the complaints that publishers receive, grayness is the most common. To make a publication "brighter," the following solutions are most common:

- Use of a larger type size, say, 10-point rather than 9-point
- Use of a normal rather than a condensed body type
- Use of more paragraph indentions
- Insertion of space between lines

The last solution is known as *leading* (pronounced "ledding") or *leading out*. The term comes from the practice of inserting strips of lead between lines of type in the days when type was cast from a molten lead alloy. An 8-point type that has no space between the lines is said to be *set solid*—and sometimes the descenders of one line will touch the ascenders of the line below it—while an 8-point type that has one point of leading is said to be set "eight on nine," sometimes written *8/9*.

Classifications of Type

There are many approaches to classifying type, none of them precise. The classification that follows parallels those of leading authors in the field of graphic arts.

The broadest taxonomy of types places them into six categories: roman, sans serif, square serif, text, script, and decorative.

Roman faces are familiar to us because most of our reading matter is set in roman. Their chief characteristic is the *serif*—a small cross-stroke at the end of each main stroke—as shown in this illustration of 72-point Caslon.

Roman gets its name from the similarity of its capital letters to the alphabetic characters chiseled by stonemasons on the early public buildings of Rome. In 1490, an imaginative Frenchman, Nicholas Jenson, combined these characters with the smaller, Carolingian minuscules to create the complete uppercase and lowercase alphabet that we know today. (The terms *uppercase* and *lowercase* stem from the early typographers' habit of storing small letters in a case below that of the capital letters.) Jenson's typeface, known today as Cloister Old Style, is a classic example of *oldstyle* roman, known for its blunt serifs. Other examples of oldstyle roman are Garamond and Caslon.

Improvements in the process of casting type led to refinements in type characters. The next major subgroup of roman typefaces, known as *transitional roman*, is characterized by its pointed serifs and rounded *fillets*, which are the connecting strokes between the serifs and main strokes. Commonly cited examples of transitional roman are Bulmer and Baskerville.

Modern roman is characterized by further refinement in design—particularly the hairline strokes, and in some cases, the total absence of fillets. Bodoni is the most commonly cited typeface. This example is set in 60-point Bodoni Bold.

fashion

Bodoni Bold is one of the most popular headline typefaces in America. In common use as body type are Times Roman, designed in 1931 by Stanley Morison for *The Times* of London; and Century, designed in 1894 by L. B. Benton and T. L. DeVinne for *Century* magazine, a leading publication in its day.

As the world's leading type foundries became aware of improvements in statistical research methods, there evolved the concept of *legibility faces*. These were faces whose designs had been tested on human subjects and which had proven to be particularly legible, or quickly read. Two legibility faces found in American newspapers today are Regal and Ideal; slightly modified, even Century and Times Roman are available as legibility faces.

Although Garamond and many others are more elegant than the so-called legibility faces, the elegant designs generally are reserved for high-quality *bookwork*. When done in a commercial printing plant, bookwork affords a much greater degree of control over the manufacturing process.

It is difficult to formulate rules about typography because as soon as the rule is formulated, someone breaks it successfully. Using Century in headlines is a good example of this: although designed as a text face, larger sizes are used tastefully in some prestigious publications.

Of the six main groups of type mentioned earlier, the next in order of importance is the group of *sans serif* faces. "Sans" being French for "without," sans serif means literally what the expression implies: without serifs.

In addition to the absence of serifs, sans serif typefaces—or *gothics*, as they are sometimes called—are often recognized for their uniformity of stroke: there is little or no variation in the widths of the strokes used to create the characters of this illustration, which is set in 36-point News Gothic Condensed.

fashion

In magazines, sans serif type plays a significant role in the titles, but only a minor role as a body type. Franklin Gothic, Tempo, Spartan, Univers, and Folio are just a few of the many sans serif designs that serve as mediums for headlines.

A word of caution in using sans serifs as a body type: because the characteristic cross-stroke on the Roman typefaces served as a delimiter on the form of each word, sans serif typefaces can be more difficult to read unless set larger or leaded out. This shortcoming of sans serif faces has caused most publications to reject it as their workhorse for body type.

Sans serif plays its most important role in brochures, road signs, billboards, magazine advertising, and labeling of consumer products.

Square serif typefaces also live up to their name: their serifs are like small, rectangular slabs. Some printers place these in the category of roman faces because they have serifs on them, and some printers place them in the group of decoratives (see Figure 6–1). When treated as an independent group, they sometimes are referred to as *Egyptians*.

Examples of square serif or Egyptian typefaces are Karnak, Stymie, Craw Clarendon, City, and Egyptian. All of these may create an "Eastern" mood for your publication, but if you decide to use them, do so sparingly at first. Stymie Bold (set in 36-point) looks like this:

fashion

FIGURE 6–1. Decorative typefaces are used to create a special effect. In this example, the typeface chosen for *feed/back*, a simple typewriter face, was selected because of the nature of the intended audience—journalists. (Courtesy, *feed/back*.)

Text faces, which are sometimes called *Old English* or *blackletter*, play only a nominal role in American publications, but many large newspapers—the *New York Times,* the *Los Angeles Times,* the *Washington Post,* the *Portland Oregonian,* the *San Francisco Chronicle,* and many more—use text faces in their *nameplates* or *flags.* In spite of this apparent allegiance to tradition, however, the use of text faces in this fashion represents a historical anomaly. As the English newspaper editor Harold Evans once said:

> The most hideous blackletter titles survive around the world from Victorian days because they are "traditional," but in fact the earliest titles, such as those of the first daily paper, *The Daily Courant* (1702), and the first evening paper, *The Evening Post* (1710), and America's *New England Courant* (1721) were all in good bold roman lower-case.

Text used as a body type is wholly unappealing, and with all the breezy sans serif faces in our environment today, it is a wonder that the blackletters have managed to survive at all. There are a few famous ones still in circulation—Wedding Text, Goudy Text, Cloister Black, and Engravers Old English, to name a few—but they are best kept in reserve for those rare occasions when you want a "gothic" mood.

Script faces look like handwriting and are used to create a "feminine" mood. Otherwise, their appeal is limited, and they are worth mentioning only for full development of our discussion of typography. The example below is called Snell Roundhand:

fashion

Decorative typefaces play an important role in magazine typography (see Figure 6–2). They are developed to reflect trends in fashion and advertising, coming and going like women's wear or styles of architecture. Broadway, for example, is usually associated with art deco and is enjoying a revival.

THE WILD WILD WEST

When the Texans took over *New West*, they promised no gunplay. Casualties now include three editors and more.

By Ken Garcia

It seemed a fitting end to a year of rampant rumor and confusion at *New West* magazine. The Northern California office staffers anxiously awaited ex-editor Jon Carroll's arrival at their Christmas party, eager to hear the real story behind his recent resignation. But Carroll never made it. He got fogged in at LAX.

Carroll's resignation signaled that the honeymoon was over between *New West* staffers and their self-appointed saviors from *Texas Monthly*. When Mediatex Inc., *Texas Monthly*'s parent company, purchased the financially troubled magazine in August, staffers greeted the news with cheers, beers and unbridled optimism. "Editor Jon Carroll, together with numerous other employees . . . issued the following closely reasoned and dignified statement for publication: Hoo-ray!" read the *Between the Lines* column on Aug. 25. Executive Editor Rosalie Muller Wright said the takeover "is great for *New West*." But with a few notable exceptions, only the head honchos at *Texas Monthly* feel that way now.

The reason: some staffers believe they've gotten a bum steer. After his first meeting with the *New West* editors, *Texas Monthly* Publisher Michael R. Levy claimed

---

Garcia, a contributing writer, most recently worked as the education reporter for the Fremont Argus.

---

there would be no immediate layoffs, and that most changes would take place through attrition. But a swift sweep followed, netting close to 15 people, including a senior and an associate editor and several people on the art staff. "It's a normal procedure in this kind of endeavor," explained Levy. "Some folks work out and some folks don't." Carroll described his own departure from the top of the hierarchy this way:

"I was not pushed out the window. I jumped."

No one was really surprised.

Ever since *Texas Monthly* Editor William Broyles Jr., went house-hunting in Los Angeles, it was suspected that Carroll would have to hand over the editing reins. But it did nothing to ease staffers' fears about job security. "There is a lot of unhappiness," said Michael Lester, a recent casualty of the layoff move. "There hasn't been as much attention to the people as the product. I think they're hoping that people here will become more optimistic in the next few months."

Broyles hopes so, too. At the present time, he admitted, "People here are nervous."

Those who have met Broyles toss around adjectives like "talented," "hard-working" and "sincere" to describe him, but a good portion of the rank-and-file still see him as an outsider. Some resentment may have been inevitable, because of the Texan's tactics following the takeover. But the new *New West* editor certainly didn't win any fans when he let staffers know that he didn't cotton to some of the magazine's methods.

While his critique of *New West*'s Oct. 20 issue applauded the excellent reporting in Nancy Friedman's cover story, "Everything They Didn't Tell Us About Tampons," he said that short shrift may have been given to the corporate side. He also thought there were too many stories which assumed an "us against them" stance where liberals were automatically "good" and conservatives "bad." He laid the law down on words he considers obscene. Calling the Oct. 20 *New West* the "fuck, cunt, dick" issue, the Oxford-scholar-turned-editor said if those words were used in the magazine, they should be written f---, c---, d---.

"I thought he was f------ kidding," said one staffer.

Broyles, whose magazine has won three national awards, explained. "I would run those [same] articles with enthusiasm. I think, though, that you need to reach out to readers and win them to your tastes. You try to persuade readers to your viewpoint with convincing arguments. You should show them as well as tell them." Asked whether he would show *New West* readers the conservative philosophy mirrored in some of his *Texas Monthly* columns, Broyles replied, "You will continue to find a diversity of viewpoints in *New West*."

But some of the changes have been met with less than enthusiasm. "Nobody ever thought we would be calling the Murdoch days the good old days," said one staffer.

Rosalie Wright's stronghold in the Northern California office is so secure that many believe her pres-

---

FIGURE 6–2. Decorative typefaces for the titles of articles are common in magazine design. Here, Souvenir creates an old-fashioned mood. Note the imaginative use of initial and *terminal* capitals to frame the two lines of the title of the article. (Courtesy, *feed/back*.)

Choosing Type

Any reliable printer has a variety of typefaces to choose from when planning a magazine. (For further, more detailed information on typefaces, consult *Type and Typography: The Designer's Notebook*, by Ben Rosen, New York, Hastings House Publishers, 1976.) The legibility of type is the most important aspect and varies widely from typeface to typeface.

Beginning editors should plan their magazines in a conventional manner for several issues, then experiment with one article. If the new typeface is legible in that article, at least as much as the rest of the articles in the magazine, consider switching to the new kind of type.

The decision to change typefaces is determined by which are most popular. Among those currently ranking high in popularity are Bodoni, Scotch Roman, Garamond, Baskerville, and Caledonia. Stanley Hlasta, a typographic specialist, said of Bodoni:

> As for magazine use, Bodoni Book is especially adaptable for house organs and external sales promotion magazines (with Futura), and for business and industrial publications dealing with insurance and finance. Bodoni blends well with Corvinius or Bernhard Modern for digests; with Ultra Bodoni for house organs; with Futura or a script face for humor publications; with the light italic or a sans serif face for architecture journals; and with a script or cursive to make an ideal chamber of commerce magazine for resort towns. Bodoni is also a good face for medical journals and for travel, art, engineering and science, and home and garden magazines.

Hlasta is obviously enthusiastic about Bodoni, but another typographer, John Biggs, said that when Bodoni is used for body type, it "is not the best type for continuous reading, and if not well printed can be positively illegible." (If Biggs' observation seems entirely negative, he did mention "if not well printed.") Biggs also approves of Bodoni when the printer takes care.

Psychologist Miles Tinker has studied legibility and believes that reading speed is the best measure, so he devised a test to compare various types. Tinker chose seven typefaces that were most frequently stressed by 37 publishers: Bodoni, Scotch Roman, Old Style, Garamond, Antique, Caslon Old Style, and Cheltenham. He also added Kabel Light, American Typewriter, and Cloister Black. In Tinker's test he found that American Typewriter and Cloister Black were read much more slowly than the other eight typefaces. He also said about the eight faces that the people who

FIGURE 6–3. Combining typefaces from three main groups of type can be done without sacrificing unity. Here, a specialty face is selected for the title of the article and an initial capital; a sans serif face is chosen for the blurb or teaser; and a roman face serves as the body type. Note the surprint of the title on the halftone. (Courtesy, *Columbia Journalism Review*, January/February 1981.)

were tested read them with ease. Tinker concluded that "typefaces in common use do not differ significantly" in legibility.

Another important item in using type is its size. Although the largest size of type may seem to be the easiest to read, it isn't always true. Try reading 15 words in 60-point type and you will instantly understand the importance of this question: How large should the ideal type be? Neither 60-point type nor 7-point type is the answer. Most of the newspapers publish 8-point as body type, while many magazines use 10-point as body type.

Almost as important as type size is the amount of space between lines. Reading 20 lines of 8-point type set solid, then another 20 lines of 8-point type with one point of leading clearly demonstrates the difference—you'll probably vote for the latter.

Finally, consider line lengths. Most newspapers in recent years have recognized that eight-column pages make the lines too short. These papers have changed to a six-column format, which makes the lines longer. Because the magazines have a much freer form, the editors may some day have to face this question: How long should the lines go? Biggs has suggested that each line should not contain more than about 10 or 12 words of average length. Perhaps the only researcher who has answered this basic question validly is Tinker, who states that 22 picas is the optimum length.

Copyfitting

Estimating

Most magazine editors describe the length of articles in terms of the number of words they contain. Editors first count a few lines on one page, then count the number of lines on that page, and multiply the average number of words by the number of lines per page. If elite type has been used, the average number of words per page is approximately 290–300; if pica type has been used, the average number of words per page is approximately 250–260. In other words, if an article runs 10 pages and elite type was used, it will be about 2,900–3,000 words long; with pica type, the length will be about 2,500–2,600 words.

Some publications retype all copy on paper with rules at the left and right, arranged so that typists cannot go over the rules. Most magazines, however, are not quite so elaborate. A good practice is to type a paragraph of an article with rules and then decide where the right margin should be.

Most magazine editors are satisfied with an estimate of the length of each article. The magazine's editor-in-chief ensures that all other editors use these estimates for the close fitting of copy.

Fitting Copy Most editors use a system of 50 characters (or letters) per line of typewritten copy. For example, setting the typewriter margins at 10 and 60 (or 20 and 70) results in 50 characters per line. Each line doesn't have to measure *precisely* 50 characters; the shorter and longer lines can be averaged, as the following typewritten sample shows:

```
The margins have been set at 20 and 70 to type this
particular bit of copy for a line length of about
50 characters.  Some of the lines will then be less.
```

As an example, here is how an editor might deal with a particular problem. The editor has 40 lines of copy that have been typed, not with 50 characters per line, but with 55. The editor follows these steps:

Step 1:
```
      40  Typewritten lines
    × 55  Characters per line
     200
     200
    2200  Characters in copy
```

Step 2:
```
         44   Lines of type
    50)2200   Characters in copy (divided by
      200        characters in type line)
      200
      200
```

Because this magazine uses 10-point type, that number is used in the third step.

Step 3:
```
      44  Lines
    × 10  Points
     440  Points of space filled
```

Because there are 72 points to an inch, that number is used in the next step.

Step 4:

```
              6.11   Inches of type
        72 )440.00   Points of space divided by number
           432
           ___
            8 0
            7 2
            ___
              80
              72
              __
               8
```

Such pinpoint accuracy need not necessarily be stressed. The editor can decide that the article uses 6 inches (or 7 inches, because the few points can be used as white space).

Other Copyfitting Methods

Retyping each piece to fit copy will guarantee excellent results, but it is a time-consuming process. If time and money are critical factors in the editorial department's schedule—as they are on any publication—other methods of fitting copy might be more appropriate. The following method will not guarantee perfect fit, but at least it will provide a rough measure of the length of each story, accurate within an inch or so of the true figure.

Select a stack of representative manuscripts and ask your printer to set the copy in the magazine's usual body type and column width. When the typeset material is returned, simply count the number of lines of typewritten copy and the number of inches of typeset copy. A little thought will enable you to produce a chart such as the following:

Format: Times Roman, 16.5 pica column width, set 8/10

No. lines typewritten copy	No. inches typeset copy
1	.19
2	.38
3	.56
4	.75
.	.
.	.
.	.
100	18.75

Copyfitting thus becomes a matter of counting the number of typewritten lines in the edited manuscript and referring to the chart.

The chief drawback of this particular method is the degree of variance in the preparation of most manuscripts—but this can be controlled by giving each author and typist a set of instructions on manuscript preparation for your particular publication. (See *Writer's Market*, edited by P. J. Schemenaur and John Brady, for a set of such instructions.)

The first step is to estimate the total number of characters in the manuscript, including spaces. Using a ruler, you can see that an elite typewriter produces 12 characters per inch. Again with a ruler, you can learn other parameters of standard typewriters—for example, that when an elite is double-spaced, it produces three lines per inch. If, for example, the average "copy area" on each page is 7.5 × 9 inches, then the total number of elite characters in a 22-page manuscript can be calculated as follows:

$$7.5 \times 12 \times 9 \times 3 \times 22 = 53{,}460$$

The next step is to estimate how many pages this will be when set in type.

Type manufacturers provide charts that indicate how many typeset characters there are per pica for each size of each typeface. Ten-point Bodoni Book, for example, has 2.8 characters per pica, so if the line length is 25 picas, then the total number of characters per line becomes:

$$2.8 \times 25 = 70$$

The type would look crowded if set solid. However, if two points of leading are added, each line will be 12 points deep (set 10/12, or "ten on twelve"). Since there are 70 characters per line, and since there are 53,460 characters in the manuscript, the total number of lines becomes:

$$53{,}460 \div 70 = 763.7$$

The total length thus becomes the number of lines, rounded up, multiplied by the depth of each line:

$$764 \times 12 = 9{,}168$$

In points, the figure is not useful; however, since there are 72 points per inch, divide by 72 to determine the length in inches:

$$9{,}168 \div 72 = 127.33$$

This copyfitting method is very accurate, and the only figure you need to look up is the characters-per-pica count of the body type being used.

Titles and Illustrations

Typographic experts firmly believe that the titles (or *headings*) and illustrations must be carefully chosen to harmonize with both the body type and the tone of the words. Satisfying all of these requirements can seem like one gigantic puzzle.

Titles

Visual unity—an important ingredient in any publication—can be achieved by standardizing titles, by-lines, and other elements, such as blurbs. Editors vary the magazine by considering each article as a separate unit, then changing the pace by using different kinds of type for various articles. Each article is a unit—and all articles together are also a unit of the magazine.

If the magazine works with a large printer who has many kinds of type, the editor will have one of the printer's typebooks. If the printer has no typebook, the editor will get proofs of the typefaces available. (Some printers might try to persuade the editor toward a narrow range of type if it is less bother, but the editor must insist on variety.)

David Merrill, designer of 20 famous magazines, told me the following:

> Generally, I believe in using display (headline) faces that have a family resemblance to the logo face to help create that personality. Most of the magazines I've done use the same for both. And again, speaking generally, the same headline face should be used consistently throughout the magazine. Lots of magazines try to give each article "personality" by changing typefaces, but I think, with rare exceptions, that that simply leaves your *magazine* without a personality.
>
> One of the exceptions is that a *Time* cover about a war shouldn't share a typeface with a Cher cover. But *Time* is unusual in the diversity of its content. I believe they are too rigid in format—there's one face for everything. That's too rigid for *them*, but would fit nicely on most other magazines.

Body copy should be readable, and the more of it there is the more readable it should be. Unless there is a reason, I can't imagine it ought to be noticeable. I think that if it calls attention to itself, you've probably selected an inappropriate typeface. Let the logo, magazine format design, and headline type determine the "look" of the book.

A cardinal rule of mine is never to use a sans serif type for anything longer than a headline or possibly a caption to a picture. Evelyn Wood (conductor of reading dynamics courses) proved that it [sans serif] is harder to read than serif faces.

When in doubt, use Times Roman 9/10. I have on at least half of the magazines I've designed or redesigned. (Or 10/11 if you're going for an older than average audience.) *Time* uses Times Roman 9/9½ because they can pack more words in each issue, but they get hundreds of letters complaining about readability every year.

Most magazines use a three-column-per-page format, each column being 13 or 14 picas wide for good reason. It's easier to read, and we're used to it, not only from magazines but newspapers as well.*

Illustrations

Long articles published in magazines are often broken up by using photographs, also known as *halftones*. Unlike a halftone, a *line shot* can be made from a simple line drawing, usually done in black. A line shot is an exact reproduction of the drawing, but it can be reduced in size to fit if needed.

Using photographs is different from using line drawings. The camera operator photographs the illustration through a screen that breaks the photograph into a pattern of small dots. Dark areas have large dots that run together, while light areas have tiny dots. The dots are so small that the human eye cannot resolve them, and much like an illusion, they form easily recognizable patterns.

When editors have both a line drawing and a photograph for the same article, they integrate them with the body type, the title, and the other elements. Put all together, they are evaluated to see if the line drawing or photograph harmonizes with the other elements.

In earlier days, halftones were known as *cuts*—a word that appears from time to time even in this book. The term is anachronistic in the modern production plant, however, because it hails from the old days when engravers with burins labored over copper plates, carefully cutting engravings. The word hung on when acids began to be used, because the final product was still an etched image. We are now two generations away from that process: everything is photographic, no acids are used, and the final product is usually *planographic* (when it's relief, it's plastic, not metal). Today, the term *line shot* has come to replace *line cut*; a line

---

*Courtesy, David Merrill.

shot is a negative with no dot pattern, consisting only of lines—including graphics, like cartoons, or simply type images. Reproduction of your personal signature would be done with a line shot.

Planning for the Press

An editor folds a piece of paper once, then again, and finally has an uncut, eight-page booklet. This demonstrates the principle of a *signature*—a group of pages printed together. Because many more pages than four can be printed, signatures may have 16, 32, or more pages. Putting the signatures together, the editor can produce magazines of many pages.

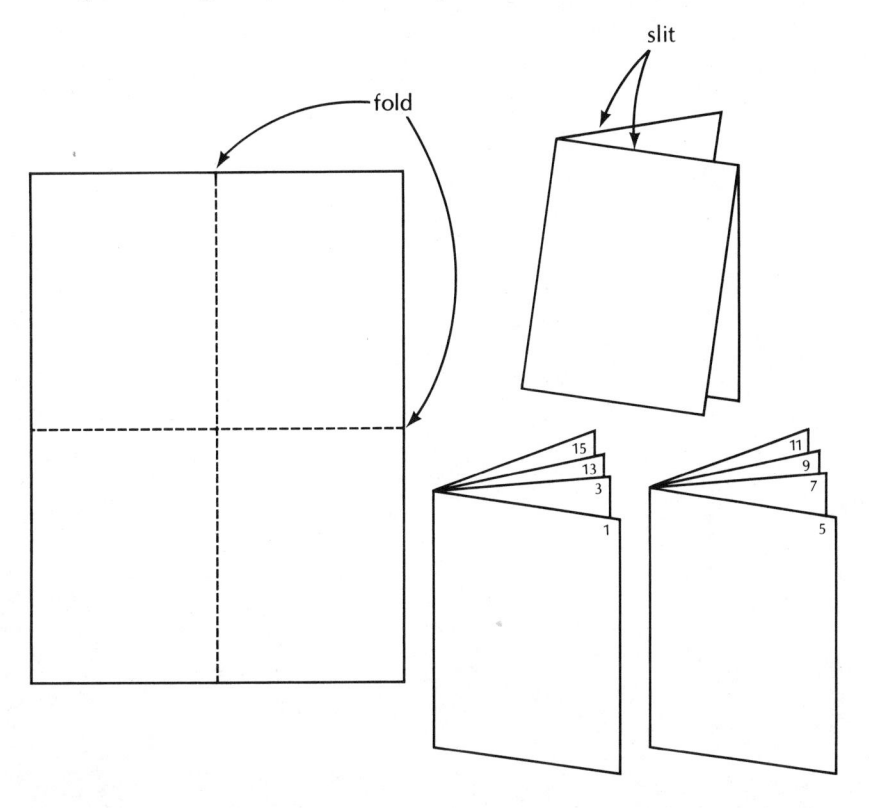

Signatures. This half-size dummy can be achieved by double-folding a page of paper that will produce an eight-page booklet. At the right, two of these signatures can be combined to result in a 16-page dummy.

We do not have "30-page magazines" because 30 is not a multiple of four. The folded sheet of paper shows that the printer must be careful in *imposition* because the pages must be printed right-side up.

The printer places the forms in a way to print four pages on one side and four on the other to make up an eight-page booklet. The editor needs to know which forms will be made up and printed first and which last, so he or she can plan the magazine and have faster production by working with the printer on the deadlines of the different forms. The less-timely articles are printed first, the most-timely articles on the last form.

Exercises

1. Collect six copies of the magazine you consider the most attractive and answer the following:
   a. In one or two sentences for each, list all the qualities of that magazine that appeal strongly to you. Consider the size, type of paper, use of color, typefaces, quality of reproduction, etc.
   b. Do the same with regard to qualities that do not appeal to you, and make suggestions for improvements.
   c. Using a magnifying glass (preferably 8× or 10×), carefully inspect the quality of reproduction. Pay close attention to edges of type characters, halftones (photos), color photos, and color tints (these will have a dot pattern). Make notes on any imperfections and suggest improvements. Try to identify the printing process used.
   d. Clip out one example of each typeface used (not including advertisements) and try to classify each face according to the broad groupings described in this chapter. Then go to a library and, using one of the many books available on typefaces, identify each face by name.

2. Collect six copies of a popular consumer magazine you consider very unattractive and answer questions a–d above.

3. Collect one copy each of the following magazines: *Reader's Digest, Time, Ebony, Graphis, Domus, U.S. News & World Report,* and *Popular Photography.* Look at them carefully with a magnifying glass. Do you see any differences? (Hint: *Reader's Digest* is printed by gravure; *Time* and *Ebony* are printed by letterpress; and the others are printed by lithography.)

4. With a ruler, determine how many characters there are per inch on a pica typewriter. How many lines are there per inch with single-spaced copy? with double-spaced copy?

5. You have been given 40 typewritten manuscript pages with an average copy area of 6.5 × 9 inches. The copy was prepared on a pica typewriter, double-spaced. Determine the total number of characters.

6. You have been given 180 manuscript pages, triple-spaced, on an elite typewriter. Average copy area is 8 × 10 inches. Determine the total number of characters.

7. You have to copyfit 30 typewritten pages, double-spaced, on an elite typewriter. Average copy area is 7 × 9 inches, and you want the material set in Old Style No. 1, 10/12, for 22 picas. Determine the length in inches.

8. You are planning a special issue, and all the space has been filled except for 25 inches. The column width is 22 picas, and the body type is 10-point Bodoni Book, set 10/12. If the typewriter margins are set at 20 and 80, how many lines of elite typewriter copy must be written to fill the hole?

9. Using the example in this chapter, estimate the length in inches of the following typewritten passage after it has been set in 10-point type:

```
           FLORIDA'S 'YANKEE' COAST


     In Florida, they tell it this way:  A new
arrival in heaven was well pleased with the place.
He found everything to his liking.  Heaven, he
decided, was all it was cracked up to be.
     Then, one day he came upon another who had
been admitted to the heavenly portals;  this man
sat in a corner with a ball and chain attached to
his ankle.
     The new citizen, puzzled, went to St. Peter
```

and asked: "How come this man has to wear a ball and chain?"

"Well," St. Peter replied: "that man's from Florida and every time we turn him loose he tries to go back."

The people who live along the 100-mile stretch of white sands that curve along the Gulf of Mexico from Pensacola to Panama City will vow and declare that the man was from Northwest Florida, not the more heavily publicized regions to the South. St. Petersburg, Miami, Daytona Beach and environs, they claim, are next door to nothing at all compared to Northwest Florida, where the sand is whiter, the water is wetter, the skies are bluer, and the fishing's better.

And there are plenty of vacationers from the Far North--Alabama, Georgia, Mississippi, and Louisiana--who will take their oath that no vacation is better spent than the one that has the tourist roosting on the Northwest Florida coast throughout his weeks-with-pay.

In fact, a Birmingham manufacturer set himself up as a one man Chamber of Commerce for "Yankee" Florida. He reasoned that the war being fought over the beaches--Daytona Beach claims "The World's Most Famous Beach," Miami beats the drums for "The Magic City's Magic Beaches," and Californians point with pride to "Beautiful Long Beach"--failed to take account of the one great property of every beach. No, not water. Sand.

A widely traveled, jovial fellow whose face is as ruddy as a beachcomber's, F.H. Mohler, started collecting sand from the ocean-side in six states three years ago. Now, he has 17 bottles of the white (some of it not-so-white) gritty stuff gathered in Florida , Georgia, South Carolina, North Carolina, Mississippi, and California. The sand from Long Beach, California, is far down the "whiteness" list; No. 16 among the 17 specimens.

Sand from Panama City and Fort Myers ran one-two, with Panama City in first place. Daytona Beach was the third-place winner. From there, the sand gets darker and darker in this order:

Bradenton, Biloxi, Ormand Beach (Fla.), St. Augustine, Myrtle Beach (S.C.), Clearwater, Sea Island (Ga.), St. Petersburg, Wrightsville (N.C.), St. Simons (Ga.), and Port St. Joe (Fla.).

Magic Miami's sands were in 17th place.

There were howls reverberating across the nation when The Associated Press filed that story on its wires, but, of course, nothing but chuckles came from Panama City, where the local drumbeaters had long been whooping up "The World's Most Beautiful Beaches."

And the same self-congratulations might have been causing Pensacola and Fort Walton to dislocate their municipal elbows while patting themselves on the back, for the glittering ring of real estate that curves around the Gulf at Panama City sits in the front yards of both Fort Walton and Pensacola. For most of the 100-mile stretch along U.S. 98 from Pensacola south to Panama City, the white stuff is banked between the highway and the shoreline for nearly the length of a football field.

Pensacola, the closest of the trio of Northwest Florida cities to Louisiana, actually suffers, tourist-wise, because of its fame as "The Annapolis of the Air."

"Pensacola? Sure, I know where that is. That's where they have the Navy air base."

Visitors to Florida can be pardoned for taking such a narrow view of it that they think of it only as Navy air town, for the U.S. Naval Air Training Station is so intimately bound up with the city that it almost serves as an alter ego. Divorcing Pensacola from the Navy station is something like splitting ham and eggs--unthinkable.

But Pensacolans are quick to point out that the military, which once seemed to be the city's be-all and end-all (and is still a huge economic factor), isn't the entire Pensacola story; just one important chapter.

Where once a simple military town sat far up in Florida's Northwest corner more or less minding its own business, there is now a four-wheeled city with deep-rooted military, recreational, industrial, and trade foundations.

Like most of the other growing cities ringed along the brilliant sands, Pensacola has been taking the high road since World War II brought thousands to the area and gave them a chance to see Florida living, Northwest-style. Once the forgotten section of the state--vaguely considered Alabaman or Georgian by Gold Coast Floridians--the Northwest has suddenly been remembered.

Although it's as Floridian as citrus fruit, Pensacola doesn't push its "vacation paradise" advertising in the same directions taken by many another coastal city. Well aware that the term "resort town" has an expensive ring to some who yearn for a vacation on the beach in the sand in the sun, Pensacolans underline the fact that theirs is a community with permanent facilities.

Your money is welcome, but it neen't come in thousand-dollar bills. And, like the other Northwest Coast cities, which reverse the "winter vacation" theories of the South Florida resorts, summer is tourist-time in Pensacola.

From Pensacola Beach down the long stretch south to Panama City, vacationers have been putting down two-week roots for more than a month. New tourist courts have been springing up like giant pastel toadstools, and some are well outside the urban areas. They begin to multiply about halfway between Pensacola and Panama City, then there is a huge cluster of cottages for tourists at Fort Walton--which calls itself "The Playground"--before once again the sea and sand are the only views to the motorist's right as he shoots south along U.S. 98.

Several miles before coming into Panama City, tourist courts and cottages burgeon again--and continue for miles.

Panama City itself is actually next-door to St. Andrews Bay, not the Gulf of Mexico, and is a few miles inland. To the vacationer, however, it's all Panama City, even though there are municipalities along the stretch before the highway slants inland to Panama City proper.

Panama City can't compete with St. Petersburg, Miami, Key West, and other South Florida locales in the year-round sunshine race, but it's not even sure it would like to have the sun beaming down all the time. Winter tourism is big business, but there are Georgians, Alabamans, Louisianians, and Mississippians who have become Panama City Floridians because they like the nip in the air at Christmas brought on by temperatures in the 40's and 50's.

The swimming season often starts late in February and lasts until November. A few of the younger (and hardier) have been seen fighting the waves in December and January.

As for prices to vacationers, they're lower in town than at the beaches of Panama City, as is true throughout the state. In Northwest Florida, the "season" runs from late in May until Labor Day.

"Yankee" Florida caters to the workingman's wallet.

In the Panama City area, particularly, a tourist family can save as much as $100 a week simply by renting a cottage on the inland side of the highway rather than the beach side. That walk across a 30-foot-wide pavement can save you enough to buy a new tire.

That offers a picture of life in the Panama City area--the nearer you are to water, the nearer to heaven. The shining stretch of sand sets up an irresistible mating-call every summer.

Economics is an important subject to the Bay County seat itself, locked in a municipal tug-o-war that will determine what the city is to be. The financial pendulum is swinging toward the ever-booming tourist trade, but industry is still in the running. Actually, Panama City is a town with a two-way stretch; it has plenty of room to grow in both directions. And it has both doors open for business.

Nor only is there plenty of room for expansion toward the beaches, but the vast plains of white sands themselves are growing. Eastern beaches have been opening up, assuring visitors they'll never have to experience the jam-packed Coney Island atmosphere, or the tinsel attitudinizing of the South Florida resorts.

The attitude tourists will find among the natives of Northwest Florida--the "Crackers"-- is illustrated by the smug reaction of a Panama Citian who heard a tourist mention Miami.

"Miami? Miami?" he said thoughtfully. "Well, there's a Miami, Florida, and a Miami, Ohio, and a Miami, Texas. Which one do you mean?

10. You have been given a 30-page manuscript with a copy area of 7 × 9 inches. The manuscript is double-spaced, typed on an elite typewriter. We would like to set the text in Bodoni Book, 10/12, with a 25-pica line length. Determine the total number of characters and the length in inches.

Chapter 7

Picture Editing and Using Color

When good writers observe either a scene or person, they can describe what they've seen in clear and striking prose. But few written descriptions can compete for truth with pictures. The ancient Chinese had another way of saying it: "One picture is worth ten thousand words."

The following paragraphs were written by Wilson Hicks, the late executive editor of *Life*, who made his high reputation through giving his attention to picture editing:

> Man, in understanding what happens around him, depends primarily on his sight, secondarily on his hearing. In journalism which makes use of words only, the words bear the entire burden of recreating for the reader an experience undergone by someone else. Printed words being visual representations of spoken words, the sense of hearing is basically related to the act of reading. The eye, in conveying the sound symbols to the brain, appropriates the word of the ear, so to speak, and performs to a very limited degree its own peculiar function which, to put it quite simply, is to see. In journalism which makes use of words and pictures, to the stimuli of sound symbols there are added the stimuli of forms of reality represented in the photograph. Together these stimuli call forth a collaboration of the two senses by which the quality of a recreated experience is enormously increased, and brought much closer to actual experience.
>
> This particular coming together of the verbal and visual mediums of communication is, in a word, photojournalism. Its elements, used in combination, do not produce a third and new medium. Instead, they form a complex in which each of the components retains its fundamental character.
>
> The intent of photojournalism is to create, through combined use of the visual and verbal mediums, a oneness of communicative result. If a fusion of the mediums could come about on the printed page, the problem could be simplified to the extent that only one perceptive act on the reader's part would be required. As noted above, such a coalescence is impossible. A fusion does occur, but not on the printed page. It occurs in the reader's mind.*

Editor-Photographer Relationships

At magazines that rely heavily on photography, the photo department obviously plays a key role. David Merrill, designer of several magazines, said that a major consumer magazine such as *Time* may have one photo (or picture) editor, two assistants, and about 20 photo researchers who

---

*Courtesy, Wilson Hicks.

gather and assign photos every week. On a smaller magazine, the art director may double as photo editor.

Most photo editors start out as photographers. Becoming a photo editor takes talent, an understanding of the technical elements, a knowledge of reproduction, and a lot of experience under someone who knows the business.

If you lack the experience and technical training, however, there are nevertheless rules of thumb that can help get you started. James Fosdick, a professor of journalism at the University of Wisconsin, offers these guidelines for instructing photographers:

1. Because big pictures have impact, get close with the camera (especially Polaroid, where enlargements are impracticable or impossible), eliminate unnecessary, distracting details (by camera angle, controlled focus, and lighting), and simplify the content of your picture for more effective communication.

2. To help ensure clear reproduction, plan for good tone separation (through lighting, background selection, and subject position), try for light subjects against a darker background, or dark subjects against a light background. Avoid "busy" backgrounds, such as flowered wallpaper and the like, unless such details (a sign or symbol) convey important story-telling elements.

3. In arranging "formal" group shots, keep subjects close together, perhaps shooting from a slight side-angle, to avoid empty space between heads. If it's a large group, arrange in rows to permit normal rectangle, keep camera and light(s) high to keep head sizes uniform and lighting even. Light high and off camera will help avoid reflections in spectacles and windows.

4. With small groups, plan an informal arrangement (for either vertical or horizontal pictures), don't have them all looking down at the table, but rather at the "group leader," suggest and rehearse group action, and break down their camera consciousness with a question or brief comment. *Then be prepared to shoot when expressions and action are at the peak.*

5. Don't overlook use of flash on outdoor shots when the sun is bright and at a high angle, producing shadows on faces. No. 5 bulb in reflector (or similar strength strobe light) will eliminate shadows for better detail in reproduction at 10 to 15 feet. Use a handkerchief or remove the reflector for close-ups to avoid overlighting with the flash. With small strobe, cover about half of the front of the flash with your fingers to reduce the intensity of the "flash-fill."

6. In photographing buildings and outdoor scenes, include people in natural positions to add interest, "scale," and meaning. If a person is prominent in the story, get him close to the camera—4 to 8 feet—with building or scene in the background. Use small lens aperture to get depth of field.
7. When making pictures in rooms with light walls and/or a light and low ceiling, consider the use of "bounce" flash to open up background detail and supplement the existing light, if necessary. Allow more exposure to make up for greater light diffusion and spread.
8. Be certain the flash is directed *at an angle* and not head-on when shooting subjects in front of a wall surface to avoid direct glare of the flash into the camera lens.

The following quotation from Mary Ord of *Sunset* magazine presents another point of view on the relationship between magazine writer and photographer, and how they can work together most effectively:

Unless a story has no prospects of photography, or the writer is taking his own pictures, the writer will be dealing with a photographer. The writer sets the scope of the story (though great photography may unexpectedly dictate a shift of emphasis), but since the photography is done before the layout, the photographer doesn't have to work within that sort of rigid framework.

The quality of the photographs makes the difference between a two-column and a two-page story, no matter how worthy the topic. So the writer chooses the photographer whom he thinks can do the job best. Some photographers are best at studio shots, some at wildlife shooting, some at house photography, and some at photographing children.

The writer tries to tell his photographer as much about his story as possible. If the story calls for going out of the studio to work, the writer tries to give the best idea he can of what the situation will be, what lighting there is, what distance the photographer may be shooting from, how much legwork may be involved in getting the shots. The writer should say if he just doesn't know what they'll find, or if he has specific shots in mind.

If all this is communicated, usually the photography comes out all right. But my first experience working with a photographer was a disaster. The story was a Christmas crafts project, and I signed up the only photographer who had any free time that week. The story required a how-to picture and one of the finished project, both to be done in the studio. For the how-to shot, nothing we tried seemed right after a half a day's work. Standing there in the studio with the lights and all, I thought, "This glamorous world of magazine work sure isn't much fun." Finally I went and got my art director to set up the shot. It turned out that this photographer's forte was wildlife shooting and he was as new to studio work as I was.

Doing your own photography is encouraged at *Sunset*. If you are competent at it, you are more useful. It is good if a writer can take at least adequate scouting photographs to help him sell his story to editors, to help determine if it is worthwhile to send a full-time photographer back, and also to show that photographer what kind of conditions he will find. Writers often do their own photography if the story is some distance away and is not of certain enough value to warrant the expense of a photographer's time.*

Although very few other magazines encourage their writers to take photographs, you as a picture editor or as a staff writer may be assigned to accompany the photographer to produce an article. If the article is primarily a visual story, the photographer should have the right (on some magazines) to chart the course. But if the published words will dominate the story, you as the editor should demand the right to shape it.

Writing to Pictures

The key principle in fusing word and picture is to write *to*, not merely *about*, a picture or a series of pictures. Many writers have discovered that they write most successfully to a single picture by performing a simple trick: imagine that the picture is the lead of a story and that the caption is a continuation that explains and amplifies the lead. It is essential, however, that the writer first determine what is obvious and what must be explained. Most captions can be written well by following these rules:

1. Remember that a caption is an explanatory paragraph that stands alone. Even if there is an accompanying story, the caption does not depend on it.
2. Excessive explanation is a mistake. The word "above" has no place in a caption running under a single picture. And, if only a man and woman are shown, a caption that explains that a man is "left, above" is ridiculous as well as superfluous. Similarly, when only two men are shown and one is identified at "left," pointing out that the other is "at right" or "right" is unnecessary.
3. The spirit of the picture dictates the spirit of the caption, although captions are, as a general rule, written in a lighter and more colloquial tone.
4. The key details related to pictures—among them, names and

*Courtesy, Mary Ord.

things that need explanation—are the key words that must come near the beginnings of captions. It is usually a mistake to start a caption with a name, but if a person is the key to a picture, the reader should not have to wait for the identification until he or she reaches the end of the caption.

5. The rule regarding tenses in captions varies from publication to publication. Generally, a caption for an action picture starts with a sentence in the present tense. This practice is entirely in keeping with the idea of fusing word and picture: the photographer has captured a moment in time—the picture can be considered a piece of "frozen time"—and the words that enhance the moment are expressed in present tense to heighten the effect. However, sentences that are not so directly related to the picture—references, for example, to the actions of the subject at another time—are usually written in the past tense. A cardinal rule is that *tense should never be changed within a sentence*. In general, the writer should make a distinction between action pictures and posed pictures—action is in the present, posed pictures are from the past.

6. Although a caption is brief, it should contain story elements so that the readers will understand the picture and its feature angle. Avoid such phrases as "Pictured above are . . ."

7. The readership of captions is quite high, and the readership will be enlarged if boldface, italics, or caps are used for the first two or three words. The first words of the first sentence of a caption replace a picture headline or overline and also save space and time. Many stories can be adequately reported with a good picture and a slightly expanded caption.

Writing to Picture Stories

Good picture stories are essays and must be *planned*. In fact, it is doubtful that a great picture story can be achieved unless its producers have arrived at a theme or central idea *before* the photographer starts work. Happy accidents have been known to result from haphazard shooting, but the weight of experience suggests that the good picture story is developed rather than stumbled on. A finished picture story is usually achieved by:

- Choosing a dominant picture
- Facing pictures toward the related text
- Avoiding "rivers of gray" caused by captions meeting irregularly near the same level
- Arranging similar captions in the same width, type, and number of lines
- Focusing simultaneously on a subject or personality as well as on a theme or mood

Writing to a picture story differs markedly from writing to a single picture. The writer must focus at once on a single picture and on continuity from photograph to photograph.

1. Think of variety when planning a picture story. Don't crowd too many pictures into the space available. It is better to use a few *good* pictures that can be seen and understood instead of a page full of thumbnail group shots where nobody is recognizable. Make it a rule to use a caption with each picture and a headline overall.
2. Provide a central copy-block that relates to all the pictures and echoes the spirit of the pictures as a group.
3. Hold captions ruthlessly to a minimum. (Readers like to leap rapidly from picture to picture.)
4. Avoid superfluous words in direction as well as in description. Captions can be related to pictures by proximity, keyed letters or numbers, or arrows.
5. A headline is advisable for a layout of two or more pictures on the same subject to "tie the package together" in the reader's mind.

What to Do with Pictures

A picture editor has a number of duties: cropping, sizing and scaling, mortising, and retouching. The remainder of this section describes each of these processes.

If time permits, the photo editor should order contact prints before the final prints are made. Contact prints are proofs of the negatives that are the same size as the negatives themselves; although small, they are easily inspected with a *linen tester*, a small 8- or 10-power magnifying glass.

Immediately reject photos that are out of focus or that contain unwanted blurs. Order prints as 8 × 10 glossies for the following reasons:

- Hundreds of photos will cross the desk in a given day and are easier to handle if the same size.
- Defects in the image are easy to spot.
- Airbrushing and other touchups, if warranted, will be easier to do.
- When the photos are reproduced on film in the mechanical department, reducing the image will *sharpen* detail; enlarging the image will *enlarge defects*.
- Although it costs a few cents more to make an 8 × 10 than a 4 × 5, time is saved in the mechanical department because reductions take less time than enlargements.

Cropping

Cropping pictures means deciding what part of a print should be reproduced in the publication. This must be done at the glossy-print stage. Many editors cut out busy backgrounds, superfluous people, and other distractions to make certain that the real focus of the picture stands out. Cropping is done by making cut-off marks in wax pencil (in the photo margins) where the editor wants the picture framed. To make certain that the editor is viewing the photograph accurately, he or she frames the picture with a rectangle formed between extended thumbs and forefingers. Although this may feel silly at first, it is an excellent technique to really see the part of the picture as *the* picture.

Keep these guidelines in mind when cropping:

1. Avoid cropping pictures in fancy and irregular shapes.
2. When using head shots, leave some space on the side the person is facing.
3. When cropping an action picture—whether a racing boat or a runner—leave space before the thrust of the action.
4. "When in doubt, crop it out" is good advice.

Begin cropping by covering up parts of the photo that contain no information or irrelevant information. What remains will have greater impact if it is sized adequately.

Scaling

Scaling a photo means determining the size it should be in the publication. To do this, editors use a device called a *proportion wheel*, or a *scale* and a *line gauge*. A line gauge is a ruler with printer's measurements on it; a proportion wheel consists of two concentric, movable wheels with scales on them. Line gauges and proportional wheels are available at printing supply firms.

If a proportion wheel should be unavailable, use the following formula:

$$\frac{\text{picture width}}{\text{picture depth}} = \frac{\text{halftone width}}{\text{halftone depth}} \qquad \frac{4}{3} = \frac{6}{x}$$

Multiplying 4 times x and 3 times 6, the answer is 4x = 18. Divide the 18 by 4x, which results in an x of 4½. That is the depth of the halftone. In addition to giving you the reproduction size, the proportion wheel also gives the reproduction size as a *percentage* of the original size. An 8 × 10 reduced by 50 percent would be (8) (.5) × (10) (.5) or 4 × 5. This information is written on a halftone order (see below) and attached to the photograph.

```
┌─────────────────────────────────────────────────────┐
│                                                     │
│                   HALFTONE ORDER                    │
│                                                     │
│   Slug _____    Original size _____   │
│                                                     │
│   Page _____    Reproduction size _____  │
│                                                     │
└─────────────────────────────────────────────────────┘
```

Tone Butting and Runarounds

Tone butting is cutting two halftones and placing them side by side. *Runarounds* are type images placed around a tone image. Runarounds are fairly straightforward and can produce a nice effect, but tone butting is easily botched and should be used sparingly.

Retouching

Circles identifying the hand of an assassin, dotted lines to show the route of a burglar, airbrushing to drop out the background—these are all photographic operations carried out by the art department. Staffed by one or two artists, this department serves the editorial department in much the same way as the photo lab does.

Preparing a Photo

Step 1. The first step in preparing a photo for reproduction is to visualize the area desired. *Cropping angles* may help, as demonstrated by Bill Harke.

Step 2. Next, measure the depth of the image area with a line gauge.

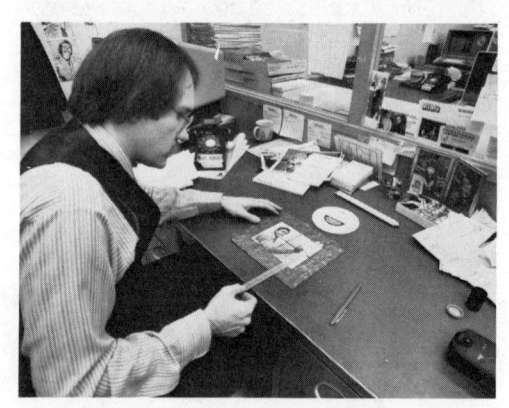

Step 3. Then find the depth of the original on the inside wheel of a proportion scale and place that figure opposite the size you want the photo to be when it appears in the magazine. A window on the inside wheel shows the percentage of reproduction.

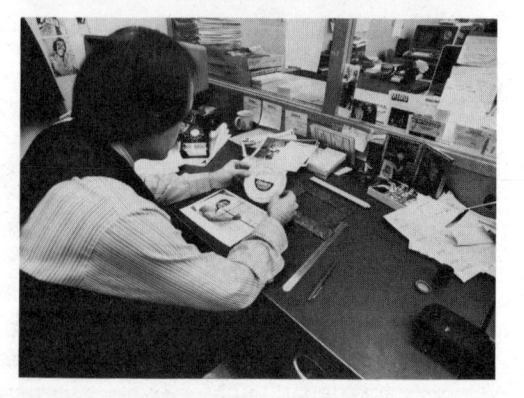

PICTURE EDITING AND USING COLOR   165

for Reproduction

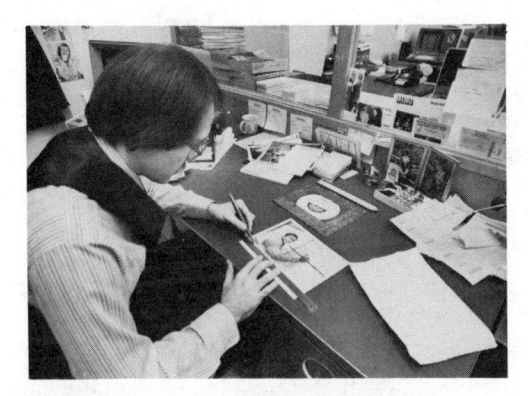

Step 4. Harke marks the margin of the photo to indicate the areas he wants cropped out of the final reproduction.

Step 5. From the desk, the photo is sent to the camera department, where process camera operator John Turner produces a screened reproduction—one with a halftone dot pattern.*

*A "halftone dot pattern" is a regular pattern of small dots of varying sizes that, when viewed from a distance, appear to form a recognizable image. The best way to understand the notion of a halftone dot pattern is to inspect a photograph in a magazine with a magnifying glass. As reproduced, the photograph is an optical illusion made possible by the inability of the human eye to resolve the pattern at a distance of more than a few inches.

Four Guidelines

Cropping, sizing, and scaling are all important functions of a good picture editor. These four guidelines should also be kept in mind:

1. Choose a *few* good pictures. It's tempting to select too many pictures, but if they are all crowded in, the result will be mediocrity. One or two outstanding pictures will perform a better job than five small, ordinary pictures.
2. Use pictures in large sizes. This is the age of television. Readers are so accustomed to pictures that striking pictures in large sizes are most impressive. Research has demonstrated over the years that most readers prefer large pictures.
3. Learn to *bleed*—to use pictures that run off the edge of the page. In some cases, pictures that bleed on all four sides are used. Bleeding a picture has a strong effect on readers.
4. Use pictures to tell a story, and be especially careful in selecting and arranging them. To make certain that you are not publishing a mere scrapbook of pictures, *begin* by believing that you are telling a story. Perceptive picture editors observe a scene or a person and write captions to describe the photograph in either rich or simple prose.

Color

Classification of Color

Many volumes have been written about color, and some colleges and universities offer courses in color theory. Full treatment of the subject is beyond the scope of this book, but a basic vocabulary of color terminology is essential for communicating with the printers of your magazine.

Several schemes exist for classifying colors. Among them are the Ostwald and Munsell systems, which commonly are taught in the classroom but which, for technical reasons, are not commonly employed by commercial printing establishments. From the commercial standpoint, the most useful system is the Pantone Matching System (PMS), which has been widely adopted by ink and paint manufacturers, as well as advertisers and commercial printing establishments. Soft drink and cigarette manufacturers, whose images depend on a specific color, may well request a PMS color when placing an ad in your publication, and failure to comply—or even poor color rendition—could result in loss of advertising revenue. A visit to your local printing supply firm, or to a well-stocked art store, can provide you with a PMS color chart. Abbreviated charts are normally provided free of charge.

Color is a powerful editorial tool and should be employed in enhancing the appearance of major articles, but it is also very expensive. The ink itself is cheap, but a separate printing plate and press unit must be set aside for each additional color; simply cleaning the press for a new color is a labor-intensive process that markedly increases the cost of production. If an advertiser has requested a specific color, however, for, say, the inside back cover, then the color will be available not just on one page, but two; if you remove the staples from the center of a magazine and inspect its *imposition* (the way it has been folded), you will see why this is so. Depending on how the magazine is imposed, 4, 8 or even 16 pages can be printed by the same color plate. In such cases, the astute editor will take full advantage of the situation by using the color on every page for which it is available. This is called a *pick-up*: the color that an advertiser paid for on the inside back cover may be picked up on the inside front cover.

Spot Color

Simply printing a solid color is known as *flat* or *spot color*. This is common as borders for entire pages, boxes around *sidebars* (short pieces accompanying another, larger article on the same topic), and outlines for halftone illustrations.

The printing of large blocks of solid color is offensive to the eye, however, and is not recommended. If a large area of color is desired, the intensity should be reduced by means of a *tint* to yield a fine pattern of small dots indiscernible by the casual viewer. Use of a tint with only black yields gray. Tints are expressed as percentages: on the dummy, for example, an editor may sketch a border and write a note beside it saying "50% blue tint." Because printers are inconsistent in their ability to produce a given percentage tint, only experience will enable the editor to order the best tint for the occasion.

Fake Color

Stock and *substrate* are the terms printers use to denote the material the magazine is printed on. Plastics and metal foils are common alternatives to the many kinds of paper available. Although white paper is the most common substrate, the use of colored stock should not be overlooked. This is known as *fake* color, because the appearance of color is obtained without the use of colored inks. Fake color has its drawbacks: pigments in the stock reduce reflectivity, so a bolder or a larger typeface should be employed to improve legibility of body types. Use of colored inks for body types severely reduces contrast and is strongly discouraged.

Process Color

The most colorful photographic reproductions in magazines are called *process color* (or *full-color* or *four-color*) reproductions. The original color photograph is subjected to a complex process in which the colors are separated into only four—magenta (process red), cyan (process blue), yellow, and black. (Technically speaking, black is not a color, but it nevertheless is commonly referred to as such.)

Based on the three-color theory of vision, the process briefly is this:

- The original photo is photographed with a red filter. Because only red light passes through the filter, blue and yellow are blocked out. This becomes the red separation negative, and is used to produce the cyan printing plate (or the cyan *printer*).
- The original is then photographed with a green filter. This green separation negative is used in the production of the magenta printer.
- A blue filter is then used to produce the yellow printer.
- A negative representing the black in the photograph is made using a yellow (modified) filter.

Either photographic prints or color slides (sometimes called *reflection* and *transmission* copy, respectively) may be used for process color separations, but photo editors generally prefer slides because of their superior color rendition. If a choice is available, 2¼ × 2¼ transparencies are strongly preferred over 35mm.

Because of the complex process involved, color separations are very expensive: a high-quality separation of one color slide may cost several hundred dollars, not to mention all the extra plates, inks, and printing units used in the reproduction.

Preseparated Color

When a cartoonist prepares artwork for the Sunday comics in a daily newspaper, the final product is *preseparated color*, or *preseparated art*.

Preseparated color comes in sets—usually three or four hand-sketched images that are used to make three or four different plates. Each plate takes a different color ink, and when these are printed in register, a colorful image is the result.

In its most sophisticated form, preseparated color is known as *keyline*, a method of carefully registered transparent overlays prepared by a highly skilled graphic artist. In its crudest form, preseparated art is available as *clip-art* and can be bought at any well-stocked art store. Newspapers use preseparated clip-art provided by subscription services that regularly print artwork to reflect seasonal moods. Clip-art appears most often in the display ads of newspapers, but when well chosen, it can provide a new dimension to the graphics of a magazine.

Duotones and Posterizations

Duotones and posterizations are not as common as the techniques already mentioned, but they are most effective and generally cheaper.

A *duotone* is much like a halftone, but an additional color—usually blue or brown—is added to give the effect of process color. Blue is particularly effective with *mug shots* (portraits). Only one extra plate in addition to the black printer is necessary for a duotone.

Technically speaking, a *posterization* is a no-screen exposure of a regular photograph. The result is a photographic image with no dot pattern, but simply a black-white rendition with no grays or midtones. This particularly dramatic effect is useful for concealing identities of photographed subjects in stories about drug smuggling and the like, but it also can be quite artistic when colors are used instead of just black and white.

Exercises

1. Look through several magazines, reading captions with the textbook at your side. Check carefully the seven rules outlined in this chapter for writing captions. When you run across captions that do *not* follow these rules of thumb, clip them out and bring them to class for discussion.

2. Find a magazine that has only a small amount of color and remove the staples. Look at the colors only. Did the editors pick up all the available color? Discuss your answer.

3. Clip five examples of each of the following and glue to 8½ × 11 sheets of white paper, properly identified:
   a. Spot color
   b. Fake color
   c. Preseparated color
   d. Process color
   e. Color tint
   f. Duotone
   g. Posterization
   h. Bleed

4. Answer the following questions:
   a. A 5 × 7 photo reduced 60 percent would be _____ × _____ inches.
   b. A wallet-sized 2¼ × 3¼ photo enlarged to 2.70 inches × 3.90 inches would be a _____ percent enlargement.
   c. If an 8 × 10 photo is reduced so that the 8-inch side is only 6 inches long, how long will the 10-inch side be?

5. Crop a horizontal photograph to eliminate extraneous material. This photograph, when properly cropped, should become a vertical. Then scale the photograph for a two-column story.

6. Assume you are the photo editor of *The Quill,* a magazine for which the following story was written. The managing editor has agreed to run the story in the next issue, and she has turned it over to you for illustration. After reading it carefully, make a list of at least five possible photos to illustrate the main points in the article. Be specific, and write them as though they were instructions to a staff photographer.

Why the Press Is the Other Government

By William L. Rivers

The Press has become the greatest power within Western countries, more powerful than the legislature, the executive, and the judiciary. One would then like to ask: By what law has it been elected and to whom is it responsible?

—Aleksandr Solzhenitsyn

The capital city of the United States of America, like the federal government it houses, was constructed according to plan. The original city, most of which still stands, is the physical equivalent of Jefferson's Declaration of Independence, of Madison's Constitution, and, in general, of the whole assortment of utopian notions that Carl Becker has called "the heavenly city of the 18th-century philosophers." As London's Crystal Palace symbolized, for all the world, the progressivism, utilitarianism, and scientism of the 19th century, so the Washington of L'Enfant, at least in certain kinds of weather, is an artwork of the Enlightenment—a perfect emblem of the 18th century's spacious, optimistic, slightly naive view of man.

As with any good work of art, every feature of official Washington has a meaning. The various presidential monuments, the Supreme Court building, and the Capitol itself reflect, massively, the founding fathers' dream of resurrecting the Roman Republic (there even are *fasci* beside the speaker's platform in the House of Representatives). A tall, cigar-store Indian perched atop the Capitol's great dome can render the general effect, for the finicky observer, less classical than kitschy. But this touch of the frontier serves to remind us that the city of Washington was designed to be the set piece of a continental empire.

By contrast, the executive mansion, at 1600 Pennsylvania Avenue, is a structure so austere and virginal that posterity has named it, simply, the White House. Beside the White House, and housing its senior functionaries, is the EOB, the old Executive Office Building—a Victorian ostentation of *nouveau riche* power in which Walt Disney might have felt more at home than Queen Victoria.

Official Washington is majestic and orderly, erratic and tasteless. Its architecture represents the impossible simplicity and systematic character of the U.S. Constitution. It also reflects the labyrinthine complications and overelaboration that were the inevitable products of the Industrial Revolution, of Manifest Destiny, of one civil and two world wars, of bread-and-circus electioneering—the inevitable products, in other words, of two centuries of human foible.

But there is another side to Washington—another government. In a high-rise building on Pennsylvania Avenue, near the old Executive Office Building, is a floor of small offices whose windows overlook governmental Washington—the White House, the Capitol, the great monuments and museums along the mall, and the gargoyled mug of the old EOB.

"Here. Look. This is the best view of Washington," says Mel Elfin, capital bureau chief of *Newsweek* magazine. If you can appreciate the incongruous, Elfin is doubly right. These windowed cubicles of one significant organ of that other government reflect not only a different organization from that of official Washington, but also a distinct view of man.

Just outside Elfin's office window is a little balcony with a few chairs and a low-slung rail to keep one (barely) from becoming hamburger on the pavement below. The balcony is covered with screaming green Astroturf, which provides a startling emphasis in the foreground to the classical travertine and brownstone edifices beyond. Some old potted petunias and a couple of tomato plants struggle to cope with what appears to be constant neglect.

Somehow, the bedraggled pots fit the scene. Everywhere in the *Newsweek* offices are similar images of an eccentricity that is born of hard-nosed realism.

Everywhere, there is also awesome disorder; for although the *Newsweek* offices are fairly plush by press standards, this week they are being renovated—new carpets, some rearranged partitions, and the addition of a kitchen and conference room.

Also being renovated is the National Press Building, some three blocks from the old EOB and *Newsweek* offices, and 14 blocks from the Capitol. Since 1908, this venerable structure has been the focal point for most Washington news operations. It was definitely showing its age. Its brickwork was crumbling, its hallways were yellowed and dingy. In the ornately plastered lobby, elevators chugged up and down like old mules about to give up the ghost, while reporters and editors muttered disagreeably about how long it took them to get up to their offices.

The National Press Building was in an advanced state of decay. It is certain that the Washington press headquarters is getting a face lift. The Other Government—the Washington news corps—has come to consciousness of its power and is gradually moving into larger, more official, less eccentric structures.

Richard Rovere once suggested that our attitudes toward national politics—and, indeed, our national politics—might have been profoundly different if the founding fathers, instead of creating the nation's capital on the mud flats of the Potomac, had set it down in the center of 18th-century Manhattan. Our federal politicians and public servants would not now be jousting in the limiting and incestuous environment of a municipality given over entirely to government. With the national government as but one sector of a complex city, federal officials could not have avoided rubbing elbows and shaking hands with the nation's literati and its social critics. The condition that resulted might have rendered American politics less peripheral and vague in the national literature, and American social criticism less divorced from the political realities.

Rovere made this point most authoritatively. In order to write about national affairs for *The New Yorker*, Rovere himself commuted to Washington from his work in New York City. He often lamented that "very few reflective, literary intelligences deal with public affairs in this country," and he attributed this problem to the singularity of concerns and the cultural remoteness of Washington, D.C. For political man, no city is more exciting, more electric, than Washington. But for those with other or broader passions, no city is so stultifying. Among the intellectual and creative elite who have been honored in Washington, few have been willing to linger longer than it took them to finish their dinners at the White House.

The result of Washington's cultural estrangement from the nation has been the elevation of Washington's journalists to a kind of academy of national sages and prognosticators. In most other world capitals—which, usually, are also highly cosmopolitan cities—the journalist must vie with the novelist, with the playwright, with the artist, and with the critic in reporting, in analyzing, and in interpreting national public affairs. In Washington, news correspondents win by default. As a result, they have acquired the authority and sometimes even the power of a shadow government.

The Washington press corps has certainly acquired the trappings of power. Privileged as no other citizens are, the correspondents are listed in the *Congressional Directory*; they receive advance copies of governmental speeches and announcements; they are frequently shown documents forbidden even to high officials; and they meet and work in special quarters set aside for them in all major government buildings, including the White House. Fantastic quantities of government time and money are devoted to their needs, their desires, and their whims. Some White House correspondents talk with the president more often than his own party leaders in the House and in the Senate, and there are Capitol correspondents who see more of the congressional leaders than do most other congressmen.

No wonder, then, that Washington correspondents feel what one presidential assistant has termed "an acute sense of involvement in the churning process that is government in America." A close view of this involvement so impressed Patrick O'Donovan, a former Washington correspondent for the London *Observer*, that he said, "The American press fulfills almost a constitutional function."

Indeed, in Washington today, correspondents who report for the news media possess a power beyond even their own dreams and fears. They are only beginning to become aware that their work now shapes and colors the beliefs of nearly everyone, not only in the United States but throughout most of the world.

For the American public, full acceptance of the media's new authority and responsibility came at the end of the Watergate crisis, when the president of the United States posed his word against that of the press and lost. But Watergate was less coup d'état than it was climax. It was the end of a long evolution that was first observed by a newsman nearly fifty years ago, during the trial of the Lindberg baby's kidnapper and killer. At that time, Walter Lippmann commented that in our democracy "there are two processes of justice, the one official, the other popular. They are carried on side by side, the one in the courts of law, the other in the press, over the radio, on the screen, at public meetings."

Lippmann's observation remains true today, yet those who would end this discussion on the question of the court verdict versus the popular verdict are missing a much greater issue. For the basic question is not just whether we have two parallel systems of justice in this country, but whether we have two governments. Do we have a second, adversarial government that acts as a check on the first and controls public access to it? Indeed we do—and this Other Government is made up primarily of the more than two thousand news correspondents stationed in Washington.

In our daily lives, we trace a path from home to work and back. Without the news media, we would know almost nothing beyond our own sphere of activity. The public's knowledge of national government depends not on direct experience and observation, but on the news media; and it is the media that set the agenda for public discussion and decision.

To a large degree, the employees of the government—including the president himself—must also depend on the reports of the news media for information about some of their most important concerns. In government, as elsewhere, each worker is circumscribed, and his sphere is small. A congressional assistant may spend much or all of one day absorbing details about the religious leaders of Iran and learning much more than is published or broadcast about the imminence of all-out war in the Middle East. But he hasn't the time to inform all of his colleagues about his new knowledge, and he is likely to know less about House debate that day than any tired tourist from North Carolina who wandered into the public gallery to give his feet a rest. Both the tired tourist and the congressional assistant must depend on the newspapers to find out what happened that day in the Senate.

In an article for a journal of political science, former Senator H. Alexander Smith of New Jersey made it clear that members of Congress are not Olympians who learn what they know in closed-door hearings and secret communiqués. They, too, must depend on the media. Senator Smith listed thirteen different sources of information for congressmen; but the news media, he wrote, "are basic and form the general groundwork upon which the congressman builds his knowledge of current events. The other sources . . . are all supplements to these media."

Even presidents, with their vast and powerful apparatus of information, often end up relying as much on the press as on their own informational systems. John Kennedy admitted that he acquired new information from the *New York Times* about his own secret sponsorship of the Bay of Pigs invasion. Eleven days before the invasion that the CIA had been shepherding so carefully, the editors of the *Times* informed Kennedy that their correspondent, Tad Szulc, had discovered the secret and that a detailed news report was imminent. Kennedy persuaded the publisher to postpone publication until after the landing in Cuba. But, during the discussions with the *Times* editors, the president picked up new information about the mounting of the invasion.

Afterward, in regret at the fiasco, Kennedy said to Turner Catledge, the executive editor of the *Times*, "If you had printed more about the operation, you would have saved us from a colossal mistake." Again, a year later, Kennedy told the publisher of the *Times*, "I wish you had run everything on Cuba. . . . I am just sorry you didn't tell it at the time." The president thus recognized the power and the value of the national news media: Reporting the coming invasion would undoubtedly have resulted in its being vetoed.

Even the strongest and most capable president requires such reporting; for he is *always* insulated from the realities of his administration by the fears and ambitions of his subordinates. He cannot possibly sort and absorb all of the vital information that is produced by government agencies and activities. Many believe that the fall of Richard Nixon was foreordained by his hatred of and isolation from the media.

The influence of the Washington press corps is also recognized in the third branch of the federal government. Justice Potter Stewart said in 1975, with something like wonder: "Only in the two short years that culminated last summer in the resignation of the president did we fully realize the enormous power that an investigative and adversary press can exert."

The courts have long been suspicious of that power, and over the years, they have waged a largely silent battle with trial reporters over the reporters' access to and publication of courtroom proceedings. Moving ponderously, the courts have attempted to close off much of the access of the news media. Moving quickly and sometimes deviously, the media have anticipated and occasionally foreclosed these efforts, very often using one courtroom and one judge against another.

The Other Government wins some, loses some. During the fifty years since Walter Lippmann's observation about public and private trials, legal maneuvers between the federal government and its courts and the national news media have resembled a very intricate and symmetrical minuet. The courts move to gag orders and to secret trials. The media, stalemated, take the issues to higher courts and begin to employ attorneys as reporters.

But the dance does not always include willing partners, and the Other Government is usually less effective than official Washington at some of the more subtle steps. Often the official government will make the news media an unwitting participant in the never-ceasing warfare among its various branches and agencies.

Twenty years ago, a young reporter was writing an article about the powerful Brooklyn congressman, John J. Rooney, who headed the House of Representatives subcommittee that controlled the State Department budget. Every year, Congressman Rooney savaged the State Department budget request by speaking against "booze money for those striped-pants cookie-pushers." He alarmed the young reporter by exclaiming angrily, "I want to keep an open mind and be fair, but if you people in the press keep harping on it, I'm afraid you'll make me whack the budget too much."

The reporter then interviewed the assistant secretary of state, who had the task of arguing in Congress for whatever budget the department thought reasonable. The reporter asked him how badly Rooney's attacks crippled the budget request. "Why, not at all," the assistant secretary answered. In fact, he explained, Congressman Rooney was "the best friend the Department of State had." By berating Old Foggy Bottom on the floor of the House, even as he was pushing a generous budget, Rooney persuaded the representatives who abhorred striped pants that he had the State Department's number. Rooney's strong words were a facade that enabled the congressman to sneak more money into the budget than Congress would otherwise have granted.

That sounded to the reporter like double talk, but no matter how many people the reporter interviewed, they were almost evenly split on the question. In the end, the reporter decided that Congressman Rooney was not a friend of the State Department; that he was, in fact, an irresponsible budget slasher. But even as the reporter was typing his article, he worried: It *could be* that Rooney is a clever ally of the State Department. Any Washington reporter can be convinced at times that Machiavelli is alive and advising congressmen.

A few months later, in 1961, the same young reporter was feeling the impact of the new Kennedy administration. Like other Washington correspondents, he was invited for the first time in history to share with a president both the crushing responsibility and the glittering aura of the greatest center of leadership in the Western world. Before 1961, the White House had been a closed preserve. Information was channeled through the president's press secretary, and some news correspondents never so much as met the White House advisers and chief assistants. A reporter who had arranged an interview with an Eisenhower assistant without going through Jim Hagerty, the president's press secretary, was so elated that he telephoned his editor in New York to say, "I broke around behind Hagerty!" The important news was not the substance of the interview but the fact that he got one.

When Kennedy took over, correspondents wandered through the White House offices in such numbers that they created a traffic problem. President Kennedy was his own most effective promoter. He practiced personal salesmanship with the élan of one accustomed to establishing the rules of the game. Kennedy made such a fetish of giving exclusive interviews that his press secretary, Pierre Salinger, once observed that he had to go to the Oval Office to find the White House correspondents.

The heady effect of this unaccustomed presidential attention is demonstrated by the behavior of our young reporter on the morning he received a call from the White House that the president wanted to talk to him. It was a snowy, miserable day. With a studied show of nonchalance, the reporter announced his coup to his colleagues, drew on his topcoat and one of his galoshes, and clumped out the door toward the elevator, leaving the other galosh on his desk.

The reporter who wrote the article about Congressman Rooney and who interviewed President Kennedy was me. I was then working for the now-defunct magazine *The Reporter*. Although I quit being a Washington correspondent near the end of 1961, I remained fascinated by the profession and by the sharpening power struggle between the Washington press corps and the federal government. Through secrecy, through the courts, through its press representatives, the government has awesome control over the public image of itself. Only the news media can exert an effective counterbalancing influence on the public's perception of government. Surely, if the government closes off freedom of access in any area, a balanced picture of government will give way to government propaganda.

Yet, there is another side to this issue. In 1978, philosopher-novelist Aleksandr Solzhenitsyn—an outsider, a Russian—observed, with considerable disapproval, that "The press has become the greatest power within Western countries, more powerful than the legislature, the executive, and the judiciary." How could he believe that? What of the effective machinations of a shrewd congressman or of a suspicious judge? What of the overwhelming power of an attractive and canny president? What of the sheer size of the federal bureaucracy and its countless daily actions and decisions, which can vitally affect the course of society? Is it possible, despite the odds, that Solzhenitsyn is on to something?

We must remind ourselves periodically that the American republic's founders granted to the press, alone among private business institutions, the task of protecting the U.S. Constitution. Contemporary Washington correspondents are well aware of this responsibility and are proud of their independence from the official government and from the biases of their editors and publishers and station owners back home.

This independence marks the sharpest difference between Washington correspondents and their local brethren and between the Washington press corps today and that of previous generations. In 1936, Leo Rosten made this statement to a group of newspaper correspondents and asked whether it was true in their experience: "My orders are to be objective, but I *know* how my paper wants stories played." Slightly more than 60% of the correspondents replied yes, indicating that they felt at least subtle pressure from their editors and publishers. In 1960, the mark came down dramatically; only 9.5% replied yes to the same question.

That difference is so dramatic that one may think there was a misunderstanding or a mistake. Another statement, which also tested freedom from home-office pressure, drew a similar response, however. Rosten asked the correspondents in 1936 whether this could be said of their work: "In my experience I've had stories played down, cut, or killed for 'policy' reasons." Slightly more than 55% of the correspondents answered yes. In 1960, only 7.3% affirmed the same statement. During the twenty years since 1960, that downward trend has continued.

Yet, as my own experiences with President Kennedy and Congressman Rooney indicate, the independence of the contemporary Washington correspondents may be something of a mirage. In any event, what truly counts is not so much the independence of the reporters as it is their service of the public interest. How well do the news media serve our interests? How much do they show us of official Washington?

Learning about the national government from the news media is like watching a tightly directed play. The director features the president at some length, the leading congressmen as secondary players, and the cabinet and justices of the Supreme Court as cameos and walk-ons. There are seldom any other entries in the dramatis personae, although there are *three million* employees of the national government. Any effort to move beyond the stage to see the undirected reality is useless. We must understand this: that the *image* of government appears to us primarily through the news media, and that the *reality* of government is often quite different from that reported by the two thousand news correspondents who help to create that image.

The public and the government are awash in a torrent of media reports. Yet, inquiring into how the news media actually serve the public yields a different perspective. Radio and television are mainly useful in signaling news events, providing the immediate—and sketchy—reports that announce happenings. More and more, we depend on television, despite the fact that our understanding is distorted by the brevity of the news reports. Broadcast journalists skim the top of the news, working with headlines, leads, and the bulletins that alert the public. Only occasionally does a documentary flesh out the news. Av Westin, a news executive of the American Broadcasting Company, has said: "I think television news is an illustrated service that can function best when it is regarded as an important yet fast adjunct to the newspapers. I know what we have to leave out; and if people do not read newspapers, news magazines, and books, they are desperately misinformed."

Newspapers cannot compete with radio and television for rapid transmission, and they cannot compete with television for the sheer impact of seeing and hearing news in the making. But a newspaper is available at any time, and it can provide a vast range of information on many subjects. The importance of the newspaper has been described best by a man who was interviewed during a newspaper strike: "I don't have the details now; I just have the result. It's almost like reading the headlines of the newspaper without following up the story. I miss the detail and the explanation of events leading up to the news."

Most magazines can treat their subjects in greater depth than newspapers, but they generally cannot cover as many *different* subjects. Even the news magazines, which attempt to cover a wide range of subjects in some depth, do not publish as much information in their weekly issues as can be found in a single issue of a large daily newspaper. Like people who write books, those who write for magazines can seek out the unreported, flesh out the information that has been presented only in silhouette in broadcasts and newspapers, and report matters that the faster media have missed in the rush to meet deadlines.

It would seem that such a division of labor would help us to learn about *everything* that goes on in the government: radio and television rapidly reporting the action; newspapers putting most of the stories into context; and the magazine writers and book authors reporting the major stories more fully, and with more grace and flavor. But this range of public affairs reports, however carefully some may be fashioned, often seems the reflection of a faulty mirror. The mirror is first held this way, then that way, but how narrowly it is focused! The presidency, the congressional leaders, the State Department, and the Department of Defense are in view. Only occasionally is mention made of such bureaus as the Departments of Energy, of Transportation, of Agriculture, or of such agencies as the Federal Communications Commission, the Food and Drug Administration, the Interstate Commerce Commission, and the many other agencies that figure so importantly in our everyday lives. Only a few such agencies ever make it to the front page, to the television screen, to the radio interview.

Protesting the narrow focus of the Washington press corps, Derick Daniels, former executive editor of one of the Knight-Ridder newspapers, argued that journalists must recognize the reader's needs and desires:

> Yes, yes, we understand that the poor slob in the kitchen is interested in the price of soap when she *ought* to be interested in Congress. But I mean recognizing squarely, as a matter of intellectual honesty, that the kitchen is really, *in fact*, just as important. . . .
> The amount of knowledge and information collected, and the studies available through the U.S. government, are nearly limitless. A single document—the yearbook of the Department of Agriculture—contains more useful information in its pages than most newspapers report in a year.

The media are thus confronted with a dilemma. It is impossible for any news organization, no matter how large, to cover fully the entire federal government every day. And even if it were possible, no one would want to sift through such reports. So the real question is not whether the media are at fault for not covering the entire government all the time, or for printing only a small portion of what is knowable about the government. The more appropriate questions are: How good is the judgment of the Washington press corps as to what parts of the government to watch and which of its actions to record or to investigate? And how good is the judgment of the Washington news bureau and their outlets in deciding what information to print and to broadcast every day?

These are two important questions—as important as any questions we can ask about our official government in Washington; for, in a sense, the two governments—the official government and the national news media—increasingly form part of a single, symbiotic unit. The major difference between the real government and the media government begins with the conscious and deliberate action by most officials to insert the image they desire into the media process. The government nearly always attempts to create an image of itself. Whether this will be successful depends on the reporter. In some cases, the image of the officials vies with the reporter's own concept of those officials. In other cases, the images are a match.

Ben Bagdikian, one of the most powerful media critics in the United States, commented on the interrelationships between government image-making and press image-making when he made a study of newspaper columnists. He talked to many federal assistant secretaries for public affairs about how they briefed their bosses and how they preferred to break government news. Bagdikian found that the secretaries were heavily influenced by what they saw in the news media, that they accepted this as what the media would respond to, and that, as a result, they fashioned their output to serve what they perceived to be the media interest. Thus, the work of the Washington columnists, Bagdikian speculated, "includes guessing what the government is doing." This produces a double-mirror effect, in which each side responds to what the other is doing, while at the same time adjusting itself to the other side's anticipated needs.

Thinking about the mirrors of politics, John Kenneth Galbraith commented wryly: "Nearly all of our political comment originates in Washington. Washington politicians, after talking things over with each other, relay misinformation to Washington journalists who, after further intramural discussion, print it where it is thoughtfully read by the same politicians. It is the only completely successful closed system for the recycling of garbage that has yet been devised."

Viewed in the rawness of this circus of political reporting, government news seems very complicated—and dangerous. It is true that since the Vietnam War and the Watergate crisis, Washington correspondents are much more suspicious of the announcements of government officials. More and more correspondents every year are asking sharp questions of officials.

The questions are important because there have been times in the past fifteen years when *no one* in the official government knew what was true. Phil Goulding, assistant secretary of defense for public affairs in the Johnson administration, once said: "In our office, the secretary's office, or the White House, we never knew how much we did not know." Again, in reference to the Nixon years and the Watergate scandal, Senator Charles Mathias has said: "The more a president sits surrounded by his own views and those of his personal advisors, the more he lives in a house of mirrors in which all the views and ideas tend to reflect and reinforce his own."

When it became evident in 1973 that Nixon had been living in a world of mirrors—that he saw only the image that he had manipulated—Dr. Edward Teller, who had developed the hydrogen bomb in strict secrecy twenty years earlier, wrote ruefully, "Secrecy, once accepted, becomes an addiction." He might also have noted that secrecy, once the routine practice and defense of the official government, had, by 1973, finally given way to the angry probings of the Other Government.

By the time the Watergate case had brought an end to the presidency of Richard Nixon, the Other Government was firmly in control. Contemplating the Washington cityscapes from the barely contained chaos of the *Newsweek* offices, one wonders if this is what the founding fathers had in mind.

Chapter 8

Layout and Design

"Good layout" or "good design" is *not* a goal in itself. This is the most important principle of magazine designing. Design, after all, is but a means to an end: communication.* The design of a magazine article must contribute to the communication of ideas within the article. Thus, the layout must be specifically designed for each article to help convey the point contained in that article. "Good looks" is more than just a goal; it is a way to get the article off the page and into the reader's mind.

Magazine journalists must know as much about layout and design as any artist, because layout and design are integral elements in communicating the content of the article.

Occasionally articles are split from the design because the layout was done by someone who hadn't read the article. This is the wrong way to do layouts. The content of the article and the layout must work in harmony to communicate the ideas involved. On smaller publications, there should be no schism between an article and its layout, because one person does the editing and the design. On larger publications, however, where an art director does all the layouts, harmonizing each article with its layout is difficult. In the first case, if the article and the layout don't work together, it is the fault of the editor; in the second case, any problems are probably caused by lack of communication.

Basic Rules of Layout

The first basic rule is that layout is not an end in itself, and so it should not call attention to itself. Readers should not look at a spread and say, "Oh, what a nice layout!" If a reader focuses on the layout rather than the article and the pictures, the layout has failed. The layout should invite the reader to take note of the pictures and the articles themselves—not their arrangement on the page.

For this reason, a magazine must follow a consistent layout style. An especially flamboyant layout might be used to call attention to a particular article. But if every layout were flamboyant, the reader would be overwhelmed with the flamboyance, and attention would be distracted from the content.

The second basic rule of page layout is to think of the double-page spread rather than one page at a time. Most readers see both pages at

---

*I am indebted to Tom Siegfried of Texas Christian University for information in the first section of this chapter. He knows layout and design in an admirable depth.

LAYOUT AND DESIGN 189

Sacramento Cartoonists / Guitar Player / Comics Protest

feed/back

The California Journalism Review

$2.00   SPRING 1980

Unions Strike Out; Synanon Strikes Back

KRON-TV management lets some employees in from the cold while Synanon sends a news service running for cover

FIGURE 8–1. A tint block in the lower left-hand corner of this cover of *feed/back* illustrates the use of a blue tint with a black surprint. The photograph of a man is a duotone (blue and black). "Feed/back" and "unions strike out" are examples of reverse type (images are not printed—and the white of the paper simply is showing through selected areas of solids). (Courtesy, *feed/back*.)

once, rather than each page separately. Layout must be designed with this in mind.

Readers see both pages at once, but the *gutter*—the space between the left-hand and right-hand pages—divides them. The most common way to tie the pages of a spread together is to bleed a picture across the gutter. The editor should plan for the gutter to fall on a portion of the picture where details are not important, because the gutter may obliterate something.

An editor should consider the value of simplicity. A complicated layout with many elements is distracting, and it is difficult for the reader to sift a message out of such a mess. To achieve simplicity, the editor must not have too many elements, and the elements must be arranged in a coherent manner.

Elements

Margins. There are two margins to consider: the margins around the page and the margins around the elements. Most magazine editors ordinarily use *progressive margins*—with the largest at the bottom, the side slightly larger at the top, and the smallest margin in the gutter.

Margins serve at least two purposes on most magazines. The first is to distinguish editorial pages from advertising pages; the second is to contain type. Type should "respect" the margins—except in cases where a magazine is attempting to achieve specific effects.

As for margins between the elements, an editor must think of consistency. Some kind of consistent system to separate elements must be

FIGURE 8–2. *How to use a layout sheet.* The layout sheet indicates outline markings with lighter lines. The heavy lines indicate heads, copy, and pictures. The large "X" shows an illustration; the arrows are used for copy.

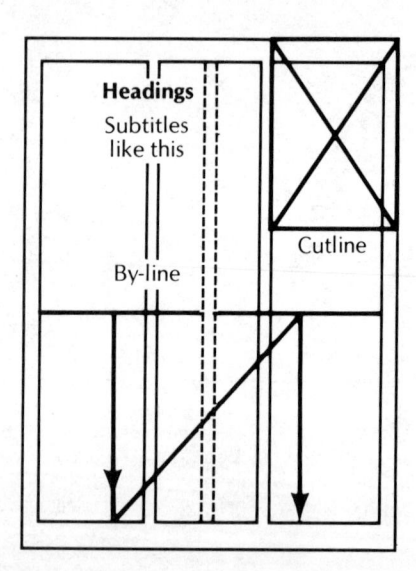

Short Stuff

- Nancy Luce was a poet who lived by herself on a farm in Edgartown, Mass., and kept chickens as pets. She wrote a book of poetry about her chickens called "Poor Little Hearts." When her favorites died, she erected gravestones for them inscribed with her own poems.
- "Old Mother Featherlegs" operated a hangout for outlaws along the Cheyenne–Black Hill Trail in Wyoming until she was murdered by "Dangerous Dick." She got her nickname from the red ruffled pantalettes she wore, which fluttered in the breeze when she rode horseback.
- Composer Lillian Hardin "Lil" Armstrong led her own all-woman band in the 1930s. And some claim she taught her husband, Louis Armstrong, music theory.

These three women are among the thousands—the famous and the little known—included in *Women's History Sources: A Guide to Archives and Manuscript Collections in the United States* (Bowker, $175), a two-volume reference set, four years in the works, edited by Andrea Hinding. The books record the achievements of women whose lives fell somewhere between fame and failure, Hinding said. "One can deduce from the books that women led circumscribed lives, but one of the things that kept us going through 10,000 manuscript pages was our own sense of all these magnificent women who survived and achieved in spite of the obstacles."

The books list 18,026 collections available as references for researchers. The material, which includes a history of 25 women educators who taught in China, papers of a Lutheran organization serving young professional and business women, and a Catholic college's collection of material on the psychological liberation of women, was obtained through a nationwide survey conducted at the University of Minnesota. There are entries in the volumes for 305 journalists, 412 physicians, 352 attorneys, 449 college teachers, 338 poets, 250 housewives, 118 novelists, 1,500 authors and 134 Native Americans.

Back to the Drawing Board

Lower test scores in math may be the result of the back-to-basics movement and increased use of minimal competency tests, according to Edward Esty, senior associate of the National Institute of Education.

Testifying before a federal hearing on declining test scores, Esty said the trend in mathematics is to teach more computation and other rote procedures and to streamline word problems to lower reading levels. In addition, he noted, "texts are organized so that word problems at ends of chapters use whatever skill was just taught in the body of the chapter, so students do not have to think through the problem to see what must be done." Higher level analytical skills, he said, are not sufficiently stressed.

At the hearing, which probed the drop in mathematics performance in the National Assessment of Education Progress over the past five years, the current teaching of math got low marks. What can be most easily tested and taught are now the teaching objectives in many schools, testified Shirley Hill, president of the National Council of Teachers of Mathematics. Many schools and teachers, she said, have "settled down to a single-minded dedication to one goal: high scores on tests of minimal skills. Short-term retention is the goal, not long-term retention and ability to apply."

Hill predicts, "We will see considerable reporting of increases on minimal competency test scores in the next few years," but at the same time, a test of the National Assessment type will likely "continue to reflect poor problem-solving performance." And such data will not be inconsistent.

Surprise Endings

First graders at Alexander Elementary School in Duncanville, Tex., were asked to come up with their own endings for some old proverbs. Some results:
Don't count your chickens . . . before you cook them.
Don't put your eggs . . . in the microwave.
People who live in glass houses . . . better not take off their clothes.
If at first you don't succeed . . . go play.
All work and no play . . . is disgusting.
Eat, drink and . . . go to the bathroom.

A similar assignment for first graders at the Arthur Dudley School in North Highlands, Calif., evoked these responses:
Children should be seen and not . . . babysitted.
Don't bite the hand that . . . is dirty.
You can lead a horse to water but . . . not to God.

14 LEARNING, FEBRUARY 1981 Art by Bill Prochnow

FIGURE 8–3. Using a *tint* may create the effect of two colors when only one is printed. Here, the background of "Back to the Drawing Board" has a gray appearance because it is composed of thousands of tiny, black dots; the rectangular block underneath is a lighter gray because the dots are even smaller. (Reprinted by special permission of LEARNING, The Magazine for Creative Teaching, February, 1981. © 1981 by Pitman Learning, Inc., 530 University Ave., Palo Alto, CA 94301.)

established; otherwise, the reader is much more likely to focus on the arrangement of the elements rather than the elements themselves.

Type. First, type usually does not have as much weight or heaviness as a picture. Thus, it is generally better not to sandwich type between large pictures, but to let type occupy the outer edges of a layout. Second, large areas of type give a gray appearance to a page and are monotonous. Large areas of type must be broken in some manner to relieve this boredom.

Also, the reader must know where to look next when he or she finishes reading a column. The reader's eye expects to read an article from left to right and from top to bottom. Good editors always lay out the page so that the order of the various sections of the article will be clear.

Pictures and Art. In most cases, pictures and art form the central part of the layout, with the other elements built around the illustrations. Consider a picture's position on the page. For example, if action in the picture is directed to the left, it should not be placed on the left side of a double-page spread, because the flow of action takes the reader off the page. In fact, the pictures are the most important element for controlling the movement of the reader's eyes over the page, and should be placed with that in mind.

As for the size of the pictures, the decision must be based on what the photograph is attempting to accomplish. If a photographer's purpose is to attract attention, then the picture must be large. If it is to illustrate or explain, it can be much smaller. In most cases, however, effective pictures are fairly large.

White space. The function of white space is to do something specific to "help" the layout. White space should *not* give the impression that a picture is missing or there isn't enough copy to fill the page.

Most magazine editors select a column width that will allow at least 28 characters per line. Also, the editors do not fill out a column by changing the spaces between the lines of type.

Other Layout Considerations

1. Consider the article as a whole, keeping in mind that each spread usually follows and precedes another spread.
2. The opening page must be provocative or entertaining.
3. The other pages must be put together to make following the copy convenient for the reader.
4. As for pages with ads, do not try to outshout the ads. A deep top margin can signal an editorial page.

Layout of an Article

Jean Bradfisch, executive editor of *Sea Frontiers*, had accepted an article from Vesta Rea–Salisbury entitled "Columbus's Arawaks." Then she had to layout the article with illustrations. Bradfisch explained, first, the process involved in illustrating an article:

"The author sends in any illustrations (photos, maps, diagrams, or sources of possible illustrations) he or she can muster, and then we read the article to see if there are any additional ones that are needed. With this article I wanted something that showed the Indians, if possible, and since these Indians are extinct, I knew it would have to be from an archive. Since Bettmann Archive seldom fails us, we called them for *anything* they had on the subject. A note is enclosed listing the clues we gave them. They replied with a wide selection of illustrations. One was used in this article, one with another article in the issue. From there, a selection was made from the pictures the author sent. (Since we do not commission photographs, we must work with what we can get—and often the selection is wanting. We do the best we can and are ever trying to upgrade our material.)" The following pages (Figure 8–4) show the article Bradfisch pasted up.

FIGURE 8–4. Courtesy, *Sea Frontiers*. © The International Oceanographic Foundation, Miami, Florida.

194 CHAPTER 8

horizon. Suddenly, something gleaming white appeared in the west. His eyes locked in on the object. He felt excitement start to mount. "Tierra! Tierra! (Land! Land!)" he yelled. At last, he thought, their objective had been sighted. Little did he know the New World had been discovered!

At that particular moment it is doubtful that anyone could think of anything but getting through the coral reef, off their caravels, and stepping onto solid shore, even if the land was nothing more than a small island called Guanahani (San Salvador) populated by a tribe of Arawaks, who were called Lucayans.

BLUFFS AND BEACHES of San Salvador (above), attractive to tourists today, were a welcome sight to Columbus. When he landed, he found them peopled by Arawaks. Culturally, these Indians were farmers but, because of the island's thin soil, had turned to the surrounding sea (right) for food.

At the time of Columbus, the Arawaks not only inhabited the Bahama Islands, but also the Greater Antilles, which consisted of Cuba, Jamaica, Hispaniola (now the Republic of Haiti and Dominican Republic), and Puerto Rico. They had originally migrated northeastward, out of the Orinoco River region of South America to escape the cannibalistic Carib Indians, who considered them a delicacy. It is believed that the Caribs gradually encroached upon the territories of the Arawaks, causing some of them to migrate into the Bahamas, their last migration point before they were eventually carried off by the Spaniards to slavery or death in Hispaniola.

A Peaceful Indian Tribe

The Lucayans, relatively peaceful Indians, had permanent villages and a well-developed aristocracy, with emphasis on songs, dances, ceremonies, and worship of images known as "Zemis." Their culture was characterized by farming, but in the Bahamas the soil was so thin they had to utilize the sea for survival.

At the time of the discovery of San Salvador, many of the Lucayan tools were derived from the sea. Celts (a prehistoric axlike tool) and chisels were made from the heavy lip of the conch shell (*Strombus gigas*). The conch was brought from the sea, and a gash was made in the side of it to sever the muscle fastening the edible snail to the shell. The heavy lip was broken from the shell and chipped to the desired shape and size. Slabs of limestone with worn spots where the side edges of the celt had been smoothed have been found at Lucayan worksites.

THOUGH THE ARAWAKS disappeared from San Salvador long ago, archaeological artifacts are evidence of their existence. Fragments of items such as carved stone Zemis, or idols, (above) and pottery bowls (right) give insight into their culture.

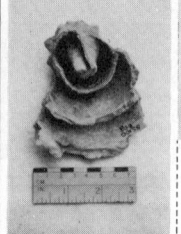

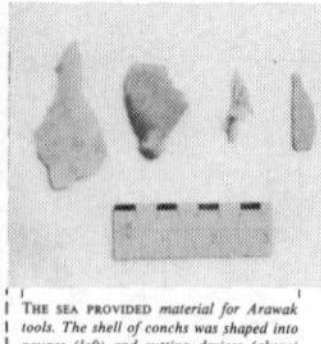

THE SEA PROVIDED material for Arawak tools. The shell of conchs was shaped into gouges (left) and cutting devices (above) for use in constructing canoes. There was no hard igneous rock on the 60-square-mile island for the making of stone implements.

Also, the limestone had curved cavities where a sharp circular cutting edge had been formed on the shell by rubbing it with a swinging motion against the stone.

The use of shell tools probably came about because there was no hard igneous rock on many Caribbean and Bahamian islands. Conch celts and chisels had to take the place of stone axes and adzes. It is also possible that the Lucayans preferred the conch tools to stone because the shell was easier to resharpen.

Large Canoes, Simple Tools

Because the Lucayans were island people, canoes were necessary to their way of life. Columbus mentioned in the records of both his first voyage in 1492 and his third voyage in 1498 that he saw canoes made of mahogany 75 feet long and 5 feet wide carrying more than 50 people. By anyone's standards the building of a craft this large was no small feat, particularly with shell tools.

The timber from which the canoe was to be fashioned was charred, chiseled, and sawed to remove an immense amount of woody material so that the walls were suitably thin. One of the early chroniclers suggests that the final smoothing of the wood might have been done with the rough skin of a shark. Fred Olsen in his book *On the Trail of the Arawak* contends that coral rasps could have been used for this job also. Coral pieces, 10 inches long and 3 inches wide, with spines worn smooth have been recovered from archaeological refuse heaps of these primitive people. It is logical to assume that the Arawaks were well aware of the advantages of smoothing the wood through coral grating, as they used this technique in preparing their food. Often, a piece of staghorn coral was used for scraping of corn and fish scales and grating sweet potatoes and cassava.

From recent excavations on San Salvador, it appears from the large quantities of shells found that clams and conchs were high on the priority list of marine foods. Studies also reveal a definite preference for parrotfishes, triggerfishes and assorted mollusks—chiton, West Indian top shells, and bleeding tooth.

A Stunning Fishing Method

The Lucayans, of course, used the sea and the brackish rivers with occasional sinkholes containing reef fishes for fishing. Their fishing methods, however, would be considered unsportsmanlike by today's standards. They used a narcotic that was produced by crushing the leaves and bark of the dogwood tree. This pulp was then placed in a bag and dragged through the water near the mangroves that grew along the creek banks. In a few seconds, the fishes would be temporarily overcome and float to the surface where they were easily collected. The marine life was only stupified briefly for, as they floated into clean water, they would quickly revive. It also should be noted that the Indians used nets and a primitive bamboo pole with a fish tooth on the point as alternate ways to fish.

Once the fish was caught, it was used in its entirety—the flesh for food and the bones for jewelry. Necklaces were also made of shells and combs were made of fish bones inserted into finely cut and polished mahogany pieces. Bracelets were made from beads of stone, fish bones, seeds, coral, shell, or a pearllike substance obtained from the shell. Delicate egg-shaped pink pearl from the conch was considered a prized treasure.

The island Lucayans were not an unattractive people, perhaps due in part to their practice of anointing their bodies with turtle-egg oil. The turtle oil acted as a skin softener, a mosquito repellent, and a vehicle for the coloring matter for body painting.

The Sea in Art and Religion

Depictions of sea life were a major part of their carvings, artwork, and idol, or Zemi, worship. The Lucayan religion was a combination of the guardian spirit concept and fetish worship, where the idol was the central figure. On San Salvador, a few Zemi made of conch have been discovered at the Pigeon Creek archaeological site. Professor Marjorie Pratt of Ithaca College, New York, and her husband, Dr. Peter Pratt of State University of New York, uncovered others made of

UNCOVERING CLUES *to the past at San Salvador, workers carry out careful excavation of the Pigeon Creek site, one of the largest archaeological digs in the Bahamas. Using grids and precise measurements (lower), archaeologists can pinpoint the location of each artifact.*

Vesta Rea-Salisbury

the island limestone. The Pigeon Creek site is one of the largest reported in the Bahamas. It covers several acres, and has been under excavation since March 1973 by the College Center of the Finger Lakes and by the Pratts specifically.

Other depictions of the Indian sea interest are present on upright stone slabs that had been carved with petroglyph. Most of these show line drawings of fish surrounded with decorative designs.

Over the years there have been a few archaeological finds of significance on San Salvador. Several years ago, the Academy of Natural Sciences in Philadelphia had a wood *duho*, a ceremonial seat used by the chief, or cacique. It had been carved in the form of a sea turtle and, it is said, had been removed from a San Salvador cave in 1828 by a loyalist farmer who

EXCAVATION OF A MIDDEN, *an accumulation of refuse that surrounds a dwelling place, reveals that clams were an important food in the Arawak diet. Other evidence suggests that conchs and reef fishes also served as staples.*

was struggling on the island after the American Revolution.

At the time of Columbus, the Lucayans used the blowing of the conch shell to announce the death of a native or a warning of danger. The horn could be heard all over the island and summoned people from the fields and from the sea at great distances. The old celts that had once been used as tools have been uncovered by the present-day inhabitants of San Salvador and in some cases are worn around their necks as good-luck pieces.

People travel weekly to this remote island to view the three possible places Columbus could have landed. Few are aware of the Indians that greeted the Great Navigator or of what his landfall did to the Indian civilization. With his arrival, the sea and the Lucayans, who had struggled together over centuries, would now feel the irreversible effects of civilization. The "virtuous savage" would be gone forever, and the majestic sea would have to labor for survival against pollution and destruction.

Laying Out a Magazine

Despite the many layout possibilities (and the fact that so much depends upon your taste and the taste of your readers, several general principles should be observed:

1. *Keep the layout consistent.* A carefully chosen type style for the heads, the subheads, and the initial letters will make an impressive difference. After consistency has been established, changing the typeface to accentuate the mood of the piece will be easier.

2. *Square up elements.* Line up the top edges of halftones (photos or cuts) that are similarly placed on one page. Also, "square" items with the margins. For example, if there are two "tones" (printers' slang for halftones) at the top of the page, do not make one 4 inches deep and the other 4½ inches deep. But if you should have a halftone that measures 5½ inches deep and another halftone beside it that measures 3 inches deep, remember that the reader's eye will not automatically square them because of the obvious visual difference.

3. *Distribute elements.* Bunching the title, blurbs, tones, and by-line at the beginning of the story creates an imbalance. In some cases, it creates columns of unbroken type. To avoid that, and to visually break up the text of the article, place the elements around and across the spread.

4. *Do not have the elements fighting each other.* Place gray and white between the strong elements. For example, if there is a large tone on the right-hand page, do not place a smaller tone next to it on the left-hand page. White space makes the page seem airy, and an airy page is easy to "get into," so feel free to make use of white space.

5. *Think about the sizes of the pictures.* Avoid placing small halftones under large ones. Avoid a "hanging system" in which the small cuts seem to be suspended from the larger cuts.

6. *Try to be unusual.* Once you feel comfortable with the process of layout, ask yourself these questions: Should I use a wider column at the beginning of this article? Should I box this page? Should I place this article on colored stock? Should I use a ragged margin on the part of an article where the writer quotes someone else at length?

Use your own sense of creativity to design an attractive magazine. This will ultimately determine whether or not it has an inviting appearance.

One of the most popular methods for laying out part of a magazine is known as *columnar layout*, which uses either two or three columns per page and elements that conform to the columns. There are several advantages in using this method, including:

- People are used to it
- It corresponds to standard ad sizes
- It is efficient for laying out copy rapidly

Although graphics have been overused, used cleverly they can play down the pattern and play up the content. Again, the pattern should *not* call attention to itself, but should facilitate communication.

Two- or three-column layout is the most popular, but you can experiment with four- or five-column layout. This style allows for some variety in picture size and helps the editor avoid splitting pages by forcing a bleed picture across the gutter.

Dummying Your Magazine

A *dummy* is a map of your magazine. Many publishers use thumbnail layout sheets (Figure 8–5) to plan the positioning and appearance of the major articles and to fit the advertising and regular features into the allotted number of pages. The advantage of the thumbnails is that they allow the art director and the editor to evaluate each edition at a glance.

Once the general organization of the magazine has been finalized, the actual dummying can begin. Essentially, the dummy is a guide for the printer during paste-up of the publication and is necessary to avoid miscommunication and costly delays. Because most publications are highly standardized, dummy forms are used (Figure 8–6). Arrows and squiggly lines usually denote positions of text matter, boxes usually denote photos or borders, and display types are identified in shorthand. The dummy can be either a hastily put-together or a finely detailed model of your final product, so you can use it either way.

Set aside adequate time to construct the dummy. Remember that it will go to the printer, who most likely has made up many different magazines without much direction and who will probably work on whim if you do not carefully specify design directions.

FIGURE 8–5. *Thumbnail layout sheets.* All magazines, of course, can mimeograph thumbnail layout sheets in half-size. Observe that the pages are grouped as spreads, with page 1 and page 16 as single pages.

LAYOUT AND DESIGN 199

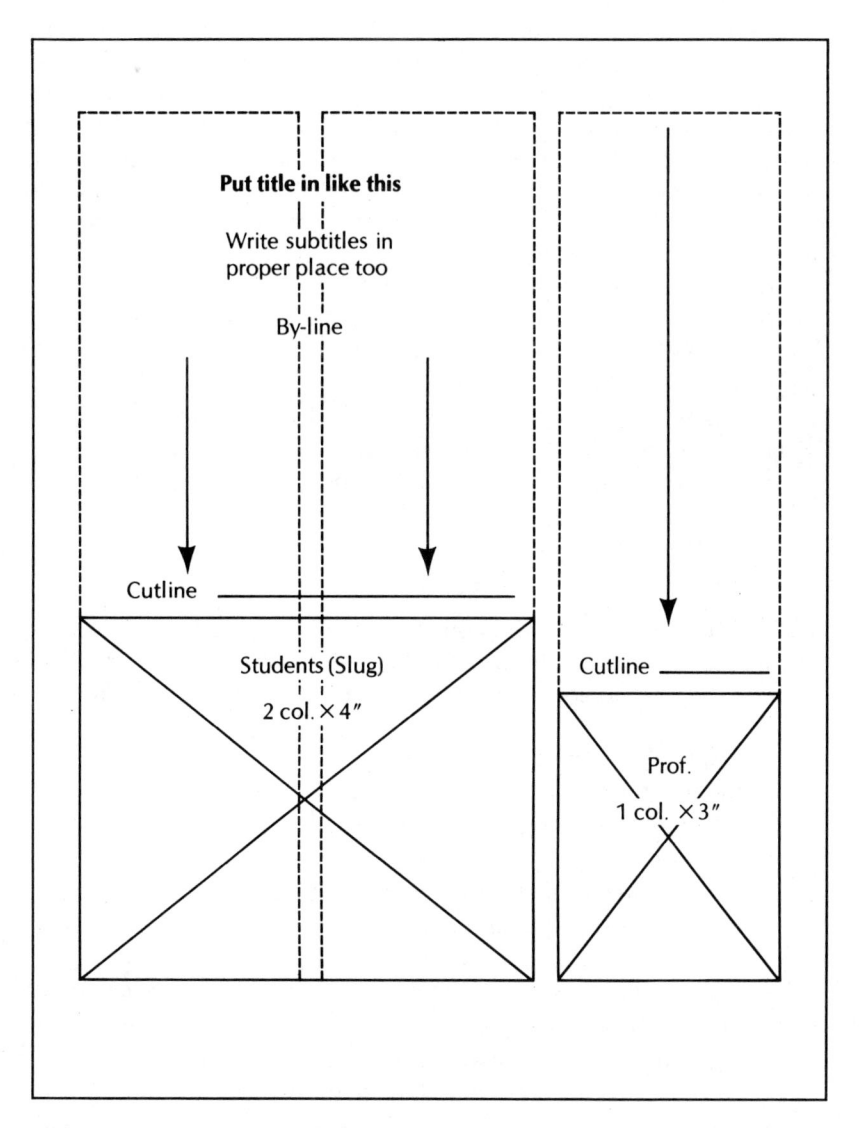

FIGURE 8–6. *Layout.* This shows a half-size layout for an 8½ × 11 magazine. A cut 4 inches deep and 4¾ inches wide is drawn 2 inches deep and 2⅜ inches wide. The printer will be informed by instructions shown above.

Covers

Some editors think first of the cover, or *wrap*, of their magazine, because it can attract or repel prospective readers. Some editors do not tie their covers to any particular article inside. For example, *Advertising Age* has no real "cover"; the articles begin near the top of the first page, leaving room only for the name of the magazine. The *Reader's Digest* cover is its table of contents. Most magazines, however, do give as much attention to the cover as to the articles inside, because it acts as a kind of banner to attract the reader's eye.

The least expensive covers are composed only of type—articles can begin on the cover or article titles can act as a lure. Nonetheless, a picture should always be used unless the magazine is aimed only at intellectual readers.

Although people have been used on all of the following covers (Figures 8–7 through 8–9), observe the great differences between them. *Learning* used real people, *feed/back* and *The Quill* used paintings.

Back Covers

The back cover must also be considered. Will it contain an advertisement? Will it be blank otherwise? If there is no advertisement, the back cover can be used to good advantage by doing one of the following:

1. Extend the front cover to the back cover by using one large picture. Make certain that the center of interest is on the front cover; the details of the picture should begin near the edge of the front cover and continue onto the back.
2. Like the *AP World*, the back cover can be used as an extension of the magazine by picturing one or more of the people who appeared in the magazine. The picture can cover about half the page, including a short caption, and the rest of the page can be an appealing white or a subdued color.
3. Use the back cover as an advertisement for the next issue by printing in bold type some of the titles that will be featured.
4. If your magazine is struggling with finances, the back cover can make an appeal for contributions and/or subscriptions.
5. If the magazine represents an organization (such as the American Newspaper Publishers Association), the back cover can list upcoming organizational meetings for several months or the coming year.

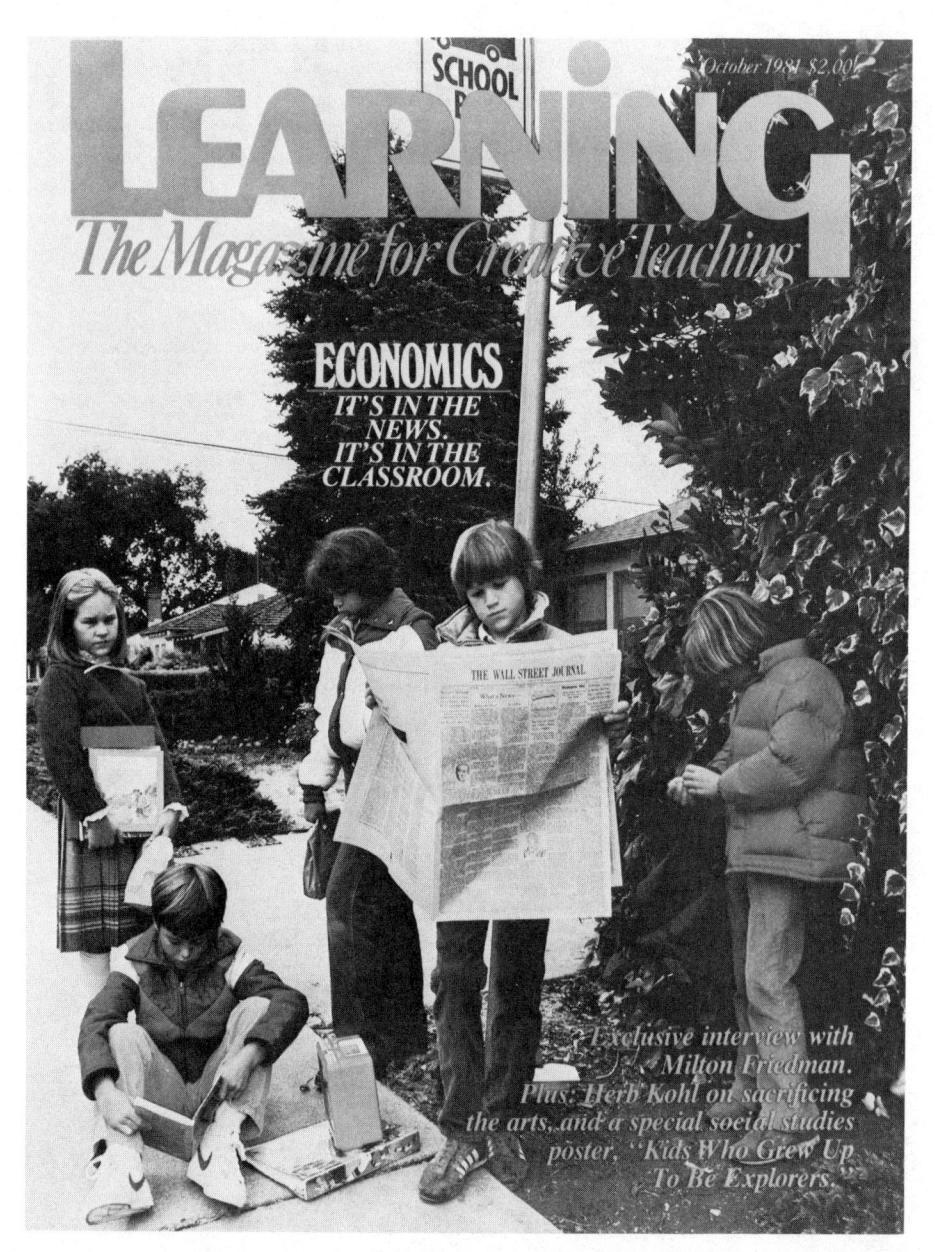

FIGURE 8–7. Reprinted by special permission of *LEARNING,* The Magazine for Creative Teaching, October, 1981. © 1981 by Pitman Learning, Inc. Photography by David Hale.

FIGURE 8–8. Courtesy, *feed/back*.

FIGURE 8–9. Courtesy, *The Quill.* Cover illustration by Susan Randstrom.

Inside Covers

The front cover is the most important eye-catcher, but the inside covers, both front and back, are also critical. What goes there? Visit a large news stand for 20 minutes or so and leaf through the many magazines. You will find that the inside covers express an astonishing range of information. For example,

1. *Reader's Digest*. The inside front cover of this magazine is a large ad, while the inside back cover features a part of the magazine such as "Quotable Quotes." During different months, advertisements may run in both inside covers.
2. *The Quill*. About a fourth of the inside front cover is devoted to an ad, with the rest of the page given over to "Editor's Notes." Part of the inside back cover is a continuation of the magazine's editorial pages, and about half is devoted to "*Quill* Classifieds."
3. *Chaparral* (Stanford quarterly humor magazine). Because students work hard at selling ads, the inside covers are composed of at least two ads. The inside back cover usually has at least four ads.

As you can see, inside covers vary widely. One rule is to bow to the advertisers regarding placement of ads on the inside covers, because they support your magazine and because the back cover sells for a premium rate.

The late Harold Ross, editor of *The New Yorker*, drew a line between the editorial department and the advertising department and literally would not allow the advertising staff to enter the editorial department. But year by year, *The New Yorker* has led all other American magazines in advertising revenue. Leafing through the magazine, it seems almost choked by ads, and both inside covers always carry them. (*The New Yorker* is, however, one of the most carefully edited magazines in the world.)

The Lead Article and Center Spread

Choose the lead article for your magazine with great care. Some readers may read (or scan) the *back* of the magazine first, but most begin with the first article. Ideally, the lead article should combine information first and entertainment second.

> *General Organization of Magazines*
>
> Front cover (picture, table of contents, large type, ad, etc.)
> Front inside cover (full-page ad, small ad with editorial matter, etc.)
> Table of contents
> Masthead
> Postal permit
> Departments, columns, and letters (in some magazines)
> Lead article
> Secondary articles
> Center spread (ad, pictures, article, etc.)
> Jumps (in some magazines)
> Departments, columns, letters (in some magazines)
> Cartoons, fillers, reviews (in some magazines)
> Back inside cover (full-page ad, small ad with editorial matter, etc.)
> Back cover (extension of the front cover picture, extension of editorial matter, picture and caption, ad, etc.)

The *center spread* is the two pages in the middle of the magazine. If the magazine is saddle-stitched, or stapled through the center, it tends to fall open at this point. Special attention is given to the center spread, because these are the only two pages in the magazine that can be treated as a single printing unit. Some magazines sell the center spread to advertising (which usually costs the advertiser much more). Think about the advantages of the center spread. It is the third most important opportunity, following the cover and the lead article, to display your ingenuity.

As a final note, remember that the message comes first, but the visual design is part of that message. The text and the illustrations *must* work together. Each article must work with the design, the flow, and the message of the entire magazine.

Remember, too, that the magazine is a unit. Any article is only one unit in the whole, as the photograph is only one unit in the article, the paragraph only one unit in the text, the sentence only one unit in the paragraph, and so on, down to the final period.

The editor must combine all the necessary pieces, organize them, and present them in a clear and logical manner. What is the message? Which articles, which words say it best? Which word order? Which pictures? Which picture order? Each decision contributes to the final product, the finished magazine. The sense and the beauty of it—both verbal and visual—must be considered, must work to make it as aesthetically pleasing as possible.

FIGURE 8–10. *Lead article.* The editor originally considered leading with this article, but then decided to feature it later in the magazine. Some readers might have been puzzled about reading a first article on a left page. ("Milton Friedman Talks About Economics And Teachers: An Interview," by David Grady. Art by Dick Cole. Reprinted by special permission of *LEARNING, The Magazine for Creative Teaching,* October, 1981. © 1981 by Pitman Learning, Inc., 530 University Ave., Palo Alto, CA 94301).

Should teachers be teaching economics to kids? At least one leading economist has some decidedly unconventional views on that subject. When David Grady, an editor of Learning, *interviewed Milton Friedman, the Nobel Prize winner expressed deep misgiving about whether public school teachers are likely to promote the kind of economic thinking that he, for one, favors. Moreover, he argued the question should really be: When are we going to change our school system to make it compatible with the American belief in free enterprise?*

Milton Friedman Talks About Economics And Teachers

A Nobel Prize–winning economist argues that good economics education depends on much more than choosing the "right" materials.

AN INTERVIEW BY DAVID GRADY

GRADY: Dr. Friedman, for some time there has been an argument that goes something like this: increasingly the issues facing our democracy are economic issues; if we don't use our schools to produce a more economically literate population, we endanger the democracy, because people won't know enough to deal with the issues intelligently. In your view, should teachers be striving to produce more economic literacy among their students?
FRIEDMAN: I believe that it would be highly desirable to have a greater degree of economic literacy in the population at large. But I can't say whether teachers should make the children more economically literate unless I can first answer the question: What are the chances that what they teach will be good economic literacy instead of bad economic literacy? Everything that goes under the name of economics is not good economics.

In my view, most teachers have two characteristics: they have had no exposure to economics as a serious subject, and they are working in an institution—the public schools—which is fundamentally socialist in character. I find it hard to believe that the people in a socialist institution can teach the kind of free-enterprise economics that I believe is really needed in our society.
GRADY: My guess is that most teachers will be absolutely stunned to hear you say that. They feel that if they even remotely approached teaching socialism—assuming that they wanted to—they would be run out of town on a rail.
FRIEDMAN: Do you know the statement—was it in a play by Molière?—"For 40 years I have been speaking prose without knowing it"? Many teachers have been "speaking" socialism without realizing it. And they aren't the only ones. Many of our top businessmen who proclaim themselves staunch defenders of free enterprise are speaking socialism—over and over again.
GRADY: Can you give me an example?
FRIEDMAN: A very obvious recent example is Lee Iacocca, the head of the Chrysler Corporation. If you ask Mr. Iacocca if he believes in private enterprise, do you have any doubt that he would say, "Of course. Private enterprise is absolutely fundamental to the preservation of our society"? But what did he *do*? He went to the government and asked to be bailed out. That's practicing socialism while preaching free enterprise.
GRADY: Why do you say the public schools are a socialist institution?
FRIEDMAN: What's our definition of socialism? Governmental ownership and control of the means of production. Who owns the public school buildings? Who pays the salaries of the public school teachers? When I describe the public schools as socialist, I am simply being descriptive.
GRADY: But weren't the public schools set up on behalf of free enterprise? Wasn't the goal to provide all the citizens of the country with the education they needed to be full participants in a system based on individual freedom?
FRIEDMAN: As is so often the case, what we have is a fascinating story in which people do something that turns out to have an opposite effect from what they had intended. Horace Mann and the others of the nineteenth century who promoted public schools and compulsory education were strong believers in individualism and free enterprise. If you had told them that they were planning to introduce socialism in America—that would have been heresy to them. And yet, in fact, that's what they were doing.

Now so long as this relatively small, essentially socialist institution was responsive to the bulk of society, which was essentially pro individualism and free enterprise, it was possible for the schools to teach the principles of free enterprise. It was possible because they existed in a highly decentralized system under which there was effective local control of the schools and under which the parents had a good deal to say.

But then, around the turn of the century, came the well-meaning reformers—particularly in the large cities—who saw that local control meant great diversity in the schools—some good, some bad. Their movement was directed at consolidating local schools and replacing elected or politically appointed boards of education and superintendents by supposedly professionally trained people, that is to say, graduates of schools of education.

At first their reforms took hold in the cities. Then, increasingly—and inevitably—control moved to the state capital, and now, in recent years, it has been moving to Washington. As a result, public schools are no longer a decentralized socialist institution responsive to local mores. They are much more centralized and thus far less likely to promote free enterprise.
GRADY: What, in your view, would be necessary to change the current situation to one that favored the teaching of free-enterprise economics?
FRIEDMAN: From my perspective, the only way to improve economic literacy in the United States is to change the structure of the school system in a way that eliminates collectivist and socialist elements. But please understand that I believe much more is at stake than whose economic ideas are being taught in the schools. In my opinion, it is precisely those collectivist and socialist elements that are responsible for the deplorable record our school system has been developing. There is no disagreement among anybody, I believe, that the school system in America has been failing in its basic mission to an increasing extent over the past 10, 20, 30 years. Although there are still some excellent schools in the system, they exist for the most part only in the affluent suburbs, where parents still exercise a large degree of control.
GRADY: You and your wife, Rose, advanced a similar argu-

Art by Dick Cole

LEARNING OCTOBER 1981 45

208 CHAPTER 8

FIGURE 8–11. *Center spread.* The top illustration shows the initial layout of the picture and the article; the bottom one shows how they were finally published. This is a center spread, in which the layout person uses the entire two pages for the picture, ignoring the gutter between pages. (Cameras in the Courtroom 1982, illustration by Andy Thomas.)

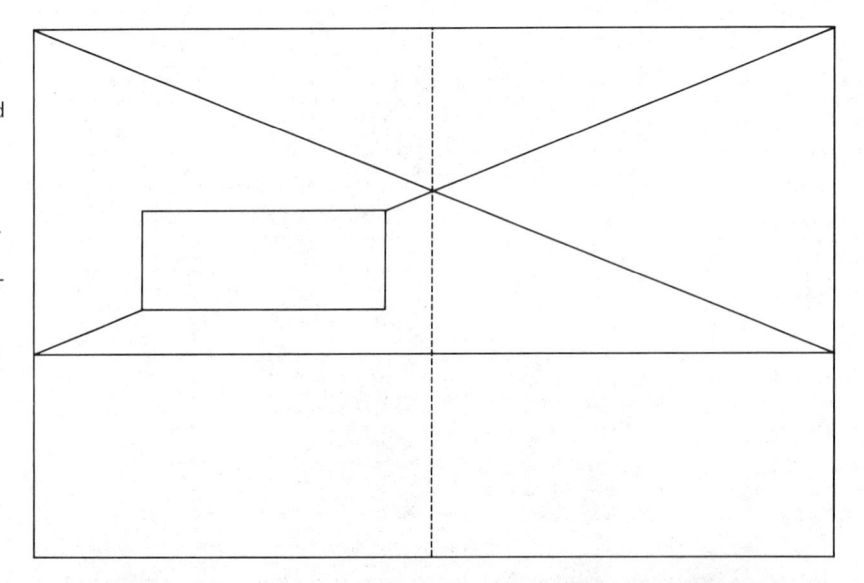

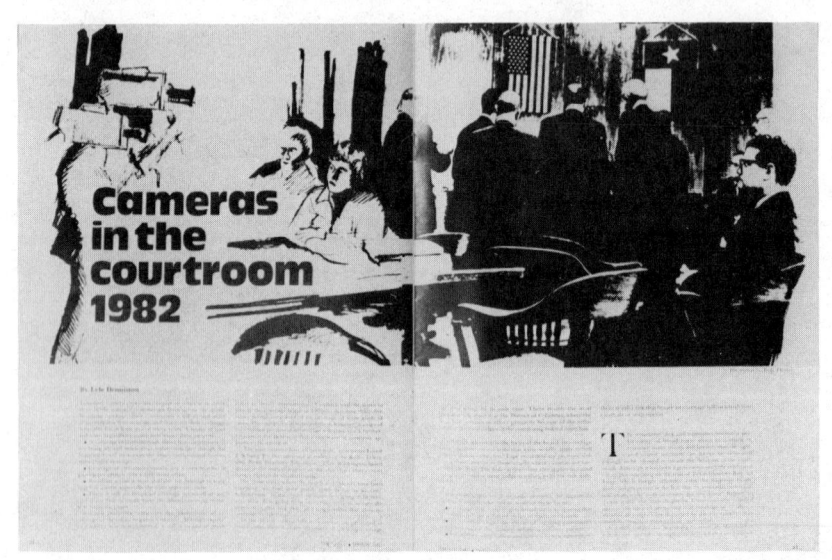

Exercises

1. Select a magazine you think is poorly designed. Review the magazine carefully, identifying those qualities of design that are unappealing to you. At the next class, present a critique of the magazine. Be specific in your criticisms, noting concrete examples of the shortcomings.

2. Select two major consumer magazines and determine the following:
   a. Page size
   b. Method of binding (stitched, sewn, or glued)
   c. Column widths, in picas, and number of columns per page
   d. Gutter widths, in picas
   e. Margins, in picas
   f. Column depth, in picas
   g. Uniformity of display types
   h. Overall use of white space (not much or a lot)

3. Select two scholarly journals and repeat exercise 2.

4. Select six different major consumer magazines and identify how each used the following:
   a. Front cover
   b. Inside front cover
   c. Page one
   d. Lead article position
   e. Center spread
   f. Last page
   g. Inside back cover
   h. Back cover

   Do you see any patterns?

5. Repeat exercise 4 using six different scholarly journals.

6. Returning to the magazine you critiqued in exercise 1, disassemble the magazine and rearrange the design elements in a two-page spread. The titles need not reflect the content of the redesigned pages, and the text need not flow. The purpose is simply to alter the visual impact. Cut and paste the design elements onto a piece of bristol or posterboard.

7. Look carefully at the layout of "Arawaks." Then answer the following questions:
   a. Is the general layout original or predictable?
   b. Is the display type too large or too small?
   c. Is the body type too large or too small?
   d. Are there too many illustrations or not enough?
   e. Are the many historical illustrations too old to grace a modern magazine?

8. Using this same article, cut out the body type, then the display type, and finally the illustrations. Then rearrange the layout in a way that pleases you. Show your layout at the next class meeting.

9. Before the next class, choose a magazine that you think will appeal to the other students. List five articles with titles and explain in a few sentences what the articles contain.

Chapter 9

Magazines: Law and Ethics

Freedom of the press is a highly valued ideal that springs from the philosophy on which this country was founded: that everyone should be free to speak and write his or her own thoughts. The clash of ideas, the Founding Fathers believed, would produce something called Truth.

But our lofty interpretation of freedom does contain some snags: in practice, every society restricts free expression in some way. For example, we have laws to protect citizens against defamation, to protect individual copyrights of original information, to preserve community standards of decency and morality, and to protect the states against treason.

As champions of the public's right to know, writers and editors have ironically claimed a First Amendment right to *withhold* information. In the late 1960s and 1970s, journalists found themselves the objects of a number of government subpoenas, many of them stemming from coverage of the antiwar movement, the civil rights movement, the counterculture, prostitution, gambling, drugs, and corruption in high and low places. They sought the right to withhold various types of information, including:

1. The identity of confidential sources.
2. Unpublished information provided on a confidential basis.
3. Information not included in stories or edited out before their release, such as what might be found in "outtakes" (film or tape shot but not used in a final story) or in a reporter's notes or drafts.
4. Information gathered through direct observation, such as the witnessing of a political demonstration or a crime.
5. Physical evidence, such as a letter or tape recording from an underground organization.

The use of the subpoena power to compel testimony or evidence is a well-established right of government acting on the public's behalf; indeed, the Sixth Amendment to the Constitution explicitly guarantees to criminal defendants the right to compel the appearance of witnesses on their behalf and to be confronted with the witnesses against them, although those are the only circumstances in which the subpoena power can be used. Thus, the public has a right to information not only through the mass media but through established legal processes as well.

Any false statement, written or broadcast, is considered libelous if it causes anyone to suffer public hatred, contempt, or ridicule; or if it causes one to be shunned or avoided; or if it injures one in his or her business or occupation.

In 1964, the U.S. Supreme Court decided in *New York Times Co. v. Sullivan* that even false statements that tend to injure public officials must be protected by law unless facts were deliberately misstated or unless there was reckless disregard of the question of truth or falsity. In 1971, the Court decided in *Rosenbloom v. Metromedia* that private individuals who are involved in matters of public or general concern also should be limited severely in their ability to recover damages in libel actions. Like public officials, they must prove that they are victims of actual malice or "calculated falsehood" to sue successfully, no matter how great the damage.

Focusing on magazines, consider actor Marlon Brando's actions when the *Saturday Evening Post* published an article entitled "Marlon Brando—How He Wasted $6 Million by Sulking on the Set." Brando filed a $5 million libel suit against the magazine (and lost). Also, Linus Pauling, a chemist who twice won the Nobel Prize, sued the *National Review* for $1 million, saying that the magazine had branded him falsely as a "traitor engaged in subversive Communist activities." In this case, the *National Review* won.

Magazine editors are usually safe when they print accurate reports of major official proceedings at the federal and state levels. If editors publish articles about local organizations, they must be accurate and take care that their motivation is a desire to serve the public.

The defenses against libel suits can be separated into three general categories: truth, privilege, and fair comment and criticism. The late Ben Hibbs, editor of the *Saturday Evening Post*, wrote this advice for the new editors:

> Any national publication dealing with topical matters must, I think, take its chances with the libel laws now and then. By that, I don't mean there is any excuse for carelessness, but I do mean that timidity has no place in an editor's kit bag when a real issue is at stake.

Defamation

On June 7, 1971, the Supreme Court ruled that Philadelphia radio station WIP was *not* guilty of libel when it referred to a local magazine shop owner as a "smut distributor." The shop owner, George Rosenbloom, had been arrested and then acquitted on charges of criminal obscenity. At the libel trial, Rosenbloom was awarded $25,000 in compensatory damages because he claimed that the broadcasts had put him out of business, and also $725,000 (later reduced to $250,000) in punitive damages. Had the Supreme Court upheld the libel judgment, WIP would have had to pay Rosenbloom a total of $275,000. But the Court ruled that WIP was not legally responsible.

The decision was a pivotal one for American journalism, the climax of seven years of Supreme Court decisions that had eroded the laws of libel to the point where, as the *New York Times* stated, "It is now close to impossible for anyone to collect substantial damages for a libelous remark printed in a newspaper or magazine or book or broadcast on radio or television." The phrases "close to impossible" and "substantial damages" are important qualifications; the laws of libel have not been repealed.

The seven years of change began in 1964 with *New York Times v. Sullivan*. The *Times* had published a full-page advertisement paid for by Negro clergymen in Montgomery, Alabama. L. B. Sullivan, the Montgomery city commissioner in charge of the police department, claimed that he had been libeled in the ad by false and defamatory statements about the police. Alabama courts had found for Sullivan, but the Supreme Court reversed the decision. Justice William Brennan wrote:

> The constitutional guarantees require, we think, a federal rule that prohibits a public official from recovering damages for a defamatory falsehood relating to his official conduct unless he proves that the statement was made with "actual malice"—that is, with knowledge that it was false or with reckless disregard of whether it was false or not.

This decision was based on the belief that the media must be free from the peril of huge damage suits if they are to carry out their function of reporting on public affairs. Officials began to find it difficult to sue successfully because the Supreme Court did not define "malice" as the layman usually does—simply as ill will—but as calculated lying or reckless disregard of truth.

The libel pendulum swung backward in 1974 with the Court's ruling in *Gertz v. Robert Welch, Inc.*, which narrowed the definition of a public figure and which rejected the public issue rule in *Rosenbloom*. In that case, Elmer Gertz, an attorney who was an expert in libel law, sued a John Birch Society magazine, *Public Opinion*, for the libel contained in an article about him. Despite the fact that Gertz had been active in community and professional affairs and controversies, the Court held that Gertz was not a public figure and, as a private individual, needed only to show negligence on the part of the publication, a much lighter burden than proving actual malice. Although the Court made it easier for a plaintiff to win a libel suit, the press did win some protections. The Court required a showing of negligence because there can be "no liability without fault." In addition, to prevent media self-censorship, the Court said that a private individual would have to meet the actual malice standard before he could collect punitive damages—damages that often run into thousands of dollars and that the Court criticized as being "private fines levied by civil juries" to punish the press.

The *Gertz* decision, which left the actual malice standard intact for libel against public officials and public figures, is the governing decision for libel law in the 1980s. Since *Gertz*, however, three Supreme Court decisions have put further restrictions on who can be considered public figures in libel cases. In *Time, Inc. v. Firestone* in 1976, *Hutchinson v. Proxmire* in 1979, and *Wolston v. Reader's Digest* in 1979, the Court ruled *against* the press, holding that, in each case, the plaintiff was a private individual, not a public figure.

In *Hutchinson v. Proxmire*, the Court ruled that a publicly employed scientist at a state hospital, Ronald R. Hutchinson, who received substantial funds for research on monkeys, was not a public figure. The scientist sued Senator William Proxmire for libel after the Wisconsin senator awarded the agencies that supported Hutchinson's research his Golden Fleece award for wasteful government spending. In *Wolston v. Reader's Digest* the Court ruled that the prior conviction of Ilya Wolston in the late 1950s was not enough to make him a public figure. The Court rejected the argument of *Reader's Digest* that "any person who engages in criminal conduct automatically becomes a public figure for purposes of comment on a limited range of issues relating to his conviction."

Since the *Gertz* decision, the press has had one victory. In 1977, in *Edwards v. National Audubon Society*, the Supreme Court let stand a decision that provided constitutional protection for the press when it engages in "neutral reportage" of charges. The case began when the *New York Times* carried a story on the dispute between the pesticide industry and the Audubon Society. The *Times* repeated the charges made by the Audubon Society that criticized certain scientists for their reports on the effect of DDT on birds.

The changes in Supreme Court decisions over the years indicate that the Court is quite capable of redefining its own conceptions. In addition, of course, cases differ in so many particulars that it is difficult for a journalist to be certain that a case involving his or her own errors is exactly like a case the Court has already decided.

Privacy

In cases of privacy, the freedom of the writer and the editor has been growing; the courts support the public's right to learn about their fellow citizens. You must remember when you are directing or editing a writer's work that the writer is *not* free to invade privacy at will. When privacy is at issue, the courts weigh the public interest against the interest of the person who believes that his or her privacy has been invaded. When it can be shown that issues or matters of general concern are involved, the courts tend to rule in favor of the magazine.

In an issue of the *Ladies' Home Journal*, the editor decided to publish an article titled "Love." With the caption reading "Publicized as glamorous, desirable, 'Love at first sight' is a bad risk," it pictured a man and woman sitting at a counter, his arm around her and his cheek against hers. The man and woman, who are husband and wife, sued the magazine. They said that their privacy had been invaded, and that they had been depicted as loose, immoral persons engaged in the "wrong kind of love."

The California Supreme Court ruled that it is no invasion of privacy if a pose is voluntarily assumed in public and the ordinary sense of decency is not shocked. Six of the justices agreed on these words, which provide a guideline for editors:

> Plaintiffs' sitting romantically close to one another, the man with his arm around the woman, depicts no more than the portrayal of an incident which may be seen almost daily in ordinary life. . . . The right to be let alone and to be protected from undesirable publicity is not absolute but must be balanced against the public interest in the dissemination of news and information consistent with the democratic processes. Moreover, the right of privacy is determined by the norm of the ordinary.

In a famous case, a one-time child progidy named William Sidis was the subject of a profile in *The New Yorker*. Angered by the publicity that had enveloped him when he was a child, Sidis, who had lost his passion for mathematics and was leading an obscure life as a bookkeeper, sued on the grounds that *The New Yorker* had invaded his privacy. But the Court ruled that he had been a public figure and still was.

Because most of the articles are written and edited with the cooperation of those who are prominently featured, few magazines have been threatened with suits based on the right of privacy. Writers and editors who become involved in such suits usually recognize while researching, writing, or editing articles that danger looms, and this gives them time to seek legal help.

Public or Private Figures?

The Supreme Court also made it more difficult for the media to distinguish between public and private figures. In 1967, *Time* magazine reported among its "Milestones":

> Divorced by Russell A. Firestone, Jr., 41, heir to the tire fortune: Mary Alice Sullivan Firestone, 32, his third wife, a one-time Palm Beach schoolteacher; on grounds of extreme cruelty and adultery; after six years of marriage, one son; . . . .

Although the divorce court's language was unclear, the divorce decree did not include adultery. Indeed, Mrs. Firestone could not have been awarded alimony under Florida law if adultery had been the grounds for divorce.

The question for the U.S. Supreme Court was whether Mrs. Firestone was a public or a private figure. In *Gertz* the Supreme Court had noted that some people "occupy positions of such pervasive power and influence that they are deemed public figures for all purposes." But, the Court said, "more commonly, those classed as public figures have thrust themselves to the forefront of particular public controversies in order to influence the resolution of the issues involved."

Although Mrs. Firestone had called press conferences on the subject of her divorce, the Court ruled that she was not a public figure because the dissolution of her marriage through judicial proceedings was not the sort of "public controversy" referred to in *Gertz*. The Supreme Court seemed to put itself back into the dilemma of deciding what public issues were of legitimate interest to the public—a dilemma the Court said in *Gertz* it wished to avoid.

The Supreme Court sent the *Firestone* case back to the Florida courts to decide what standard of responsibility Florida would impose on the media—and whether *Time* had met it.

Firestone and *Gertz* reaffirmed the tremendous protection for the media against defamation suits brought by government officials and public figures, but the two cases also led the media into another era of uncertainty as state courts exercise the option of setting their own standards for private libel cases. Just how careful do reporters and editors have to be in New Mexico? in Minnesota? in Georgia? How many sources have to be checked? How exact must the wording of a headline be? What trade-offs on certainty of accuracy can be made under the press of the deadline?

Cameras in the Courtroom

In 1962, Billie Sol Estes, who had already been convicted in a federal court and sentenced to 15 years in prison, was tried in a state court in Texas on additional charges. Although Canon 35 of the American Bar Association was still on the books, it did not have the force of law; and Judicial Canon 28 of the State Bar of Texas permitted news photography and radio and television broadcasting at the discretion of the trial judge. Estes' attorneys argued before the pretrial hearing that television, radio, and news photography should be banned from the courtroom. But the case had attracted national attention, and the judge denied the motion. Estes was found guilty.

In 1965, the Supreme Court reviewed the case and reversed Estes' conviction in a 5-to-4 decision. The Supreme Court ruled that Estes deserved a trial without such extravagant coverage by television. The majority stopped short of a ruling that would suggest to judges in lower courts that cameras are never welcome in any trial, but it is clear that the cause of electronic communications lost ground. Then, in 1980, the judges of many courts allowed cameras into courtrooms.

Stronger Restrictions

All signs point to stronger restrictions on law enforcement coverage by all the media. The real dangers have been spelled out plainly by Nicholas Horrock, a reporter for *Newsweek*, who claims that "prosecutors, police, and other mechanics of the law enforcement business spend much of their time and effort now in endeavoring to conduct their business with as little public scrutiny as possible." Recalling his days as a cub reporter in New Jersey, Horrock told of the arrest of a Newark black for the rape of a suburban housewife. Horrock and a veteran reporter were at the police station when the man was brought in at 2 a.m. Said the veteran: "Look around—do you see any lawyers—anybody from the ACLU? Sure you don't. You and I are it."

Despite the obvious value to many defendants of journalists who are on hand to observe the quality of justice that accused persons receive, many critics of the media argue that the United States should adopt the more restrictive British system. For the most part, British journalists cannot report a trial until it has been concluded. Anthony Lewis of the *New York Times* is among those who argue that the British system could not work in the United States. Among other points, he stresses that British trials involving major crimes are commonly completed in less than two months, but similar trials and appeals in the United States often take years. Moreover, Lewis points out that police and judicial corruptions are virtually unknown in Great Britain, but experience has shown that the watchdog function is essential here. If American journalists were to adopt the British system, they would be abdicating important responsibilities.

Obviously, the collision of the First Amendment and the Sixth Amendment has been echoed in irresponsible performances by both journalists and officials. This problem continues to be a central one that cannot be solved by journalists alone.

Obscenity and Pornography

Filing a brief in *David S. Alberts v. State of California* in 1956, attorneys for the plaintiff pointed out that John Keats' *Endymion*, Percy Shelley's *Queen Mab*, Walt Whitman's *Leaves of Grass*, Daniel Defoe's *Moll Flanders*, Theodore Dreiser's *An American Tragedy*, and many editions of the *Bible* have been declared obscene at various times in various places. That being the case, a 5-to-4 Supreme Court decision in 1973 made it impossible for anyone to know in advance exactly what is obscene. More precisely, no one can be certain *where* a given work will be judged obscene.

During the 1950s and 1960s, the Supreme Court decided how it should go about ruling in cases of obscenity and pornography, even though the justices were unable to define the terms precisely. They had decided that the obscene, whatever it may be, is not part of the constitutionally protected freedom of speech and press. In *Roth v. United States*, the companion case to *Alberts*, and subsequent cases, the Court decided, according to an analysis by Justice William Brennan, that three elements must coalesce for a work to be judged obscene:

> (a) The dominant theme of the materials taken as a whole appeals to prurient interest in sex; (b) the material is patently offensive because it affronts contemporary standards relating to the description or representation of sexual matters; and (c) the material is utterly without redeeming social value.

These elements offer only a general guide, and Brennan's statement expressed a minority view. The Court was so patently unable to establish that obscenity is harmful that many attorneys came to refer to the body of obscenity law as a prohibition in search of a rationale. In short, the "dim and uncertain line" that had long marked the difference between obscenity and constitutionally protected expression continued indistinct.

But the vagueness of the period before the Supreme Court decision of 1973 seemed like bedrock certainty compared to that of the period after it. For, although the Court retained the first two elements of obscenity judgment—that the dominant theme be prurient and that the material be patently offensive—the decision changed the third. Rather than being "utterly without redeeming social value," a pornographic work is one that "taken as a whole, lacks serious literary, artistic, political, or scientific value." Most important, the decision held that what is obscene should be decided locally. Chief Justice Warren Burger wrote, "People in different states vary in their tastes and attitudes, and this diversity is not to be strangled by the absolutism of imposed uniformity."

Justice William O. Douglas dissented sharply, warning that the new test of obscenity "would make it impossible to ban any paper or any journal or magazine in some benighted place." He added, "To send men to jail for violating standards they cannot understand, construe, and apply is a monstrous thing to do."

Douglas' opinion was echoed by a great many media spokesmen, especially book publishers, magazine writers and editors, and filmmakers whose work circulates widely and who had become accustomed to the old standards, which had encouraged a more permissive atmosphere. Many expressed the widely held opinion that the Supreme Court should have established a standard restricting what is available to minors, leaving it to adults to make their own decisions about what they buy and see.

Magazine copy editors should know this: in the absence of a definite decision from the Supreme Court, it is possible for every community to establish its own standard. The laws of obscenity can only be surmised. Almost all large newsstands today carry *Playboy, Penthouse,* and the like.

Magazines and Copyright Law

Most magazines are protected by copyright laws. When a magazine buys an article, it purchases specific rights to publish the article or to authorize others to publish or reprint the article. Some magazines give reprint royalties to writers, but others do not. It is important for editors and writers to understand exactly what the free-lancers are selling when they sign contracts and receive payments for articles.

A writer who produces an article working under contract to a magazine is considered to have written a "work made for hire." In such cases, the magazine is considered the "author" for copyright purposes and is thus entitled to initial ownership of the copyright. Staff writers (who may be listed as "editors") also work under this condition.

Because most publishers are fair-minded and because few articles have a life beyond first publication, the magazine seldom pays its authors to copyright their own work or to worry about which rights they are giving up. Once most articles have been published, rights to them are no more valuable than used theater tickets. But enough authors have had cause to rue the cost of once-careless habits to suggest that knowing the law and reading contracts carefully can be important. Consider this excerpt from a magazine contract:

> In consideration of the sum of $_____ (in payment of which we herewith enclose our check), the author grants to _____ Publishing Company, its licenses and assigns forever, all rights in and to the material and all rights of copyright and renewal of copyrights therein, including, but without limitation, the exclusive right to publish the material in magazine, newspaper and book form, and to use it in dramatic, motion picture, radio, and television productions anywhere. The rights herein granted include the right: to edit, revise, abridge, condense, and translate the material; to publish the same in one or more installments; to change the title thereof; to use the author's name, biography, and likeness in connection with the publication, advertising, and promotion of the material; and to make such other promotional use of the material as _____ Publishing Company may determine.

Most magazine editors wonder just how much a writer can quote from a copyrighted article or book. This issue centers on the doctrine known as "fair use," and as one panel of distinguished judges pointed out: "The issue of fair use is the most troublesome in the whole law of copyright."

The copyright doctrine we now have is imprecise at best. There are no fixed rules to dictate exactly how much a writer may quote. Most publishers tell their authors to obtain written permission to quote any substantial amount of copyrighted material, and that in any case the author must obtain permission to quote a passage as long as 300 words—or 400 or 500, varying with the publisher. Quoting a sentence or a paragraph seldom infringes on copyright. The pivotal question is whether the quotation represents substantial use—and especially whether quoting, whatever the length, may prejudice the sale or diminish the need for the original work.

Many magazines carry notices that not a word may be reproduced.

The masthead in *Reader's Digest* states, "Reproduction in any manner in whole or in part in English or other languages is prohibited." However, publications *cannot* pass their own laws. Those issuing such warnings are subject to the rules of fair use just like everyone else.

Editors should know that general facts cannot be copyrighted, and a writer can paraphrase almost at will. Copyright is not a prison for ideas, words, phrases, and the phrasings themselves. Conceivably, copyright can be infringed by paraphrase—if the writer paraphrases at length and so deftly that a court might rule unfair use—but that danger is remote.

If you are perplexed by the complexities of law, you should study one of these books on communication law: *Mass Communication Law* by Donald M. Gillmor and Jerome Barron; *Law of Mass Communications* by Harold L. Nelson and Dwight L. Teeter; and *Rights and Writers* by Harriet F. Pilpel and Theodora S. Zavin.

Editors' Ethics

In an article entitled "Cry Rape," four professors at Washington and Lee University described a very difficult and complex case. Read the following five paragraphs from the story, which was published in *Quill*:*

> Twenty-nine-year-old Gaspar Farquardt is dead. He was beaten to death because he had raped a 16-year-old girl. He was killed by the rape victim's father.
>
> There is no mystery here. The father told the police all details of how Farquardt broke into the house, held the girl and her youthful companions hostage for several hours, and raped the girl. He told how he arrived home and, in rage, beat Farquardt to death with a poker.
>
> The police have reluctantly charged the father with murder.
>
> It's a "good" story. But what should the story contain?
>
> Is this the time we break the rule about never publishing the name of a rape victim? How can we print the whole story, giving sufficient background to explain the motive for the killing, without revealing the girl's name? Even printing the name of the father—as we would the name of anyone else accused of murder—would reveal the girl's identity. If we do not suggest the motive for the killing, this probably justifiable homicide would be presented as a brutal beating death. . . .

The article ended with this:

---

*Courtesy, Dr. Louis W. Hodges, John K. Jennings, R. H. MacDonald, and Hampden H. Smith III.

Here is a case in which situational ethics cannot handily be counted upon to provide the answer. Clearly, there are several ways to go, each with its own pitfalls. What is not so clear is which is the better way in terms of causing the least harm while at the same time keeping the public informed on matters of vital importance to society.

"Sometimes," according to one of the editors, "you must decide about what to do—and you will always be *wrong*." Another editor agreed, saying that if you decide to publish everything known, you will be attacked by some people, and if you decide *not* to publish anything, rumors will fly. Although this case has *no* generally accepted solution, other cases in this chapter do.

Code of Ethics and the Editor

The first rule in the Code of Ethics established by the American Society of Journalists and Authors (ASJA) is this:

> The writer shall at all times perform professionally and to the best of his or her ability, assuming primary responsibility for truth and accuracy. No writer shall deliberately write into an article a dishonest, distorted, or inaccurate statement.
> Editors may correct or delete copy for purposes of style, grammar, conciseness, or arrangement, but may not change the intent or sense without the writer's permission.

On many magazines, the editors often ignore this. On many other magazines, however, the editors pay attention to the ASJA because its membership contains more than 500 free-lancers who provide most of the articles in their magazines. The Code of Ethics of ASJA also states:

> The practice of written confirmation of all agreements between writers and editors is strongly recommended, and such confirmation may originate with the editor, the writer, or an agent. Such a memorandum of confirmation should list all aspects of the assignment including subject, approach, length, special instructions, payments, deadline, and kill fee (if any). Failing prompt contradictory response to such a memorandum, both parties are entitled to assume that the terms set forth therein are binding.

The following letter of agreement has been recommended by the ASJA.

LETTER OF AGREEMENT

Originating with the writer (to be used when publication does not issue written confirmation of agreement).

Editor's name and title　　　　　　　　　　　　　　　　　　　　*Date*
Publication
Address

Dear *Editor's name:*

This will confirm our agreement that I will research and write an article of approximately *Number* words on the subject of *Brief description*, in accord with our discussion of *Date*.

The deadline for delivery of this article to you is *Date*.

It is understood that my fee for this article shall be $ *Amount*, payable on acceptance, for which sum *Publication* shall be entitled to first North American publication rights in the article.[1] If this assignment does not work out after I have submitted a completed manuscript, a kill fee of $ *Amount* shall be paid to me.

It is further understood that you shall reimburse me for routine expenses incurred in the researching and writing of the article, including long-distance telephone calls, and that extraordinary expenses, should any such be anticipated, will be discussed with you before they are incurred.[2]

It is also agreed that you will submit proofs of the article for my examination, sufficiently in advance of publication to permit correction of errors.

This letter is intended to cover the main points of our agreement. Should any disagreement arise on these or other matters, we agree to rely upon the guidelines set forth in the Code of Ethics and Fair Practices of the American Society of Journalists and Authors.

Please confirm our mutual understanding by signing the copy of this agreement and returning it to me.

　　　　　　　　　　　　　　　　　　　　　　　　　　Sincerely,

　　　　　　　　　　　　　　　　　　　　　　　　　　(signed)

Publication　　　　　　　　　　　　　　　　　　　　　*Writer's name*

by _____
　　　Name and Title

Date _____

[1] If discussion included the sale of other rights, this clause should specify basic fee for first North American rights, additional fees and express rights each covers, and total amount.

[2] Any other conditions agreed upon, such as inclusion of travel expenses or a maximum dollar amount for which the writer will be compensated, should also be specified.

Exercises

1. You are an editor of a campus magazine. You have learned that a young man who enrolled in your university is a former Hollywood star. Your source said that he has had a nervous breakdown because of the pressures of stardom. His dorm supervisor refused to help your magazine writer interview him. What advice would you offer the writer, who is new to the magazine world?

2. You are the articles' editor of a professional magazine and have responded favorably to a query from a writer. You have told the writer that the magazine will pay her $500 if the article is accepted, zero if it is not. When the article comes in, it is barely acceptable. Your editor-in-chief said that the magazine cannot pay any more than $250 for that article. What would you say on the telephone to the writer?

3. This chapter included a story about the death of Gaspar Farquardt (page 222). Read again that entire story; then be prepared at the next class meeting to explain what you would do if you were an editor.

4. In 1981, Janet Cooke won a Pulitzer Prize for a story she had published in the *Washington Post*—only to surrender her prize and resign from the *Post* when the editors learned that she had fabricated much of her story and had lied to her editors about much of her college background. Describe what you, as editor-in-chief, might do to decline publishing her story if you only suspected that part of it was fictional.

5. As this chapter described, "the judges of many courts allowed cameras into the courtrooms." Because the courts have been more and more in favor of allowing cameras in the courtroom, it is likely that, by 1990, most of the courts will be abristle with cameras in highly publicized cases. Describe what you would say to a new photographer for your magazine if he or she were about to go to a courtroom.

6. If you favor or disfavor certain magazines such as *Penthouse, Playboy*, or *Hustler*, write what you would say to the managing editor of such a magazine if he or she offered you a job.

Appendix A

How Newsweek *Is Prepared for Publication*

Sunday

Early Sunday morning—11 floors above a quiet Madison Avenue—a *Newsweek* copy editor releases the last page for printing, checks the clock, then lists the time in the last blank space in a special log. Another issue of *Newsweek* is closed.

This moment, to be repeated 51 times in the coming year, marks the end of a complex, tightly coordinated week in the life of one of the nation's leading news magazines.

Soon, the giant presses at *Newsweek*'s seven domestic printing plants from Connecticut to California start to churn out the new issue. Film for Newsweek International's Atlantic and Pacific editions is airborne for printers in London, England; Zurich, Switzerland; Tokyo, Japan; Hong Kong; and Sydney, Australia. A Daytona, Florida, plant begins

Appendix A courtesy of *Newsweek*, Inc.

printing International's Latin American edition. By the time the presses stop, 3.6 million copies will have been printed and sent on their way to subscribers and newsstands around the globe.

For six days, nearly 500,000 words have poured into the magazine's news desk from 70 correspondents. Hundreds of rolls of film have been processed, pictures selected and rejected, layouts drawn and redrawn to add maximum impact to as many as 178 separate geographic and demographic editions and three international editions. The manufacturing department has arranged for the millions of printing impressions and tons of paper necessary to complete this one issue.

Researchers, writers, and editors have labored over the issue's 7,000 lines of editorial content (about 49 pages). For six days, the efforts of hundreds of men and women around the world have been directed at one specific goal: to inform, enlighten, and entertain more than 20 million readers worldwide.

This is the story of one of those six-day marches toward closing. It is neither more nor less typical than any other week, for news is as unpredictable as the people who make it.

The pace is slower this Sunday, but in less than 36 hours, it will begin to pick up again.

For some, it already has. One of *Newsweek*'s Washington bureau staff photographers follows the President to church hoping to catch good informal pictures of the President and first family. A foreign reporter in Africa trudges through the bush accompanying rebel guerrillas on a night patrol and in Los Angeles a correspondent who has been up all night on a police stakeout is just getting to bed.

Monday

Traffic bustles now past *Newsweek*'s headquarters at 444 Madison Avenue in New York's midtown. Manufacturing and traffic already are coordinating the printing, binding, and nationwide distribution of over 3 million copies of the current issue. Advertising copy, layouts, and shooting scripts are rapidly coordinated to promote the current issue in newspapers and on television and radio.

The back-of-the-book sections (such as Science, Education, Sports, Theater, and Medicine) work on the upcoming issue, sifting suggestions sent in the previous week from the editorial bureaus and weighing advance information about the week's expected events. Researchers start culling the library files for pertinent information and interviewing background sources. Writers and editors do background reading and interviewing of their own and determine which of *Newsweek*'s far-flung bureaus should be tapped for additional information. Some sections that are not likely to be affected by news developments, such as Books and Movies, will be written, edited, fit, and released to the printers by Tuesday for the "Early Form"—pages that are printed ahead of the rest of the magazine.

As the 70 men and women in *Newsweek*'s ten domestic and 14 overseas editorial bureaus arrive at their offices Monday morning, each may have one or two stories, assigned in advance, in various stages of completion. High-speed data terminals have transmitted new queries over the weekend from New York, their chatter growing more insistent throughout the week as the editors schedule additional stories, postpone others, and request photos or needed information. Bureau correspondents work what are probably the longest hours in the news business—on call virtually 24 hours a day, seven days a week. In the days ahead, they will cover breaking events, interview sources, and dig for background color and insights—completing the files (reports from the field) in answer to New York's queries. Their efforts are supplemented by some 200 stringers, reporters from daily newspapers and other news organizations who make their free time and expertise available for special assignment. Today, the bureau chief—who traditionally covers his region's politics himself—assigns the new queries, and correspondents make preliminary telephone contacts, appointments, and travel reservations.

In Livingston, New Jersey, the center of *Newsweek*'s vast subscription-fulfillment operation, the morning brings the first batch of more than 100,000 pieces of mail that will flow in during the week-renewals, inquiries, new orders, payments, changes of address, and, yes, occasional cancellations.

Tuesday

At 10:30 a.m., *Newsweek*'s top editors convene the story conference, the first overall planning session for the upcoming issue. The Editor presides, assisted by the Managing Editor, Executive Editor, and Assistant Managing Editors. Also present: seven senior editors—one each representing National Affairs, International, and Business, and four who divide the back-of-the-book sections; the heads of the Cover, Photo, and Editorial Art departments; the Chief of Correspondents, News Editor, and Chief of Research; editors of the overseas editions; and, when in town, bureau correspondents. Occasionally, a top executive from the parent Washington Post Company will also drop in. Each senior editor has met previously with his or her writers and arrives at the conference armed with a list of stories for the week. The Editor calls on each in turn. The exchange of ideas is swift and informal, the repartee rapid-fire, preliminary decisions made quickly: which stories should have priority, what sections should handle them, how long they should be.

The "news hole" (for the magazine's editorial content) in any issue remains constant—about 49 pages—regardless of how many pages of advertising are scheduled. Only a blockbuster story, such as presidential resignation, will expand it. Experienced news judgment guides the editors as they carefully weigh the relative importance of each story suggested and decide how to divide the editorial pie. Entire sections are omitted each week to meet the more pressing space needs of others. At the story conference, choices are also made to determine which editorial pages—plus Top of the Week, *Newsweek*'s contents page—will carry four-color photos that week. Color can be added to virtually every section of the magazine, thanks to *Newsweek*'s run-of-press color capability that sets the pace in the newsweekly field.

Newsweek International editors, fresh from their own story conference, report to the domestic editors on plans for their next issue. International sometimes plans an entirely different cover subject from that of the domestic edition and different cover art for each of its three geographic editions.

The story conference over, the editors push ahead. Stories are assigned to specific writers; the appropriate research and reporting is ordered. At the news desk, the tide of queries to be sent to domestic and foreign correspondents begins to swell. By Saturday, reporters will file over half a million words in response, yet only about 45,000 actually will appear in *Newsweek*.

The photo department moves into full swing. Photo staffers, each assigned to a specific part of the magazine, review picture requirements with senior editors and writers, then start the search for the photographs that will best illustrate each story. *Newsweek* has seven full-time photographers (three in New York, two in Washington and one each in Chicago and Los Angeles) and also relies on wire services and photo agencies in the U.S. and abroad. Often the magazine calls upon proven free-lance photographers as well. In a typical week, the photo lab will process about 200 rolls of film and make hundreds of prints—only about 100 of which will appear in *Newsweek*.

Momentum builds everywhere. In the editorial art department, work begins on maps, drawings, charts, and graphs for the upcoming issue. Close by, the cover department discusses, selects, and begins processing possible covers for this week and weeks to come. Manufacturing/traffic prepares the newsstand draw (the number of copies each distributor or newsstand dealer will get) for the following week and bills for the previous one. Today, manufacturing also returns last week's editorial and ad materials, analyzes overall printing production and quality, reviews paper inventories, and prepares for printing the next issue.

By afternoon, the first of next week's Early Form begins to arrive at the Pre-Press Center in Carlstadt, New Jersey.

The Washington photographer prepares for a major policy address by the President tonight before a joint session of Congress. *Newsweek* has requested special permission from the White House to photograph the President as he puts the finishing touches on his remarks. Calls to key Administration officials and a White House contact expedite approval: the photographer has 90 seconds, precisely timed by a press-office representative, to snap a good picture of the President at work. Meanwhile, in Moscow, *Newsweek*'s bureau chief records official reaction to a State Department policy change and in Hong Kong a correspondent interviews the chairman of a shipping company for part of a business story. In Chicago correspondents canvas the city to check on consumer confidence during an inflation spiral and in Nashville a correspondent sits in on a recording session for background on a hot new music talent.

Wednesday

The pace quickens at the Pre-Press Center, where offset film for color and black-and-white ads is ready to be shipped to the printing plants.

In New York, the top editors gather again. First, in the daily meeting, they review the week's plans and change them as necessary. Then, in their weekly cover conference, the main topics of conversation are future covers and color projects. Some cover stories are pegged to regularly occurring news events—elections, theater openings, or seasonal peaks in sports. Others are planned in anticipation of significant developments, such as a major U.S. Supreme Court decision. Editors constantly watch for personalities and social trends that *Newsweek* can examine as they gain importance—but before other news organizations catch on to them. Often, however, even long-planned covers must be scrapped or postponed at the last minute, upstaged by breaking events.

The average *Newsweek* cover story requires about three weeks of reporting and writing, much of it squeezed in among other deadline assignments. However, cover pieces on breaking stories sometimes are pulled together in days—even hours—through round-the-clock efforts by a team of researchers, reporters, writers, and editors. They work closely with cover, photo, and art departments, while makeup experts and copy desk editors fit the finished product smoothly and accurately in the magazine.

One of the fastest cover efforts in *Newsweek* history took place after the election of the late Pope John Paul I. The new pontiff's name was announced on a Saturday shortly before noon, New York time. By 3 p.m., reports on his career, the politics behind his selection, and the reaction of the world's Roman Catholics had poured in from correspondents at home and abroad. Writers and editors in New York distilled the information into 16 columns of text, including four-color photographs transmitted via satellite from Rome. Just 14 hours after the first word had been received, the story, complete with the only color cover photo of the new Pope, was released for printing—in time for the normal production schedule.

On Wednesday, many back-of-the-book writers begin the long grind toward Friday deadlines. They and their senior editors stay in close touch with the bureaus throughout the week to make sure that information necessary for each story comes in on schedule. As the files arrive, Tuesday's story-conference decisions are reviewed. Does a story, coming up even stronger than expected, merit more space? Or perhaps the story just isn't there. Should a new piece be substituted, or its allotted space given to another section that needs more?

Copy begins to trickle to the copy desk—first stop in the complex system that is at the heart of the entire editorial operation. At *Newsweek*, copy is stored and set by state-of-the-art computerized copy-processing equipment, tailor-made to suit the magazine's special requirements. First, a story is typed into the computer on a VDT machine—video display terminal—which combines an expanded typewriter keyboard with input to the memory bank of the computer. Once in the computer, the story can be summoned again and again for editing and changes in space requirements.

Twenty printouts of each story are spewed out by the computer. Some go to noneditorial personnel, such as the publicity director, who is always alert for *Newsweek* "exclusives" to promote in the press and on radio and TV. One copy stamped "Edit" goes first to the appropriate section's senior editor, then to one of the top editors for further changes, additions, and corrections. Another, marked "Checking," goes to a researcher, who underlines every name, figure, and fact as they are verified for accuracy. All changes are incorporated into a master copy, stamped "Top," which then goes to the VDT room for storage of the revised story in the computer's memory bank.

The pressure of an advancing deadline is reflected by activity in *Newsweek*'s Editorial Library. Researchers comb extensive files—some 260,000 envelopes containing nearly everything important ever published on thousands of topics and individuals.

The library's crack staff tracks down obscure facts and sources and arranges to borrow or purchase unstocked books and publications as needed.

Correspondents around the world have begun to flesh out the week's files. Meanwhile, they continue to work on longer-term projects and pursue ideas for future stories by keeping up with the regional media; business, government, and community leaders; other expert sources; and contacts at business and social functions.

By the weekend, a typical file includes a mix of face-to-face interviews, phone conversations, and facts, figures, and other data culled from authoritative books and reports. Ideally, the file is sent to New York in polished form, ready for publication, though correspondents know full well that only the best material actually appears in the magazine. Mostly generalists, *Newsweek* correspondents must be prepared to tackle almost any subject on a moment's notice. No matter what the story, however, they focus their efforts on putting the writers and editors in New York—and ultimately the readers—on the scene with them so that the news comes alive in the finest *Newsweek* tradition. From now through Saturday, the bureau chief and correspondents can expect to spend at least one night working well after midnight, handing typed copy, page by page, to a telecommunications operator.

Thursday

While manufacturing/traffic confirms its prearranged schedules around the world, pages of editorial color pictures are selected at a series of showings for the top editors. The photos are then turned over to manufacturing quality control for shipment to photoengravers who use the latest laser scanners to prepare first-rate reproductions.

There are anxious moments in the photo department, as staffers make sure that all the proper pictures have been ordered, will arrive on time, and that the massive quantities of film being flown in, or otherwise transmitted, from all over the world are edited and organized for the editors' consideration.

For back-of-the-book staffers, it is a major writing day. Most of these news sections will finish their stories today—or, at the latest, by tomorrow noon—to meet their Friday-night deadlines.

Sometimes back-of-the-book sections must work later, however, to accommodate breaking news. Sports may have to wait for the result of a significant game on Saturday. Justice discovers that a major Supreme Court decision unexpectedly has been handed down on Friday morning, forcing a later-than-usual start on the story. But in an ordinary week, lights burn bright late into Thursday night as back-of-the-book writers and editors rush to have their copy written, edited, and fitted by Friday.

By afternoon, work begins on the following week's issue as the bureaus start sending new story suggestions to back-of-the-book editors in New York.

Thursday is the Washington bureau photographer's busiest day. There's a photo session with the director of Office of Management and Budget at the Government Printing Office, where the Administration's new budget is churning off the presses. Then off to American University for a photo to accompany a story about a professor with radical ideas on child rearing. The rush continues into the evening, ending with a reception for visiting students from the People's Republic of China.

The foreign correspondent in Africa travels hundreds of miles over mountainous terrain to file on the only open telex in the country. A file from a correspondent in Paris arrives on time while the Moscow bureau chief delays his transmission until he gets one more exclusive interview. Telephone and telex traffic is heavy all night.

Friday

The scheduled deadline nears. To the unpracticed eye, the unique combination of talents and machinery required to produce a worldwide newsweekly is now operating with a coordination that appears almost effortless. The skills of hundreds of experienced men and women—editors, writers, researchers, reporters, artists, technicians—are combining to work as one critical unit. In the hours that lie ahead, a new issue of *Newsweek* will be born.

At approximately 10:30 a.m. *Newsweek*'s top editors and staff reconvene for the run-through—a preliminary look at a dummy copy of next week's issue. The cover is reviewed, appraised, and if need be, changed. Then, the Editor himself examines each page in a loose-leaf binder. As he does, the Editorial Art Director flips through similar layouts mounted on boards that show, as completely as possible, the planned placement and subjects of photos and artwork with each story. Questions are fired at appropriate editors about the status and length of stories, adjustments are made in layout and space requirements, photos are discussed and changed if necessary. Early Form page proofs, complete and in place in the dummy, give a clearer picture of the issue that is taking more definite shape with each passing hour. Stories and photos are considered and selected for highlighting on the Top of the Week page. The meeting is concluded in a mere 55 minutes—but is re-enacted in the evening and again the following morning to keep pace with changing developments.

Back-of-the-book writers and editors begin to wrap up their sections, making final changes and fitting them into the allotted space. National

Affairs and International sections are starting to take shape, as the bulk of the files pour in from the bureaus. Decisions are still being made, and plans altered, to suit the changing news. Another group of four-color pages goes to the photoengraver. Press and bindery schedules have been confirmed. Traffic completes plans for distribution.

Activity in the bureau starts to peak. The bureau chiefs begin to cross finished files off the assignment list as they are transmitted to New York. With closing still more than an entire day away, reporters continue to update files with late developments and handle last-minute requests for information or clarification. Friday is also suggestion day for new National Affairs stories from the bureaus.

Covering antiabortion demonstrators at the White House and at the Capitol consumes nearly five hours for the photographer. Other appointments follow, yet by 6:15 p.m. caption material is properly prepared, and a messenger picks up the day's film and heads for the airport in time for a flight to New York. Files from correspondents around the world crowd the telex lines.

The work in New York goes on late into Friday night. Often, as many as two dozen editors, writers, and other staffers check into a nearby hotel to catch a few hours' sleep before Saturday's last push begins.

Saturday

Writing, editing, and fitting continue as the magazine moves toward its deadline. Stories are updated, rewritten, and sometimes killed. Researchers, still hard at work checking the accuracy of the stories in their sections, read the finished versions back to the bureaus for corrections and comments from the reporters who covered the stories. *Newsweek's* fast offset printing capabilities enable stories that are written as late as Saturday to appear in Monday's issue—with new photos and new layouts—even a new cover as needed.

Saturday changes can be difficult—on Saturday night, even more so. Such a revision was made after the Patty Hearst verdict, which came in about 7:30 p.m., New York time. The editors, aware that the verdict might be announced, had ordered back-up covers of Miss Hearst's likeness with two alternative slashes—*Guilty!* and *Acquitted!*—to be run off at four plants just in case. Time limitations made the reporting and writing job enormous, imposing daily newspaper pressure. Yet it was finished on time and, in fact, the editors were able to update it on Sunday with interviews of the jurors.

This week, there are a minimum of complications. As each story nears its final stages, the VDT machines direct the electronic typesetters to produce entire pages, complete with captions, black-and-white photos, and some two-color artwork. These pages are reread, checked carefully against earlier versions, checked against the makeup department's instructions on layout, and finally, transmitted to Carlstadt, New Jersey. Here the pages are prepared for shipment or satellite transmission to the printing plants.

As back-of-the-book editors put final touches on this week's stories they have already made up their story schedules for the following week.

In Washington, the photographer is off to shoot a crucial briefing by the Administration's budget experts—a story slated for special prominence in the forthcoming issue of *Newsweek*. Two rolls of black-and-white film are shot for the story, two more in color for possible use the following week. A Chicago correspondent files his story just before deadline. The Moscow bureau chief is on the telephone at 3 a.m. to discuss his file with the International section editor.

In the bureaus, the high-speed printers finally fall silent for a few hours. The staffers go home, where they will tune in to the news from time to time until Monday.

It's already Sunday in some corners of the world—time for some to begin a new workweek.

Sunday

A copy editor in New York checks the clock, then fills in the last empty slot on the page-release log: 12:23 a.m.

It's a day off for most of the editorial staff. Still, the copy desk, VDT and wire rooms, and manufacturing department are manned, just in case the news demands a change in a story already released or a big news story, unforeseen, begins to break. If necessary, the copy desk will call key editors and writers. With relatively minor developments, the editors may handle revisions by phone. But in cases of major news events, editors, writers, and researchers may return to 444 Madison Avenue to handle them properly. In a major newsbreak that obsoletes material already in type, the presses are stopped, production is delayed, and the intricate schedules for printing and distribution entirely redrawn.

Appendix B

American Society of Journalists and Authors Code of Ethics and Fair Practices

Preamble

Over the years, an unwritten code governing editor-writer relationships has arisen. The American Society of Journalists and Authors has compiled the major principles and practices of that code that are generally recognized as fair and equitable.

The ASJA has also established a Committee on Editor-Writer Relations to investigate and mediate disagreements brought before it, either by members or by editors. In its activity this committee shall rely on the following guidelines.

Copyright © 1979, American Society of Journalists and Authors, Inc. Used by permission.

1. Truthfulness, Accuracy, Editing

The writer shall at all times perform professionally and to the best of his or her ability, assuming primary responsibility for truth and accuracy. No writer shall deliberately write into an article a dishonest, distorted, or inaccurate statement.

Editors may correct or delete copy for purposes of style, grammar, conciseness, or arrangement, but may not change the intent or sense without the writer's permission.

2. Sources

A writer shall be prepared to support all statements made in his or her manuscripts, if requested. It is understood, however, that the publisher shall respect any and all promises of confidentiality made by the writer in obtaining information.

3. Ideas

An idea shall be defined not as a subject alone but as a subject combined with an approach. A writer shall be considered to have a proprietary right to an idea suggested to an editor and to have priority in the development of it.

4. Acceptance of an Assignment

A request from an editor that the writer proceed with an idea, however worded and whether oral or written, shall be considered an assignment. (The word "assignment" here is understood to mean a definite order for an article.) It shall be the obligation of the writer to proceed as rapidly as possible toward the completion of an assignment, to meet a deadline mutually agreed upon, and not to agree to unreasonable deadlines.

5. Report on Assignment

If in the course of research or during the writing of the article, the writer concludes that the assignment will not result in a satisfactory article, he or she shall be obliged to so inform the editor.

Copyright © 1979, American Society of Journalists and Authors, Inc. Used by permission.

6. Withdrawal

Should a disagreement arise between the editor and writer as to the merit or handling of an assignment, the editor may remove the writer on payment of mutually satisfactory compensation for the effort already expended, or the writer may withdraw without compensation and, if the idea for the assignment originated with the writer, may take the idea elsewhere without penalty.

7. Agreements

The practice of written confirmation of all agreements between editors and writers is strongly recommended, and such confirmation may originate with the editor, the writer, or an agent. Such a memorandum of confirmation should list all aspects of the assignment including subject, approach, length, special instructions, payments, deadline, and kill fee (if any). Failing prompt contradictory response to such a memorandum, both parties are entitled to assume that the terms set forth therein are binding.

8. Rewriting

No writer's work shall be rewritten without his or her advance consent. If an editor requests a writer to rewrite a manuscript, the writer shall be obliged to do so but shall alternatively be entitled to withdraw the manuscript and offer it elsewhere.

9. By-lines

Lacking any stipulation to the contrary, a by-line is the author's unquestioned right. All advertisements of the article should also carry the author's name. If an author's by-line is omitted from a published article, no matter what the cause or reason, the publisher shall be liable to compensate the author financially for the omission.

10. Updating

If delay in publication necessitates extensive updating of an article, such updating shall be done by the author, to whom additional compensation shall be paid.

Copyright © 1979, American Society of Journalists and Authors, Inc. Used by permission.

11. Reversion of Rights

A writer is not paid by money alone. Part of the writer's compensation is the intangible value of timely publication. Consequently, if after six months the publisher has not scheduled an article for publication, or within twelve months has not published an article, the manuscript and all rights therein should revert to the author without penalty or cost to the author.

12. Payment for Assignments

An assignment presumes an obligation upon the publisher to pay for the writer's work upon satisfactory completion of the assignment.

Copyright © 1979, American Society of Journalists and Authors, Inc. Used by permission.

Appendix C

Guidelines for Magazine Writing about Women

1. Do not use prefixes indicating marital status. First reference should include a person's title (if any) and given name; later references should include *last name only.* For example: Secretary of State George Schultz held a news conference . . . Schultz stated; Senator Paula Hawkins said today . . . Hawkins replied. Use of Mr. and Mrs. is limited to discussions that include a married couple, where the last-name-only rule might cause confusion. Miss and Ms. are not to be used at all. First names alone are also not appropriate for adults.

2. Females over the age of 18 are "women." They are not "girls," "gals," "ladies," "chicks," "broads," "lovelies," "honeys." Words like "homemaker" and "housewife" are also not synonyms for "woman"; check carefully for accuracy before they are used. "Coed" does not mean "woman" any more than "ed" means "man"; persons who attend school are "students."

3. Gratuitous physical description, uncommon almost to the point of absence in news stories about men, should also be eliminated from such stories about women. If you would not say, "The gray-haired grandfather of three was elected senator," then do not say "The gray-haired grandmother of three was elected senator." This rule does not apply with equal force to feature writing, especially profiles, in which physical description is often an essential aspect. However, care should be taken to avoid stereotypical descriptions in favor of describing an individual's unique characteristics.

4. Similar considerations apply to the mention of an individual's spouse and family. In a news story about a man, his wife and family are typically mentioned only in passing and only when relevant; the same practice should apply to news stories about women. See the examples above. Again, the practice is slightly different for feature stories and profiles, but the test of relevance should always be applied.

5. Most achievements do not need sexual identification; those that do should be so identified for both men and women. If you would not say, "Dan Rather is a male reporter," do not say "Helen Thomas is a female reporter." Instead of, "John McEnroe is one of the best American tennis players and Chris Evert Lloyd is one of the best American tennis players," say, "John McEnroe and Chris Evert Lloyd are two of the best American tennis players," or, "John McEnroe is one of the best American male tennis players and Chris Evert Lloyd is one of the best American female tennis players."

6. Avoid sins of omission as well as those of commission. If, for example, an expert is sought in a given field, or if an example is needed to make a point, women should be used in these cases as a matter of course—not simply as "oddities" or representatives of "a woman's viewpoint."

7. "Man," used alone and in words like "chairman," is a sexually exclusive term and should be avoided when possible. "Man-on-the-street," for instance, can easily be changed to "person-on-the-street" or "ordinary person"; "chairman" to "chairperson." The federal government has begun to change its job titles to reflect this attitude; persons formerly called "mailmen" are now "mail carriers."

8. Women's professional qualifications or working experience should always be acknowledged, to forestall the common (and incorrect) expectation that most women are full-time housewives.

9. "Feminist" is the correct term to describe a woman committed to equal rights for women. "Women's libber" is an unacceptable pejorative.

10. Headlines seem to be particularly susceptible to the use of stereotypical, simplistic language. As in other areas, play on these stereotypes is to be avoided.

11. When you have completed a story about a woman, go through it and ask yourself whether you would have written about a man in the same style. If not, something may be wrong with the tone or even the conception of your article. Think it through again.

Glossary

Analysis An article that is a critical examination, usually designed to explain an event.

Angle An aspect or emphasis played up by a writer, as in "woman's angle"; emphasizing elements that will interest women.

Art Any illustration.

Assignment A writing or editing task.

Back of the book Last section of a magazine, usually made up of materials that appear after the main editorial section.

Bleed Running a picture off the edge of a page.

Blurb A short, appreciative description of a story or article.

Book Generally, a synonym for magazine.

Caption Synonymous with *cutline*.

Center spread The two facing pages printed on a single sheet.

Color (1) To enliven writing; (2) to exaggerate and falsify.

Copy Any written material intended for publication.

Copy reader One who edits and otherwise processes copy.

Cover (1) To gather facts; (2) the outer pages of a magazine. The outside front is the first cover; the inside is the second cover; the inside back is the third cover; the outside back is the fourth cover.

Cover plug Special emphasis on the first cover for one or more stories.

Cut (1) An engraving; (2) to shorten copy.

Cutline The text accompanying art.

Dateline Printing of date on any page.

Deadline Last minute for turning in copy or art.

Department A regular column or page.

Descriptive The article given to describing, usually a place.

Dirty copy Written material heavy with errors or corrections.

Double-page spread Two facing pages of text or pictures or both.

Double truck An editorial or advertising layout covering two pages made up as a single unit.

Dress The appearance of a magazine.

Dummy The draft of a magazine showing positions of elements. A diagram dummy is careful and complete. A hand dummy is roughly drawn. A paste-up dummy is made up of proofs of elements pasted in their positions. A positive blue dummy shows blueprints in rotogravure form.

Duotone Art in two colors.

Edition All identical copies.

Ed page Editorial page.

Essay review A feature article that reviews a book, a movie, a play, etc. within the larger context of the subject of the book, movie, or play.

Fat (1) Oversize copy; (2) type that is too wide.

Feature (1) To play up or emphasize; (2) an article, usually human interest, related to news but not necessarily news.

Filler Copy set in type for use in emergencies.

Format The size, shape, and appearance of a magazine.

Free-lance An unattached writer or artist.

Front of the book The main editorial section.

Galley proof An impression of type that is held in a shallow metal tray, or galley.

Ghost writer One who writes for others without receiving public credit.

Gutter The space between left- and right-hand pages.

Hack A writer who will work on any assignment for any publication.

Handout Publicity release.

Head Name, headline, title of a story.

Headnote Short text accompanying the head and carrying information on the story, the author, or both.

Hokum Overly sentimental copy or art.

Hold Not to be published without release; HFR, or "hold for release."

House ad An advertisement for the magazine in which it appears or for another issued by the same publisher.

House magazine (also known as house organ or company magazine) Internal house publications are issued for employees; external house publications may go only to company-related persons (customers, stockholders, and dealers) or to the public.

HTK Head to come: a note to the printer that the headline is not accompanying the copy, but will be supplied later.

Human interest Feature material designed to appeal to the emotions. Also called personality sketch.

Impure pages Those carrying commercial *puffs*.

Indicia Mailing information data required by the post office.

Informative A feature article that informs readers, normally about a place or a process.

Island Position of an advertisement surrounded by reading matter.

Jump (1) Running a story from one page to another; (2) the portion jumped.

Jump head The title or headline over the jumped portion.

Jump lines Short text matter explaining the destination or course of the continued text.

Jump the gutter Titles or illustrations that continue from a left- to a right-hand page.

Layout Positioning of text and art on layout sheets.

Legend Explanation of an illustration.

Makeup Planning or placing elements on a page or a group of pages.

Markup A proof on which changes are indicated.

Masthead Information, usually on the editorial page, on publishing, company officers, subscription rates, and the like.

Must Copy or art that must appear.

Name plate (also known as flag) The publication's name on the cover.

Narrative A feature article that is storytelling in that the events are tightly transitional.

Outline The gist of an article.

Pad To increase length.

Page-and-turner Text running more than a page.

Page proof An impression of type that makes up a page.

Pic Picture.

Piece A synonym for story.

Pix Pictures.

Play up To emphasize.

Policy A magazine's viewpoint.

Position Where elements of a magazine appear.

Profile A feature article that describes a person.

Puff Praising publicity release.

Pulps Magazines printed on coarse paper stock.

Punch Vigor in writing or editing.

Query   A letter summarizing an article idea and asking whether the manuscript might be considered for publication.

Rejection slip   A printed form accompanying a manuscript returned to its author and rejected for publication.

Reprint   (1) To print a story that has appeared in another publication; (2) a separate printing of an article after publication.

Review   A magazine carrying literary stories, critical articles, and commentary.

Running foot   Identifying information (magazine title, date, and so forth) appearing in the bottom margins in some magazines.

Running head   Same as the *running foot* except that it appears in the top margins.

Shelter books   Magazines that focus on housing or related subjects.

Slant   Generally, synonymous with *angle*.

Slicks   Magazines printed on glossy paper and having large (usually mass) circulation.

Slug   Word or words placed on copy as a guide to the printer.

Spread   A long story, often with many illustrations.

Standing head   A title regularly used.

Tail-piece   A small drawing at the end of a story.

Tight   An issue with little space left for additional materials.

Trim   To shorten.

Typo   A typographical error.

Vignette   A very short sketch or story.

Wide open   An issue with plenty of room for additional material.

Index

Abbreviations, in headlines, 106
Acceptance of article, 29–34, 242
Accuracy, importance of, 242
"Actual fact," use of term, 83
Aderhold, Evelyn, 22
Adjectives, avoiding, in headlines, 105
Adverbs, avoiding, in headlines, 105
Advertisers, place in new-magazine planning, 18
Advertising:
    ethics in accepting and placement of, 225–226
    shift from magazines to television, 3, 5–6
Advertising Age, 200
Agreements, written, 223–224, 243
All-capital articles, marking, 62
Allen, Frederick Lewis, 12
Alliteration, use of, 94
Amateur writers, editing work of, 38–39
American Heritage, 4
American Newspaper Publishers Association, 200
American Society of Journalists and Authors, 36
    Code of Ethics and Fair Practices, 223, 241–244
An American Tragedy, 219
American Typewriter type, 135
Analysis, defined, 249
Angle, defined, 249
Antique type, 135
Apostrophe, use of, 55, 58–59
AP World, 200
Arawaks, sample article about:
    layout of, 193–195
    writing and acceptance of, 29–34
Arntz, James, 64–66
Art. *See also* Photographs. Picture editing. Picture stories.
    defined, 249
    placement of, in layout, 192
Art associate, duties of a, 22

Article critique, editorial, 38–40
Article rejections, 37–38
  reasons for, 28
Articles, in headlines, 106
Assignment, defined, 249
Associated Press, 87
Associate editor, duties of a, 20, 22
The Atlantic, 7, 225
Attribution, in headlines, 106
Audience, for magazines, 2–4
Audubon Society. *See* National Audubon Society.

Back cover, design of, 200
Back of the book, defined, 249
Baker, Sheridan, 60
Barron, Jerome, 222
Bartlett's Familiar Quotations, 73
Barzun, Jacques, 54
Baskerville type, 130, 135
Benson, John, 35
Benton, L. B., 130
Bettmann Archive, 193
Bible, 219
Biggs, John, 135, 137
Binding, defined, 123
Blackletter type, 133
Bleed, 166, 190, 249
Blurb:
  defined, 249
  writing, 114
Bodoni type, 130, 135
Body type, defined, 127–128
Book, defined, 249
Book Review Digest, 73
Books, number published yearly, 1
Bookwork, 130
Brackets, use of, 55
Bradfisch, Jean, 20, 29–34, 193
Brady, John, 140
Brando, Marlon, 213
Brennan, Justice William, 214, 219, 220
Broadcasting in courtroom, 218
Broadway type, 133
Buckley, William F., Jr., 8
Bulmer type, 130
Bureau of Land Management, Department of Interior, 228
Burger, Justice Warren, 220
Business papers, 9

Business Week, 102, 103
By-line, author's right to, 243

Cable broadcasting systems, number of, 1
Caledonia type, 135
California, 16, 102, 108
California Journal, 15
California Journalism Foundation, Inc., 15
Camera coverage in courtrooms, 218
Cameras in the Courtroom 1982, 208
Camera work, defined, 122
Campus magazine, beginnings and operation of, 13–17
Capitalization:
  all-cap articles, marking, 62
  in headline, 106
Cappon, R. J., 87, 88
Caption:
  defined, 249
  writing, 159–160
Cardoza, Judge, 54
Carson, Dan, 16
Caslon Old Style type, 135
Caslon type, 129, 130
Center spread:
  defined, 249
  design of, 205, 208
Century, 130
Century type, 130, 131
Chaparral, 204
Cheltenham type, 135
Chemical printing, 125
The Chocolate News, 1
Christian Anti-Communist Crusade, 227
Churchill, Winston, 42, 82, 93–95
Ciardi, John, 54
City type, 131
Classifications of type, 129–134
Class magazines, 7–8
Cliché, 85
Clip-art, 169
Cloister Black type, 133, 135
Cloister Old Style type, 130
Code of Ethics and Fair Practices, ASJA, 223, 241–244
Cole, David, 13, 14
Cole, Dick, 206
Collier's, 3, 82

INDEX

Colon, use of, 55
  in headlines, 106
  with quotation marks, 55
Color, 166–169
  classification, 166–167
  defined, 249
  duotones and posterizations, 169
  fake, 167–168
  preseparated, 168–169
  process, 168
  spot, 167
Color separations, 168
Columbia Broadcasting System (CBS), 228
Columbia Encyclopedia, 73
Columbia Journalism Review, 15, 17, 136
"Columbus's Arawaks":
  layout of, 193–195
  writing and acceptance of, 29–34
Columnar layout, 197
Comma, use of, 55
  in headlines, 105
  with quotation mark, 55
Committee on Editor-Writer Relations, ASJA, 241
Communication, as purpose of design, 18
Company, place in new-magazine planning, 18
Company publications, 9
Competition, place in new-magazine planning, 18
The Complete Stylist and Handbook, 60
Composition department, 122
Computerized magazine editing, 68–72
Concept, place in new-magazine planning, 17
Condensed face, 128
Congressional Directory, 73
Congressional Record, 73
Consistency:
  in layout style, 188, 196
  in type faces, 141, 196
Contact prints, 161–162
Contemporary Authors, 74
Control:
  editorial, 226–227, 228
  photographic, 227

Copy, defined, 250
Copy editing and copy editors, 52–75
  with computer, 68–72
  editorial research, 72–75
  examples of work, 64–68
  functions of, 55–60
  marking copy, 61–64
  newspaper vs. magazine, 53–54
Copyfitting methods, 137–141
Copy marks, 61–62
  examples of use, 66–67
Copy reader, defined, 250
Copyright law, 220–222
Coronet, 3
Corvinius type, 135
Cosmopolitan, 6, 108
Cover:
  defined, 250
  designing, 200–204
    back, 200
    examples, 201–203
    inside, 204
Cover plug, defined, 250
Craw Clarendon type, 131
Crewes, Frederick, 60
Critique of article, editorial, 38–40
Cropping angles, 164
Cropping photos, 162, 164–165
Crow, Elizabeth, 22–23
"Cry Rape," 222
Current Biography, 74
Cut, defined, 142, 250
Cutline, defined, 249, 250

The Daily Courant, 133
Dash, dashes, use of, 55
  in headlines, 105
Dateline, defined, 250
David S. Alberts v. State of California, 219
Deadline, defined, 250
Deck, defined, 109
Decorative type, 129, 133, 134
Defamation, 213–215
Defoe, Daniel, 219
Denver, John, 89, 90
Department, defined, 250
Descriptive, defined, 250
Design. *See* Layout and design.
DeVinne, T. L., 130
Dialogue, paragraphing of, 92

Diamond, Edwin, 1
Dirty copy, defined, 250
Disagreements, between editors and
    writers, 35–40
  article rejections, 37–38
  critiquing an article, 38–40
Display type:
  defined, 127–128
  use in design, 141
Dobell, Bryon, 14
Doctor blade, 126
Double-page spread, defined, 250
Double truck, defined, 250
Douglas, Justice William O., 220
Downstyle capitalization, 106
Dreiser, Theodore, 219
Dress, defined, 250
Dummy:
  defined, 250
  using, 197–199
Duotone, 169, 250

"Early Form," 233, 235
Editing:
  paragraphs, 89–91
  sentences, 86–89
  words, 82–86
Edition, defined, 250
Editor:
  functions of, 12–23
  importance of, 41–42
  relations with photographer,
    156–159
  relations with writer, 28–42
  as writer, 40
Editor & Publisher, 8, 102
*Editor & Publisher International
    Yearbook,* 74
Editorial assistant, duties of a, 22
Editorial need, place in new-magazine
    planning, 17
Editor-in-chief, duties of a, 19–20
"Editor's Notes," 204
Ed page, defined, 250
Edwards v. National Audubon Society,
    215
Egyptian type, 131
Electrostatic printing, 123
Ellipsis, use of, 55
Em space, 128
Encyclopedia Americana, 73

Encyclopedia Britannica, 73
Encyclopedia of American History, 74
Endymion, 219
Engravers Old English type, 133
Environmental Program for the
    Future, 228
Esquire, 14
Essay review, defined, 250
Estes, Billie Sol, 218
Estimating, to copyfit, 137–138
Ethics, editorial, 222–224, 241–244
Evans, Harold, 133
The Evening Post, 133
Exclamation point, use of, 55
Executive editor, duties of a, 20
Expanded face, 128
Extended face, 128

Facts on File, 74
"Fair use," 221, 222
Fake color, 167–168
Fat, defined, 250
Feature, defined, 250
Feed/back, 13–17, 132, 134, 189,
    200, 202
  beginnings of, 13–16
  present operation, 16–17
"Feminist," use of term, 247
Field and Stream, 228
Filler, defined, 250
Fillet, defined, 130
Financial projections, place in
    new-magazine planning, 18
Firestone, Mary Alice Sullivan, 217
Firestone, Russell A., Jr., 217
First Amendment right to withhold
    information, 212, 219
Fischer, John, 12, 39, 226
Flag, 133, 252
Flat, defined, 123
Flat color, 167
Folio type, 131
Forest Service, U.S., 228
Format, defined, 250
Formula, place in new-magazine
    planning, 19
The Fortieth Floor, 82
Fortune, 6, 40
Fosdick, James, 157
Four-color reproductions, 168
Fowler, Henry W., 60, 89, 90

Franklin Gothic type, 131
Free-lance, defined, 251
Frome, Michael, 228
Front of the book, defined, 251
Full-color reproductions, 168
Fund for the Republic, 226

Galley proof, defined, 251
Garamond type, 130, 135
General magazines, decline of, 1–2, 3–4, 5–6
Gertz, Elmer, 214
Gertz v. Robert Welch, Inc., 214–215, 217
Ghost writer, defined, 251
Gillenson, Lewis, 3
Gillmor, Donald M., 222
Gothic type, 131
Goudy Text type, 133
Gowers, Ernest, 95
Grady, David, 206
Graphic arts, 122–144
  copyfitting, 137–141
  planning signatures, 143–144
  printing processes, 123–127
  titles and illustrations, 141–143
  typography, 127–137
Gravure printing, 122, 126–127
Gruner & Jahr, 23
Grunwald, Henry R., 41
The Guinness Book of World Records, 74
Gutenberg, Johan, 124
Gutter, 190, 251

Hack, defined, 251
Hadden, Briton, 6, 7
Hale, David, 201
Halftone dot pattern, 165
Halftones, 142
Harke, Bill, 164, 165
Harper's, 1, 7, 12, 102, 108, 226
Head, defined, 251
Headings. *See* Headlines. Titles.
Headlines:
  counting, 103–104
  defined, 102–103
  grammar rules, 106–107
  practices to avoid in writing, 107
  writing, 60, 104–106

Headnote, defined, 251
Head schedule, 114
Hearst, Patty, *Newsweek* treatment of verdict, 239
Hicks, Wilson, 156
Hlasta, Stanley, 135
Horrock, Nicholas, 218
Hutchins, Dr. Robert, 226
House ad, defined, 251
House magazine, defined, 251
Human interest, defined, 251
Humor, in headlines, 107
Hutchinson, Ronald R., 215
Hutchinson v. Proxmire, 215
Hyphen, use of, 55
  with prefix, 56

Idea, author's proprietary right to, 242
Ideal type, 130
Illustrations, using 142–143. *See also* Picture editing. Picture stories.
Impure pages, defined, 251
Indicia, defined, 251
Industrial and Business Journalism, 8
Inside covers, design of, 204
"Instructive Mistakes," 35
Intaglio, 126
International Council of Industrial Editors, 9
International Oceanographic Foundation (IOF), 19, 20

Jargon, 85–86
Jenson, Nicholas, 129, 130
John Birch Society, 214
John Paul I, Pope, *Newsweek* treatment of election, 235–236
Jung, Carl G., 38
Jump, defined, 251
Jump lines, defined, 252
Jump the gutter, defined, 252

Kabel Light type, 135
The Kandi-Kolored-Tangerine-Flake Streamline Baby, 14
Karnak type, 131
Keats, John, 219
Keyline, 169
Knowland, Joe, 14
Kobak, James, 17, 18

Ladies' Home Journal, 216
Lady Windermere's Fan, 35
Lapham, Lewis, 1
Larsen, Roy, 2
Lasch, Robert, 225
Law, 212–222
   cameras in courtroom, 218
   copyright, 220–222
   defamation, 213–215
   libel, 212–215
   obscenity and pornography, 219–220
   privacy, 216
   public vs. private figures, 217
Law of Mass Communications, 222
Lawrence, David, 7
Layout and design, 188–208
   basic rules, 188–192
   covers, 200–204
   defined, 252
   dummying, 197–199
   lead article and center spread, 204–208
   magazine layout, 196–197
   sample layout, 193–195
Layout sheet, using, 190
Lead article, choosing, 204, 206–207
Leading, leading out, 129
   choosing, 137
LEARNING, The Magazine for Creative Teaching, 191, 200, 201, 206–207
Leaves of Grass, 219
Legend, defined, 252
Legibility, of type, 130, 135
Leicester, L. Anthony, 29, 31
Letterpress printing, 122, 123–124
Lewis, Anthony, 219
Libel, 212–215
Liebes, Bud H., 13, 14, 15, 16
Liebling, A. J., 16
Life, 156, 227
Line cut, defined, 142
Line lengths, choosing, 137
Linen tester, 162
Line shot, 142, 142–143
Lithography, 122, 124–126
"Little magazines," 5
Look, 3, 5, 40
Los Angeles Times, 133
Lowercase type, 130
Luce, Henry R., 6, 7, 227

Ludeke, 110
Ludlow, Lynn, 13, 14, 16

Magazine:
   defined, 5
   number begun each year, 1
   number existing, 1
   origin of term, 5
   types of, 5–9
Makeup, defined, 252
Managing editor, duties of a, 20
Margins, in layout, 190, 192
Marital status, indicating, 245
Marking copy, 61–64
   example, 66–67
Markley, Susan M., 22
Markup, defined, 252
Mass Communication Law, 222
Mass magazines, 5–6
Masthead, defined, 252
Measurement of type, 127–129
Merrill, David, 141, 156
Millay, Edna St. Vincent, 54
"Milton Friedman Talks About Economics And Teachers: An Interview," 206–207
Modern English Usage, 60, 89
Modern roman type, 130
Moll Flanders, 219
Money, 6
Morison, Stanley, 130
Mott, Frank Luther, 5
Ms., 6, 18
Mugshot, 169

Nameplate, 133, 252
Names, checking, 74–75
Narrative, defined, 252
The Nation, 7
National Association of Printers and Lithographers, 126
National Audubon Society, 215
National Review, 7, 8, 213
Negative assembly, defined, 123
Nelson, Harold L., 222
New England Courant, 133
New material, inserting, 64
New Republic, 7, 114
"News hole," 234
News magazines, 6–7

INDEX 261

Newspaper copy editing, compared to magazine, 53–54
Newsweek, 6, 7, 107, 218
   preparing an issue for publication, 231–240
New York, 6
The New Yorker, 53, 60, 86, 112, 204, 216
New York Times, 133, 214, 215, 219
New York Times Co. v. Sullivan, 213, 214
The New York Times Index, 74
Nouns, in headlines, 105

Obscenity, 219–220
Offset lithography, 122, 125
Ogilvy, David, 225
Old English type, 133
Oldstyle roman type, 130
Old Style type, 135
Omission of words, in headlines, 106
Ord, Mary, 158
Ortho film, 122
Ostwald color classification system, 166
Outline, defined, 252

Page head, writing, 112–113
Page proof, defined, 252
Pantone Matching System (PMS), 166–167
Paragraphs, editing, 89–91
  professional example, 93–95
  student example, 91–92
Parents, revival of, 22–23
Paste-up, defined, 122
Penthouse, 220
People involved, place in new-magazine planning, 18
Period, use of, 55
  in headlines, 105
Perkins, Maxwell, 12
Photographer-editor relationships, 156–159
Photographs. *See also* Picture editing. Pictures and art. Picture stories.
  tips for taking good, 157–158
Photography in courtroom, 218
Photojournalism, defined, 156
Photolithography, 125

Photo-offset, 125
Pica, defined, 127
Pick-up, 167
The Pick-Up Times, 1
Picture editing, 156–166
  cropping, 162, 164–165
  editor-photographer relationships, 156–159
  guidelines, 166
  scaling, 163, 164–165
  writing captions, 159–160
Pictures and art, placement of, in layout, 192
Picture stories, writing to, 160–161
Pictures and art, placement of, in layout, 192
Pilpel, Harriet F., 222
Pix, defined, 252
"Planet Ocean," 19, 22
Plate-burner, 123
Platemaking, defined, 123
Playboy, 6, 18, 108, 114, 220
Play up, defined, 252
Plural, forming, 58
Point, defined, 127
Policy, defined, 252
Pollock, Michael, 37
Popular Mechanics, 8
Pornography, 219–220
Porter, Tim, 16
Portland Oregonian, 133
Position, defined, 252
Possessive, forming, 59
Postage rates, as threat to magazines, 5
Posterization, 169
Prefix, rules of spelling with, 56–57
Preparing copy, 62, 63
Preseparated color, 168–169
The Press, 16
Presswork, defined, 123
Printing processes, 123–127
  gravure, 126–127
  letterpress, 123–124
  lithography, 124–126
Privacy, law, 216
Private vs. public figures, 217
Process camera, 122
Process color reproductions, 168
Production:
  defined, 122
  process at *Newsweek,* 231–240

Professional magazine:
  beginning a, 17–19
  editing a, 19–22
Profile, defined, 252
Progressive margins, 190
Proportion wheel, 163, 164
Prospectus, for new magazine, 19
Proxmire, Senator William, 215
Public, of magazines, 2–4
Public Opinion, 214
Public vs. private figures, 217
Puff, defined, 252
Pulps, defined, 252
Punch, defined, 252
Punctuation:
  in headlines, 105–106
  marks, use, 55
Purdy, Ken, 40

"Quality magazines." *See* Class magazines.
Queen Mab, 219
Query to editor:
  defined, 253
  importance of, 37
Question mark, use, 55
The Quill, 104, 110, 200, 203, 204, 222
"*Quill* Classifieds," 204
"Quotable Quotes," 204
Quotation marks, use, 55
  with colon, 55
  with comma, 55
  in headlines, 105–106
  with period, 55
  with semicolon, 55

Radio stations, number of, 1
Ragged headline, avoiding, 107
Random House Handbook, 60
Randstrom, Susan, 203
The Razor's Edge, 1
Reader's Digest, 4, 18, 200, 204, 215, 222, 225
Rea-Salisbury, Vesta, 29–34, 193
Redundancy, eliminating, 82–83
Reflection copy, 168
Regal type, 130
Rejection of article, 37–38
  reasons for, 28

Rejection slip, defined, 253
Repetition:
  avoiding, in headline, 107
  effective use of, 93, 94–95
  eliminating, 83–84
The Reporter, 82, 108
Report on assignment, author's need to, 242
Reprint, defined, 253
Researcher:
  duties of, 4, 22, 232
  editor as, 72–75
Reverse type, 189
Reversion of rights, 244
Review, defined, 253
Rewriting of article, 243
Riggio, Robert J., 22
Rights and Writers, 222
Rolling Stone, 6, 18
Roman type, 129–130, 136
Rooney, John J., 108
Rosen, Ben, 135
Rosenbloom, George, 213–214
Rosenbloom v. Metromedia, 213
Rosenstiel School of Marine and Atmospheric Science, 19
Rosette pattern of color reproduction, 126
Ross, Harold, 39, 60, 204
Roth v. United States, 219
Rotogravure, 126
Runarounds, 163
Running foot, defined, 253
Running head, defined, 253

San Francisco, 16
San Francisco Bay Area Journalism Review, 13, 14
San Francisco Chronicle, 133
San Francisco Examiner, 13
San Francisco State University, 13
Sans serif type, 129, 131, 136, 142
Saturday Evening Post, 3, 213, 227
Saturday Review, 2, 54
"Say," use in writing, 84
  alternative expressions, 84
  synonyms, 84
Scale, 163
Scaling photos, 163, 164–165
Schaefer, Faith, 20
Schemenaur, P. J., 140

INDEX

Schwarz, Frederick C., 227
Scientific American, 4
Scotch Roman type, 135
Screen process, 123
Script type, 129, 133
Sea Frontiers, 29, 193
    duties of editors, 19–22
Sears Roebuck, 225
Sea Secrets, 20, 22
Sellers, Leonard, 16
Semicolon, use, 55
    with quotation marks, 55
Senefelder, Aloysius, 124
Sentences, editing, 86–89
    professional example, 93–95
    student example, 91–92
Serif, defined, 129
Set solid, 129
Set width, 128
Sevareid, Eric, 228
Shelley, Percy, 219
Shelter books, defined, 253
Sidebar, 167
Sidis, William, 216
Siegfried, Tom, 188
Signature, 143–144
Silkscreen printing, 123
Simplicity in writing, importance of, 82
Sixth Amendment right of subpoena, 212, 219
Size of type, choosing, 128, 137
Slant, defined, 253
Slicks, defined, 253
Slug, defined, 122, 253
Smith, Dr. F. G. Walton, 19, 30, 32
Smith, F. May, 20
Snell Roundhand type, 133
Sources, use of, 242
Souvenir type, 134
Spartan type, 131
Specialized magazines, 4, 8–9
Specialty type, 136
Specialty work, printing for, 124
Specifications, for heads, 114
Spelling, rules of, 56–59
Sports Illustrated, 4, 6
Spot color, 167
Spread, defined, 253
Square serif type, 129, 131
Standing head, defined, 253
Stein, Robert, 4

Stock, 167–168
Stringers, 233
Stripping, defined, 123
Style, copyediting for, 60
Stymie type, 131
Subhead:
    defined, 109
    writing, 110–112
Substrate, 167–168
Subtitles, writing, 109–110
Suffix, rules of spelling with, 57–58
Sullivan, L. B., 214
Sunset, 158

Tail-piece, defined, 253
Teeter, Dwight L., 222
Television:
    effect on general magazines, 3, 5–6
    effect on magazine advertising, 3, 5–6
    stations, number of, 1
Television News Index and Abstracts, 74
Tempo type, 131
Text type, 127–128, 129, 133
"The Thinking Man's Medium," 2
Thomas, Andy, 208
Thumbnail layout sheet, 198
Thurber, James, 60
Tight, defined, 253
Time, 6–7, 60, 68, 82, 141, 156, 217
Time, Inc., 2, 41
Time, Inc. v. Firestone, 215, 217
The Times Atlas of World History, 74
The Times of London, 130
Times Roman type, 130, 142
"Timestyle," 7
Tinker, Miles, 135, 137
Tint, use, 167, 191
Tint block, 189
Titles:
    choosing type for, 141–142
    defined, 102–103, 107–108
    subtitles, writing, 109–110
    writing, 60, 108–109
Tone butting, 163
Trade Gothic type, 128
Transitional roman type, 130
Transmission copy, 168
Trim, defined, 253
Turnbull, Arthur, 8

Turner, John, 165
TV Guide, 4, 6
Type:
   choosing, 135–137
   classifications of, 129–134
   measurement of, 127–129
   placement in layout, 192
   size, choosing, 128, 137
Type and Typography: The Designer's Notebook, 135
Typo, defined, 253
Typography, 127–137
   choosing type, 135–137
   type classifications, 129–134
   type measurement, 127–129

Ultra Bodoni type, 135
Unit, defined, 103
Unit of thought, paragraph as, 89–91
United States Daily, 7
U.S. News & World Report, 6, 7
Univers type, 131
Updating article, 243
Uppercase type, 130
Upstyle capitalization, 106

Verb head, 106
Verbs, in headlines, 105, 106
Vignette, defined, 253

Warren, Ridge, 82
Washington Post, 133
Webster's Third New International Dictionary of the English Language, 74
Wedding Text type, 133
Wenner, Jann, 18

White, E. B., 86
White, Theodore, 3, 82
White space, function in layout, 192
Whitman, Walt, 219
Who's Who in America, 74
Wide open, defined, 253
Wilde, Oscar, 35, 36
Winters, Bill, 35, 36
Withdrawal of article assignment, 243
Wolfe, Tom, 14
Wolston, Ilya, 215
Wolston v. Reader's Digest, 215
Women, guidelines for writing about, 245–247
"Women's libber," avoiding term, 247
Wood, Evelyn, 142
Words, editing, 82–86
   professional example, 93–95
   student example, 91–92
Wrap. *See* Covers.
Writer-editor realtionships, 28–42
   accepting an article, 29–34
   article rejections, 37–38
   critiquing an article, 38–40
   disagreements, 35–40
   need for editor, 41–42
Writer's Digest, 15
Writer's Market, 5, 140
Writing with a Purpose, 60

Xerography, 123
Xerox Corporation, 123

The Years with Ross, 60

Zavin, Theodora S., 222